Learning to Legislate

The Senate Education
of Arlen Specter

Learning to Legislate

The Senate Education of Arlen Specter

Richard F. Fenno, Jr.
University of Rochester

CQ PRESS

A Division of Congressional Quarterly Inc.
Washington, D.C.

Cover design: Paula Anderson
Cover photo: R. Michael Jenkins

Copyright © 1991 Congressional Quarterly Inc.
1414 22nd Street, N.W., Washington, D.C. 20037

Printed in the United States of America

Library of Congress Cataloging-in-Publication Data

Fenno, Richard F., 1926-
    Learning to legislate : the Senate education of Arlen Specter /
  Richard F. Fenno, Jr.
      p.   cm.
    Includes index.
    ISBN 0-87187-628-0 -- ISBN 0-87187-629-9 (softback)
    1. United States. Congress. Senate. 2. Legislators--United States--Case studies. 3. Specter, Arlen. I. Title.
  JK1161.F46   1991
  328.73'0731--dc20   91-4038
                              OCLC: 23766048   CIP

Contents

Preface

Every newcomer to the United States Senate knows how to win an election. A few know how to govern. The rest have to learn. Some never do. All, however, must adjust to a new institution. All must undergo some kind of transition from the activity of campaigning to the activity of governing. The transition period is a good time to watch the development of their careers. And it is a good vantage point from which to study the Senate.

Political scientists have long believed that if we could see the Senate through the eyes of its newest members—as they were learning about the institution—we, too, could learn about the senators and the Senate. In the 1950s and 1960s, students of the institution discovered that an "apprenticeship" prescription—listen and learn, wait and watch, be seen and not heard—dominated the early experiences of freshmen senators. This apprenticeship norm became for political scientists a defining characteristic of the Senate. Likewise, the choice between compliance and noncompliance with the norm became a defining characteristic of each senator's career.

In the 1970s and 1980s, apprenticeship disappeared—both as a norm and as a practice. But new senators still go through a period of learning and adjustment. Apprenticeship may be gone, but adjustment remains. Thus scholarly attention to the early adjustment experiences of Senate newcomers can still help us to understand both the Senate and the careers of its members. Such, at least, is the premise of this book.

The book embraces the first six-year term, 1981-1986, of Senator Arlen Specter, Republican of Pennsylvania. It begins and ends with the examination of his election campaigns. But it centers on the adjustment experiences of his first two years. For much of that period, I lived in Washington and was able to follow his governing activity at close range. That was particularly true of the events connected with the career-criminal legislation that forms the centerpiece of the book. The discussions of his campaigns were also informed by personal observation. I traveled with him in Pennsylvania on five occasions—in September and October of 1980, in June 1982, in November 1985, and in October 1986.

My dominant perspective, therefore, comes from over the shoulder of Arlen Specter. In that sense, it is a limited one. It is enlarged somewhat, as readers will soon discover, by the perspectives of the members of his staff. My account of Specter's major legislative effort depends heavily on the staff members who were involved in it. I shall speak often of "the Specter enterprise," by which I mean to include the senator and his closest aides. The perspective of the book is, most accurately, the perspective of the Specter enterprise. In fact, the increased influence and size of senators' staffs are among the most important features of the contemporary Senate.

My perspective has been enlarged, further, by the accounts of journalists and reporters—some of them national, most of them Pennsylvanian. But the reader should be reminded, still, that the perspective of the book remains limited by a decision not to talk with other active participants. A well-rounded picture of the electoral and legislative events encompassed here has been sacrificed for the value of a detailed, close-up, and first-hand account.

For whatever value the book may have, therefore, my largest debt is owed to Sen. Arlen Specter. He was accessible, open, and willing to let me learn along with him. He leavened our relationship, too, with an exceptional degree of personal kindness.

To the members of Senator Specter's staff, I owe a very great debt for their willingness to talk with me and to make available to me many resources I needed to write the book. I especially want to thank Paul Michel and Gordon Woodrow for their time, their knowledge, and their patience. I thank also, for their many varieties of willing help, Bruce Cohen, Bill Loughery, Jonathan Levin, Dan McKenna, Kevin Mills, Sylvia Nolde, Yvonne O'Connor, Lonnie Taylor, and Jim Wagner. A special thank you, too, goes to Shanin Specter.

Three political science friends, Chuck Jones, Tom Mann, and Dave Weimer, helped by reading the manuscript; and I am indebted to them for their advice. I thank Rich Forgette and Steve Wright for their research assistance. For CQ Press, Dave Tarr, Nola Healy Lynch, and Jamie Holland performed the tasks of encouragement and editing with their usual easy expertise. Janice Brown turned notes into manuscript and turned manuscript into more manuscript with the talent and good humor on which I have depended for many years. Rosemary Burnham applied some finishing touches. And Nancy's support, as always, kept the whole thing afloat. Last, I thank the Russell Sage Foundation, whose financial assistance made possible much of my observational research.

Introduction

The careers of U.S. senators can usefully be studied in terms of a sequence of political activity that dominates and shapes their political lives. In this sequence the activity of campaigning for election in the home state is followed by the activity of governing in Washington, which is followed, in turn, by a campaign for reelection at home. This campaigning-governing-campaigning sequence corresponds closely with the six-year senatorial election cycle. And, of course, the sequence repeats itself every six years for as long as a senator survives in office.

To be sure, the stages are not rigidly separated; campaigning and governing activities intertwine. But the activities can be distinguished. In campaigning the main goal is to get elected; in governing the main goal is to help make good public policy. The dominant concerns of a senator's political life, running for office and running the country, rise and fall in rough correspondence to a sequential flow of this sort— enough so, we believe, to provide a secure underpinning for the narrative and analysis of this book.

Senate newcomers all find themselves somewhere in the transition from campaigning to governing. When we look closely at what they are doing, however, each senator's experience has its own finely grained texture. Between the end of a successful election campaign and the completion of a major governing accomplishment, each senator goes through a time of adjustment to the new institution and its environment. To make a close-up study, therefore, we need to refine and expand our overarching Senate career sequence to make it the campaigning-*adjusting*-governing-campaigning sequence. That is the flow of the senatorial career we will study in this book.

The adjustment period, as we define it, begins soon after the election and ends when the new senator records a substantial legislative accomplishment. The period typically lasts about two years. During this period there will be both an "adjustment from" what went before and an "adjustment to" the new institution. What a person must adjust *to* depends somewhat on what he or she is adjusting *from*.[1]

First, the fledgling senator must adjust from an election campaign. When the results are in and have been digested, each senator-elect will develop an interpretation of what happened and why. That electoral interpretation will form a basis for his or her subsequent governing behavior and therefore will affect his or her adjustment period.

The campaign is, however, only the most recent experience from which a newcomer must adjust. Before that, each person will have enjoyed another adult career of greater or lesser length and of greater or lesser impact. That pre-Senate career will call for some—greater or lesser—adjustment from. How much of an adjustment will depend on how closely the newcomer's previous line of work—its familiar routines, its rewards, its criteria for success—matches the new line of work as a senator.

A former member of the House of Representatives, we might expect, would experience less of an adjustment from than someone who had never served in a legislative capacity at any level. For the former legislator, there would be quantitative changes in familiar experiences— more demands, more power. But for the person from a different background, the changes would be qualitative—in procedures, autonomy, incentives, resources, and external scrutiny, for example. If these qualitative differences do not make adjustment to the Senate more difficult, they may at least help prolong it. In any case, a sequentially grounded analysis of a newly elected senator's behavior compels us to take into account the pre-Senate career.

The U.S. Senate presents two faces to every newcomer. One is individualistic; the other is communitarian. The first is captured by descriptions of the Senate as one hundred prima donnas or as a colony of movie stars; the second is characterized as the club or the small town.[2] Neither of these Senate faces, we might add, is characteristic of the House of Representatives. The degree to which one face or the other dominates will vary from time to time.

In recent years the more prominent face of the Senate has been its individualistic one. The contemporary institution is a collection of entrepreneurs, each one in business for himself or herself, each one with a personal agenda and goals. Each senator is richly endowed with resources to aid in individual pursuits—a multiplicity of committee positions, a large and loyal staff enterprise, strong links to external policy networks, publicly observable decision-making, easy access to national media outlets, and very permissive parliamentary procedures. It would be possible to write a book about each of these characteristics. Indeed, a superb book has recently been written about all of them: Barbara Sinclair's study, *The Transformation of the United States Senate*.[3] The transformation of which she writes is the change from what was once a predominantly communitarian Senate to what now is a predominantly individualistic one.

In the 1950s and 1960s, students of the Senate characterized the body as self-contained and inward looking. They found, among most senators, a marked concern for the collectivity—how it processed its work, how its members got along with one another, how it maintained itself in the face of outside pressures. It was not that the individual senator had no leeway. It was simply that the more striking emphasis was on an encirclement of constraints that kept the individual attentive and responsive to the collectivity, to the community. There was an apprenticeship for newcomers, a restrictive system of committee assignments, carefully circumscribed committee jurisdictions, and narrowly defined, committee-based specializations, a deferential "get along, go along" attitude toward leaders, a "give a little, take a little" philosophy in closed-door decision making, a "be a work horse not a show horse" attitude toward publicity seeking, and a sparing use of prolonged public dissent. Senators knew each other, spent time with each other, and expended a lot of their energy on matters of institutional maintenance.

Helped by the occasional levying of sanctions against violations of these informal understandings, this somewhat collegial, somewhat hierarchical, somewhat conservative community maintained itself—until changes in the outside world intruded. A steady influx of policy-oriented activist senators; an explosion of new, complex, and controversial issues; a proliferation of aggressive interest groups; a revolution in information and communications; an exponential enlargement of staff; and a decline in the influence of electoral parties combined to produce the transformed Senate. It has become a less collegial and less hierarchical Senate, one in which members spend more time enveloped in their staff enterprises than with one another and one in which deference to leadership has been replaced by issue-to-issue entrepreneurship. The Senate is altogether more egalitarian and outward looking than it once was.

Party leaders are especially acute observers of the change. Veteran Democratic party leader Robert Byrd, who watched the change, commented: "Going back to my earliest years in the Senate, I think there was . . . more of an establishment-minded feeling. There was more cohesiveness on the part of political parties than there has been in recent years. The emergence of the individual has been a kind of phenomenon." [4] Republican majority leader Howard Baker added that individual senators no longer pay much attention to their colleagues:

> They don't care, because they go outside and someone will listen with a TV camera. . . . It makes it difficult to lead. . . . If Lyndon [Johnson] were here today and tried to crack the whip [a senator] would simply go out on the Capitol steps before the TV cameras and raise hell . . . [and] that man would be a hero. [5]

A long firsthand reportorial account in 1982 was summarized in its title: "In the Senate of the 80s, Team Play Has Given Way to the Rule of Individuals." [6]

These descriptions portray the contemporary U.S. Senate. It is the kind of institution which contemporary newcomers can easily make an adjustment to. It is, after all, the institution created by their recent predecessors. And it is an institution that is largely the product of an external world with which every newcomer is familiar. Each newcomer has already campaigned successfully in that world for a year or so.

Present day campaigns, like the present day Senate, are described as highly individualistic, candidate-centered campaigns. With the bonds of party as much attenuated outside the Congress as they are inside (perhaps even more so), each candidate recruits his or her own supporters, raises his or her own money, frames his or her own issues and develops his or her own strategy. There are, still, a few party-dominated campaigns—mostly relics of a bygone era. For most new senators, however, electoral success will have been entrepreneurial success, and the Senate will be a collection of independent achievers. To that degree, adjustment to a world of individual ambitions, personal agendas, and customized resources should not be difficult.

But what about the communitarian face of the institution? How much of it remains? And how easy will a newcomer's adjustment be to that side of things? The exaggerated emphasis on internal conformity and the narrow circumscription of an individual's activity is gone. But while the concern for institutional maintenance is no longer as noteworthy as the ease with which individuals can disregard or disrupt it, a residue of community feeling exists and occasionally reveals itself.[7] At the very least, passing legislation calls for collective effort.

It is the job of leaders—committee, subcommittee, party—to superintend the governing process. But a good deal of cooperation is required among self-interested legislators at all decision-making junctures to make the legislative process work. When all is said and done, the Senate is a collective operation; it is not a one-person operation. On the basis of the need for collective action, therefore, some communitarian sentiments remain. And the Senate, it is important to note, still rewards its members for institution-minded behavior.

The transition from independent-minded winning candidate to independent-minded senator, therefore, is not as automatic as it might seem. That is, the activity of governing may call for a somewhat less individualistic outlook than does campaigning. In the Senate, the newcomer becomes one among equals rather than the indisputable head of the recent campaign. Face-to-face coalition building calls for different forms of persuasion than does influencing mass publics during the campaign. Inside the institution, interpersonal bases of trust must replace the image-based sources of trust that dominated the electoral effort. Arguments that may have been simplified for public consumption must now be complexified for close-range argumentation with peers. It appears, then, that it is the communitarian or the collective face of the Senate—however much it may seem obscured—that requires the greatest "adjustment to" for most newcomers.

From one perspective, candidate-centered campaigns reinforce the individualism of the Senate, and adjustment is easy. From another perspective, candidate-centered campaigns may hinder adjustment to the collective effort necessary to succeed at governing. Individualism comes naturally to successful campaigners; but communitarian action must be learned—or so, at least, we speculate.

Assuming that the contemporary Senate is preeminently an individualistic institution, we might expect to gain a better understanding of its workings by studying the activities of individuals. This book deals with the first six years in the Senate career of Arlen Specter, a person who came to the Senate without previous legislative experience. It focuses most sharply on his two-year adjustment period. It chronicles an adjustment to the individualistic aspects of the Senate that was quick and natural and an adjustment to the communitarian aspects of the Senate that was less natural and took longer.

The senator's adjustment experiences are framed by his electoral experiences at the beginning and at the end of the six-year career segment. Chapter 1 examines his election campaign and his earliest adjustment experiences. Chapters 2 and 3 analyze his later adjustment experience, his governing style, and his governing accomplishments. The analysis centers on his major legislative effort. Chapter 4 examines his successful reelection campaign. The analysis is guided throughout by the campaigning-adjusting-governing-campaigning sequence.

NOTES

1. A more extensive discussion of adjustment, along the same lines as this one, is Richard F. Fenno, Jr., "Adjusting to the U.S. Senate," in *Congress and Policy Change*, ed. Gerald C. Wright, Jr., Leroy N. Rieselbach, and Lawrence C. Dodd (New York: Agathon, 1986).
2. An elaboration of this distinction will be found in Richard F. Fenno, Jr., "The Senate Through the Looking Glass: The Debate over Television," *Legislative Studies Quarterly* (August 1989): 313-348.
3. Barbara Sinclair, *The Transformation of the U.S. Senate* (Baltimore: Johns Hopkins University Press, 1989). For comparative purposes, the classic

description of the earlier Senate is Donald Matthews, *U.S. Senators and Their World* (New York: Norton, 1973).

4. Irwin B. Arieff, "House, Senate Chiefs Attempt to Lead a Changed Congress," *Congressional Quarterly Weekly Report*, September 13, 1980.
5. Helen Dewar, "Is 'The World's Greatest Deliberative Body' over the Hill?" *Washington Post National Weekly Edition*, December 10, 1984.
6. Alan Ehrenhalt, "Special Report: The Individual Senate," *Congressional Quarterly Weekly Report*, September 4, 1982. Ehrenhalt has further explored this theme of several levels of American legislative institution in an excellent study: Alan Ehrenhalt, *The United States of Ambition* (New York: Random House, 1991).
7. For example, see Fenno, "The Senate Through the Looking Glass."

1

Campaigning and Adjusting

INDIVIDUALISM AND ADJUSTMENT

Arlen Specter came to the Senate in 1981, at the age of fifty, after a rough-textured political career during which his personal independence had been repeatedly demonstrated and its value ultimately vindicated. He was a lawyer in a prestigious Philadelphia firm when he entered Pennsylvania politics, as a Democrat. But he became a Republican when that party showed greater receptivity to his public service ambitions. As he explained, "I have always been more interested in working in the public sector—especially in elective office—than in the private sector. A greater intensity of interest and a greater sense of accomplishment come from the public sector." In 1965, at the age of thirty-five—after having been an assistant district attorney and an assistant counsel to the Warren Commission—he won election as district attorney of Philadelphia.

Two years into his term, he ran for mayor of Philadelphia and was defeated. Two years after that, he won reelection to a second term as district attorney. In 1973, however, he failed to win reelection for a third term. Three years later, in 1976, he lost a primary contest for the Republican nomination for U.S. senator; and two years after that, he was defeated in the Republican primary for the Pennsylvania governorship.

In neither of the last two races was he the choice of his party's leaders. Their opposition, together with his career record of two wins and four successive defeats, would have dispatched most ordinary politicians to the sidelines. But in 1980 Specter entered his third statewide primary. And once again he ran against the choice of his party's statewide leaders and of his own Philadelphia leader. As he told a group of black ministers afterward, "I don't discourage easily. In fact, I don't discourage at all." He told a reporter at the same time, "I've had a lifelong ambition to be in the U.S. Senate." [1]

Finally he won a primary; his primary victory was followed by a 51 percent general election victory in November. When asked on election night what his three losses had taught him, he answered, "I learned character; I learned tenacity; I learned steadfastness. And I did not take it as a personal defeat." [2] His election to the Senate was a triumph of one man's persistence.

Arlen Specter came to the Senate, we shall argue, viewing the upcoming business of governing through strongly individualistic lenses. Overwhelmingly, the lesson of his pre-Senate career and his electoral experience had been the importance of individual effort. He wanted, he said, to have an impact on the Senate, to be a policy maker there. His experience left him with a predisposition to seek this goal independently. To the degree that his predisposition ran with the grain of a highly individualistic institution, his adjustment problems would not be great. On the other hand, he faced the problem of balancing his tried-and-true individualism against his desire for success in an institution that had a substantial collective component. That part of his adjustment would be more problematic.

His adjustment played itself out in several Senate contexts. One of them was his effort to pass his first piece of legislation—his career-criminal bill. He introduced it in October 1981; it passed the Senate a year later; and it was signed into law as the Armed Career Criminal Act two years after that. For Specter, the three-year saga—which included a presidential veto—was both a learning experience and a personal accomplishment. For us, the story provides a vehicle for examining one independent-minded freshman's trial-and-error adventures in adjusting to the life and work of the U.S. Senate.

THE PERSISTENT PROSECUTOR

On the campaign trail in the fall of 1980, it quickly became clear that candidate Arlen Specter was somewhere in the middle of a long political career and that his previous experiences had heavily influenced his present demeanor. A complete life story would doubtless begin with his family's Jewish roots, the emigration of his father from Russia, the family's struggle in the depression, the young man's intellectual prowess, and his rising status in the legal profession. [3] But our concern with his political life can usefully begin with his formative years as district attorney of Philadelphia. The political style he displayed as we campaigned in eastern Pennsylvania in 1980 was the same style he had long since established as DA. Or so it appeared to an outside observer—since Specter talked constantly about his earliest years in office and since his presentation of himself seemed not to have changed much from the pattern highlighted in his political reminiscences. Both "then" as he reported it and "now" as I perceived it, he came across as serious and smart, energetic and aggressive, and, above all, independent.

Over and over, his conversations revealed his self-image as a hard-working, hard-charging, hard-nosed district attorney. He loved to relive his cases, highlighting both their technical complexity and his fearlessness in the face of adverse political consequences. Consider this reaction, for example, to a newspaper endorsement: "They opposed me in [one of my DA races] because I locked up a *Bulletin* reporter for wiretapping. They have been against me ever since until this month. . . . [Now] they need a Philadelphia senator. So they swallowed and endorsed me." Or this account upon his return from a meeting with union officials to secure their endorsement:

> There I was, asking for their endorsement. One of them I had indicted and another I had sent to jail, when I was DA. . . . When I saw him, [the first one] said, "You indicted me; you tried to convict me; you didn't have any evidence," and so forth. I said to him, "I indicted you because I had the evidence. You were found not guilty, and that's that. But I did my duty as I saw it."

He told a group of reporters of his proudest accomplishment as DA—the reform of the magistrate court system in Philadelphia:

> I headed the commission to investigate the magistrate's system. It was rotten. We recommended its abolition. And I indicted some of the magistrates. I remember going to a rally shortly afterward. I walked in and all the magistrates were there—some of them I had indicted, and I had recommended that the jobs of the others be abolished.

He reflected on his treatment of "special interests" when he was DA: "I prosecuted the corrupt contractors who built the City Center. I prosecuted the people who were spraying asbestos around in the building. I locked up people who had contributed to my campaign."

Each commentary was embroidered with a discussion of the legal intricacies of the case.[4] When he ran for DA, he and his running mate (for controller) had as their slogan: "They're younger, they're tougher and nobody owns them."[5] The self-portrait that emerged on the campaign trail in 1980 was the same: that of a relentless, incorruptible, and altogether formidable prosecutor.

Specter's Senate campaign brochure delivered the same message to the voters. Its cover consisted of a photograph of the candidate; its second page presented a word picture of him. It was headed "Arlen Specter: On the Record." The text began: "Arlen Specter has a proven record of fighting for people. Before he was elected District Attorney of Philadelphia, the office was run on political considerations, rather than on merit. During his eight years in office Arlen Specter turned that situation around." It continued under three subheadings: "Arlen Specter Fought For Consumers," "Arlen Specter Fought Crime," and "Arlen Specter Fought Corruption." The burden of each subsection stated that

> when he saw people being ripped off by businesses ... he
> prosecuted six large supermarket chains for dishonest advertis-
> ing. . . . He initiated reforms that put more police on the street,
> set up a 24 hour a day police court and increased the conviction
> rates for murder and rape. . . . Arlen Specter's investigations led
> to the prosecution of some of the most important people in
> Philadelphia—people of both political parties. . . .

His public presentation of himself matched the private one. It featured the same prosecutorial stance. And it contained the same underlying message that one person's individual effort makes a difference.

Journalists who had followed Specter's career, early or late, con-firmed this reality behind the image of the independent prosecutor. But a demonstrated independence can lead to another, less flattering inter-pretation. Journalistic portraits identified also a pattern of self-promo-tion that played counterpoint to the pattern of public-minded indepen-dence. In this other view, District Attorney Specter was very much concerned with political consequences. In its otherwise laudatory en-dorsement of him, one Philadelphia newspaper admonished:

> Mr. Specter's eight years' stewardship of the district attorney's
> office produced a generally acceptable level of professionalism,
> but was marred by a demonstrated tendency toward investiga-
> tions and indictments of a clearly advantageous political na-
> ture, many of which produced little in the way of final results.[6]

A reporter for another Philadelphia paper commented similarly: "Call-ing Specter driven is like calling Shakespeare well-spoken. . . . As DA, he was frequently accused of being more concerned with Arlen Specter's future than with the law." [7] And a profile in a third local paper said: "The rap against Arlen Specter has always been that he is too ambi-tious. . . . 'He's one of the most calculating persons I've ever known,' says one veteran GOP Specter watcher. 'I don't think he ever says hello without calculating what the impact is.' " [8] One reporter said privately, "The people at my paper think Arlen is a jerk. It's a combination of the ambition image and the loser image."

Occasionally, reporters would express the opinion that the Senate candidate had mellowed, since his early days.[9] On the campaign trail, one newsman said to Specter, "The last time I saw you, you were an aggressive district attorney trying to get subpoena power for law enforcement officers. But now you seem to be more mellow. How come?" Specter answered: "I'm ten years older. As a thirty-five-year-old district attorney I guess I did come on like gangbusters. But you come to realize you can't get everything done that you want to get done. So I guess I've matured." There was, then, some recognition among observers that the person running for the Senate was not quite the same person as the officeholder had been, that he had learned. There was some evidence, therefore, that he might change in the future as well. But this view of his personality was not the dominant one.

Valid or not, the dominant view of Specter as ambitious, intense, driven, and calculating lingered in the atmosphere in 1980. His opponent used it against him, charging in debate that Specter "during his time as district attorney brought wholesale indictments against people for the purpose of political gain, to use it as a springboard, hoping that he would win reelection and using it as a springboard for governor . . . with dismally few convictions." [10]

When Specter addresses this less flattering view of his independence, he reaches back to his immigrant roots. "I plead guilty to all that," he says. "I've been accused of being ambitious, and when I was growing up ambition was not only a good word in our household, it was an indispensable word." [11] To the degree that these journalistic opinions have validity, they only strengthen our case for the marked individualism of the prospective U.S. senator.

As he campaigned, the impact of Specter's district attorney experience on his political thinking was visible everywhere. Grappling with his most difficult issue—abortion—before the Pennsylvania Catholic Conference, for example, he invoked his experience as DA to argue against a constitutional amendment.

> When I was DA, I led the opposition to a constitutional amendment to overturn the *Miranda* decision. I reargued the case in the Supreme Court for the National District Attorneys Association. That was a terrible decision. It hampered me in all my law enforcement activities. I was in violent opposition to the decision. But I would not support a constitutional amendment to overturn it.[12]

Characterizing his campaign in a meeting with the editors of the *Scranton Tribune*, he said:

> I've campaigned here more than anywhere except Pittsburgh. . . . People want to know "What will Arlen Specter do

for us, how reliable is he and how much commitment does he have?" When I was DA, I created the record I'm running on—tough sentencing, long court hours, open house. I think that record is known here. One of the things I've been trying to stress is a sense of urgency. That distinguishes my campaign from my opponent's.

After his appearance at a black ministers' meeting in Philadelphia, he commented on his strong support among the city's black citizens:

I feel especially comfortable in the black community.... I believe I can be an important spokesman for blacks—with programs like "greenlining." I know 4th and Bainbridge, 8th and Market. I have good relations with the black community. I appointed more black Assistant DA's than ever before. I helped them with my reforms on bail procedures, prisons and consumer fraud. I boarded up nuisance tap rooms in black neighborhoods.[13]

In the 1980 election, he received an unusually large 38 percent of the vote in the black community of his hometown.

When I asked him who his strongest supporters were, he answered in terms of his performance as DA.

My strong supporters are people across the board—black and white, rich and poor—who are within reach of Philadelphia television, who know the job I did as district attorney. That support has dissipated some in the six years since I have been in office. Then there is a second tier, who have heard of the job I did.

Experiences and lessons from his eight years as DA informed nearly every aspect of his campaign. For a markedly public, political DA, the transfer was a natural one. His private conversation, his presentation to others, his political analysis left little doubt that inside the Senate candidate were the guiding perspectives and predispositions of a lawyer, a district attorney, and a public prosecutor.

When asked directly by reporters about the differences between himself and his opponent, Specter answered in terms of individual effort. "Sure there's a difference. I'm campaigning harder than he is." [14] Specter emphasized his effort in terms of both activism and substance. With a lawyer's thoroughness he had prepared what he called a comprehensive set of position papers—thirty-two in all. They contained detailed prescriptions for such bread-and-butter problem areas as coal, steel, transportation, and agriculture. He carried a set to every editorial board meeting and left it there. He used these issue papers as the bases for his public pronouncements. But in a strategic sense, he used them to help make the essential contrasts with his opponent—who had none.

When the editors of the *Patriot-News* began to ask him about "the issues of the campaign," he broke in:

> Before I get to the issue differences, let me tell you what I think the most important difference is. It's the intensity of my campaign and the evidence it gives of my willingness to work hard. I've campaigned in all sixty-seven counties; my opponent has not. I've produced a sheaf of position papers three inches thick; my opponent has not.... I'm trying to convince the people of Pennsylvania that I'm a serious, hard-working guy.

Privately, he spoke of his opponent as

> vague on issues. When you research him, there's nothing there. He has no position papers. He meanders during the campaign and ... changes priorities.... We've stayed one step ahead of him during the campaign.... He has been copying everything we do.... Each debate, he takes the position I took in the last debate.

Confident of his mastery of the issues and of his prosecutor's quickness on his feet, he pressed at every opportunity for more and more debates with his opponent. "If I could get all the people of Pennsylvania into one room [to listen to a debate] I could win the election." [15] An observer of one debate described Specter's debate style as "bright and brittle as always, wowing 'em with detail, six answers to every question." [16] His favorite book has long been Clarence Darrow's *The Story of My Life*. And he has long relished verbal sparring, in private as well as in public.

Specter believed that his comparative advantage lay in a contrast in styles between himself and his opponent: "When I say I've been in sixty-seven counties, people say, 'That guy is out there working hard.' It makes a nice contrast with [my opponent], who hasn't done that and who is not known as a highly energized, hard-working person." Publicly and privately, media scorekeepers agreed with this comparison. [17] And the style Specter wished to convey bore a considerable resemblance to the prosecutorial style he had, apparently, displayed earlier—tireless, intense, and in total substantive command.

THE CAMPAIGN FOR THE SENATE

Specter's Democratic opponent in the Senate race was fifty-six-year-old Pete Flaherty, a two-time mayor of Pittsburgh who had been his party's unsuccessful standard bearer in campaigns for the Senate in 1974 and the governorship in 1978. The parallels with Specter's career enticed political reporters to frame the contest, somewhat mockingly, as a battle in which one of the two big-time losers would at long last win something.[18] In more serious terms, they framed the contest geographically, as the Philadelphia-dominated eastern region versus the Pittsburgh-dominated western part of the state, with swing regions in between. Specter's natural constituency would be in the east, Flaherty's natural constituency lay in the west, and they would compete in the northeastern and central regions of the state.

This regional interpretation of Pennsylvania politics was a standard one. In 1980, it underlay the handicapping of the scorekeepers and the strategy of the candidates.[19] In one reporter's summary, "If . . . Flaherty wins heavily in western Pennsylvania and Specter wins in the east, the race may be decided in central Pennsylvania where Republicans dominate or in the northeastern coal regions." [20] The thinking in the Specter camp was that the candidate would be strongest in the Philadelphia suburbs but would do much better in Democratic Philadelphia than the usual Republican candidate, that the strategy would be to try to hold Flaherty down in the southwestern area, and that the team would campaign especially hard in the northeastern (Scranton, Wilkes-Barre) part of the state.

In every newspaper interview near his eastern base, Specter was encouraged to argue that the state needed a senator from the east to balance the incumbent (John Heinz) from the west. But, in every case, Specter demurred—not because he thought the argument wrong, but because he believed that the western area felt much more strongly and more parochially about the matter. Therefore, any exacerbation of the issue would create hostility in the west without any compensating benefits in the east. "I don't want it to develop into an east-west contest, because the west shows more togetherness on it than the east," he would tell the editors. Or "I cannot portray an east-west battle, because it would portray a battleground that is not good for me. I think the issue of balance is appropriate. But I don't want to get into an east-west battle because the west is . . . more attuned to that." So the geographical cleavage was central to everyone's calculations. But it did not surface as an issue in the campaign.

Of equal importance as a potential point of conflict were matters of ideology. But it is noteworthy that the campaign did not get framed in ideological terms, either privately or publicly. The contestants had few sharp differences. "Ideological yardsticks simply won't yield much ink in the Senate race this fall," prophesied one writer; both candidates "have staked out similar, moderately conservative positions on most domestic and foreign policy issues." [21] After viewing the TV ads of both candidates, another reporter concluded that "the commercials do little to put distance between the candidates. If anything, they emphasized that Specter and Flaherty differ over few issues even in detail; both are fiscal conservatives and social moderates." [22] Other journalists came to the same conclusion: "Both men hail from the same area of the political spectrum: Specter is a moderate Republican and Flaherty a conservative Democrat";[23] "[they are] a Democrat who often sounds like a Republican and a Republican who often sounds like a Democrat";[24] "[they are] safely middle of the road in a state that eschews extremists." [25] The policy issue on which they had a sharp, discernible difference was that of abortion, with Specter taking a general pro-choice position and opposing a constitutional amendment to outlaw abortion and with Flaherty taking the opposite stance.

The absence of ideological issues reinforced Specter's comparative advantage in the area of political style—that he was more conversant with substantive matters, that he campaigned harder, that he was more energetic and tenacious in going after what he wanted—and he tried to make style the issue between the candidates. He presented himself as someone who, on the basis of these individual attributes—displayed as DA and as candidate—would make a difference in the Senate and, therefore, would make a better senator than his opponent.[26] As his TV ads summed up: "He's solid. He's decisive. He will produce for Pennsylvania."

His media endorsers helped by seeing things that way, too. The *Philadelphia Bulletin,* describing him as "bright, well organized, hard working and ambitious," concluded that "Specter seems to have a stronger grasp of issues, knowledge of Pennsylvania and imagination in representing the state in Washington." [27] The *Philadelphia Daily News* recalled how he took unpopular stands in his mayor's race and concluded that his "ability to take a position and keep it is the major reason we endorse Specter for the Senate. . . . We just get the feeling . . . that his positions can be depended upon." [28] The *Philadelphia Inquirer* described him as "the more promising" of the two candidates: "Mr. Specter's most salient characteristics are energy and ambition. At his best he is aggressive, forceful and capable of intense concentration on complex challenges. He is a man of intelligence, decisiveness and imaginative- ness." [29] The *Patriot-News* said that "this is a contest of character. And there is nothing wrong with that. . . . Specter's strength is that he can speak and act informedly and confidently, just this side of being outspoken . . . [he] would make a solid U.S. Senator right now and perhaps a great one in time." [30] In all these commentaries, it was Arlen Specter's personal qualities and his individual effort that were used to justify the editor's preference. He had succeeded in setting the individualistic standards by which he would be judged.

Like Specter's career itself, his 1980 campaign ran an uphill course. In May he was 10 points (51-41) behind his opponent in Democratic polls;[31] in June he was 18 points (53-35) behind in radio station KYW polls. He stayed well behind—"10, 12, 15 points"—throughout the summer. As his top campaign aide put it: "When we began, we were 13 points down in the polls. After a summer of campaigning, in all sixty-seven counties of the state—a summer when Flaherty did nothing but go to Europe—would you believe it, we were 18 points down." When I arrived in mid-September, the same staffer commented, "We are down 10-12 points. It's tough, very tough. Flaherty has very high [name] recognition in the state." Flaherty had, after all, run two full-scale general election campaigns in the state. And the Democrats did have a 700,000-person registration advantage, however deceptive that might be. Flaherty's initial name recognition advantage over Specter had been 92 percent to 63 percent; but that had by mid-September been narrowed to 93 percent to 83 percent. It was a promising sign.

So, too, was the early September KYW poll showing the 18-point margin of June to have shrunk to 7. The figures were 40-33, with 27 percent undecided. Specter's advisers believed that these results reflected a movement from Flaherty to "undecided," a group now waiting to be plucked. The KYW poll, said Specter, "is the first change we have seen in the trend. Our two months of street campaigning in the summer produced no change whatever." The day before I had arrived, September 14, a poll by the Pennsylvania State Education Association, which had endorsed Specter, showed the race to be 41-39. Specter's reaction to the poll was upbeat. "Yesterday, by all objective indications, we turned the corner.... [We are] neck and neck, with Flaherty two points up." However, a *Philadelphia Daily News* poll at the end of October showed Flaherty still ahead 48-43, with 9 percent undecided.[32] Specter did not pull ahead until the last few weeks of the campaign.

Reporters believed that the outcome would be close. But they did not find this contest between two well-worn and ideologically similar contestants to be very exciting. One wrote, "The contest has been one of the sleepiest in recent memory as neither Specter nor Flaherty—both two-time losers for statewide office—has aroused much interest, even among professional politicians."[33] "Pa. Senate Campaign: It's Silent Running" read a September headline. And in September: "Flaherty, Specter Debate in Phila., But [Moderator] Emerges as the Star."[34] Philadelphia's Channel 6 evening news report on the Philadelphia Chamber of Commerce debate stated that there were "no fireworks" and that "the race has failed to capture the interest of the Pennsylvania public." Postdebate comment on Channel 10 called the campaign "the cleanest in years," said it was "neck and neck," and concluded that it would probably boil down to "east versus west" or "a contest of personality." In its last week, it was still called a "lusterless six month race ... which has sparked a public interest perhaps more closely associated with Halloween apple-bobbing contests than crusades for the United States Senate." [35]

Media portraits of the campaigning Arlen Specter were far more modest than the candidate's self-portrait would have suggested—or than would appear in his later endorsements. His campaign would have to rely on self help, with little publicity from the sidelines. "Yes, Arlen Specter is on the campaign trail ... again," began one profile. "He's been there before: The 'boy wonder' of the Republican party in the '60s—flashy district attorney, politician of the future—then the stumbles and falls of the '70s—the bitter campaigns, the narrow defeats—from 'can't miss' to 'sure loser.' " [36]

Another profile, headlined "Specter Seeks Image: Old Problem Bedevils Senate Hopeful," began: "Things have never gone as smoothly for Arlen Specter as they should have.... He had seemingly just begun a meteoric career ... suddenly, inexplicably the golden boy of the Republican party was tarnished.... Specter is pulling out all the stops— that's the kind of guy he is. The only question now is if anybody's paying attention." [37] Scorekeepers seemed to want to chain him to his past, and their storyline dampened rather than excited interest in the race, however competitive it might be.

The crucial increment of self help in the campaign came from the paid media, and from the money to buy it. "I have been beaten in the past because I've been outspent," said Specter.[38] And he was not about to let it happen again. In mid-September, Specter's two top campaigners were obsessed with media and money. Excerpts from our dinner conversation went as follows:

—We can't afford to put our research director on the payroll. We need to save everything we can for the media....
—Are other campaigns as media dominated as this one? ...
—All we think about is the media and raising the money to pay for the media....
—Senate campaigns have become exercises in fund raising. I worry about it all the time, and that's all I worry about....
—The more I'm in the business, the more I realize how much the media dominates the whole process....
—It's like [consultant David] Garth says, "If the media doesn't show it, it's not real.".
—Our ID is up to 83 from 63. All this has come after our media

started. There's no other way you can change numbers like that.

The next day, the candidate's speculations were similar. "Our media is working. . . . The great imponderable is whether Flaherty can get on the tube with his ads and how effective they are. Barring any striking event that gets free media . . . the paid media will be decisive."

The media plan was dictated by Specter's relatively low name recognition which, he believed, was responsible for his sluggishness in the polls. Accordingly, his television ads had begun early—right after Labor Day, almost a month before Flaherty's. And they were to continue unabated, at a cost of $76,000 a week, to the end of the campaign. For that amount of money, 90 percent of the people of Pennsylvania would see four Specter ads each week. The campaigners planned to alternate six thirty-second ads—a biographical ad, a spot intended for western Pennsylvania, and policy statements on agriculture, defense, revenue sharing, and steel. "With each ad, you take another slice of the apple," explained one aide, "and you just keep slicing the apple. You don't have to worry about having *the* great ad. Just have a good ad and play it incessantly. Pretty soon, even the most sophisticated listener will be moved by it."

The financial infusion that guaranteed their early start came from a $525,000 contribution—one-quarter of their total budget—from the Republican Senatorial Committee, headed by Pennsylvania's other senator, John Heinz.[39] ("Flaherty says I'm buying the election. I say to you that after having run in so many campaigns without money, it's a good feeling. And if anybody asks me about it, I'm going to say, 'Yes, I'm buying the election, but John Heinz is paying for it.'") They spent the early money "massively," as if they had enough to continue until election day. But by mid-September they had money for only two weeks more. So their worries were prompted by the need for an additional $400,000 to keep the media campaign afloat. They were very nearly successful in that effort. To the end, the media-oriented attitude of the candidate remained the attitude of the campaign. "How else can you reach a million people?" Specter asked.

The size of the state may well be the main explanation for this overwhelming media orientation. But Arlen Specter's strong personal attachment to the media as a campaign resource certainly contributed. And that attachment, not surprisingly, stemmed from his DA experience. He talked about his first campaign, in a city with the population of Iowa. "Philadelphia has about two million. In 1965, I conducted an extensive street campaign. But there's no way you can reach that many people except by media. We spent $750,000 in that campaign . . .

$550,000 of it for media. It was mostly a media campaign. It had to be." This preference never changed.

Speaking about his most recent electoral experience, he made a similar point. "The Montgomery County Republican party is the most powerful in the state. Yet I defeated them in the Senate primary—not by much, but I defeated them. And I did it with a very minimal [$150,000] media campaign. As district attorney, I became convinced of the tremendous power of the media in communicating directly with the people." And he had been a publicity-conscious, media-oriented district attorney. He explained, "When I was DA, I was in the news all the time. I held press conferences twice a week, in the morning for the *Bulletin* and in the afternoon for the *Inquirer*."

By mid-September, his TV ads, he believed, were beginning to take hold as planned. "The campaign is beginning to take on a flavor— that I'm a serious, substantive candidate, that I know my material, that my opponent is more flighty and doesn't work as hard. My TV ads reveal this about me, I think." Face recognition had increased every-where, too. "The street noises begin to sound better. When I walk down the street—the last few days—people gawk. Tonight I could feel the difference when I walked into the room. People wanted to meet me. I was a real person. This morning I bought a new suit and everyone crowded around to help me. It's the celebrity business. Television is wonderful."

To an observer who had just come, as I had, from an organization-intensive Senate campaign (of Sen. John Culver) in Iowa, the Specter group's preoccupation with the media presented a striking contrast. In Iowa, campaign talk had centered on techniques of organization, voter identification, and getting out the vote on election day. The campaign, that team believed, would be won or lost "in the trenches." Media activity was described as "frosting on the cake"—the aim being simply to neutralize your opponent's TV by matching it in volume. In this kind of campaign, the political party (the Democratic party, in Culver's case) was expected to make a significant organizational contribution. And statewide party officials were closely tied in with every campaign effort I had observed.

This contrast highlighted the relative insignificance of the Republi-can party apparatus in the thinking of the Specter campaign. A Republican National Committee operative observed privately that "Specter has no grass-roots organization." There was almost no con-versation about "the trenches." And such talk as there was underlined the absence of a capacity for trench warfare. A top aide described his frustrating effort to bring together groups of party officials to coordinate activity.

I can't get one single county chairman to agree to a date for these meetings. I can't wet nurse them. I'm beyond asking them to meet on my date. I ask them when they want to meet. Still they won't commit themselves. Eighty percent are useless. . . . So you try to work with the 20 percent—especially the ones in the most populous counties in each media market. . . . The decision I am making right now involves money for the media versus money for people who want to open storefronts or people who want street money and sound trucks for election day. The money is going for the media.

The candidate himself was more circumspect, but his conclusion was the same.

There are maybe three hundred people around the state who are special supporters of mine, but there are 66,000 polling places. We rely on the party people to help us there. But party strength runs from strong to nonexistent. Montgomery County is strong, very strong. Delaware is strong. Bucks is pretty strong, Chester's pretty strong. But the media is the most powerful force of all. There is a committeeman in every living room in the state—the television set.

Looking ahead to the fourth of November in the trenches, a key campaigner commented, "We don't have any election day organization, and we know it."

Arlen Specter's own relationship with the Republican party was a tenuous one. The party had given him his start in Philadelphia. But three times after that, the party establishment had rejected him as its statewide nominee. And three times Specter had entered the primary to campaign without the support of his party's leadership. In discussing his entrance into the 1980 primary, in which he ran against the leadership choice, he talked about his relationship with the party. "[When] it was announced that the choice of the leadership was Bud Haabestad of Delaware County, a number of people began to urge me to get into the race," he said. And he began to recapitulate his relationship with the leadership.

I felt strongly that I had been given short shrift by the Republican party. I was once a Democrat, as you know. And the party was very willing to use that fact, to use my connections in liberal circles, in the Jewish community, in the black community and let me run for mayor of Philadelphia. They were willing to use me to pull all those groups in. But when it came to the choice plums, they reserved them for [others]. In every respect of background and schooling, I was as good as they were; but I didn't get the nod of the party establishment. Even

> though I carried Philadelphia in 1969 by 100,000 votes. Even
> though I campaigned my heart out for Scranton and Schweiker
> and Scott and others on the ticket. There was always that
> bridge. . . . Dick Schweiker said it best in 1970. He said I ought
> to be promoted—"promoted" was the way he put it—to gover-
> nor. But the party put up Broderick. Then, this year there was
> Haabestad. I'm not one to shrink from a battle or a fight. I
> thought I could beat Haabestad. So I entered the primary and
> beat him.[40]

Specter had absolutely refused to quit. And he had won by dint of
extraordinary individual effort—in spite of years of opposition by the
leaders of his own party. It was, as we have said, a triumph of his
persistence and a vindication of his independence.

The party leadership rallied behind him after the primary; he
readily acknowledged their support as a source of great strength.
Especially helpful were Senator Heinz's efforts on Specter's behalf in his
native western Pennsylvania.[41] In general, however, a residue of wari-
ness remained—on both sides. Specter was a Philadelphian in a party
whose center of gravity lay beyond the city. As one scorekeeper summed
up: "His problems are that he is perceived in the hinterlands as too
urban, too Philadelphia and . . . too Jewish."[42] He was, indeed, the first
Jew ever nominated by the Republican party in Pennsylvania for the
U.S. Senate. And he would become the first Jew ever elected to the
Senate from the state. He had a track record, too, as an independent-
minded operator in a party that valued team play.

For his part, Specter could hardly be expected to forget the years of
opposition and humiliation he had faced within the party. The leftover
bruises only reinforced a determination to remain independent; he was
reluctant to place himself in the hands of others, to rely on others, or to
incur obligations to others. And he could be expected to remain his own
man. "I'm not always in step with the Republican party," he acknowledged. But, like his fellow Republicans statewide, he moved to close
ranks. Specter campaigned, for example, with the party's presidential
nominee in Philadelphia even though he believed it would not be
helpful.

> Reagan wanted to campaign in Philadelphia. I thought I should
> be a good team player and so I agreed. We tried to arrange a
> fund-raiser, but we had such short notice we didn't raise any
> money. Our picture together, with arms raised, appeared on the
> front pages of the paper. I lost some political skin on that one.[43]

Within the city, there was a good deal of mutual support between the
party and the candidate, and they had for a long time needed each other.

In late October, the candidate flogged himself from one Philadelphia ward rally to another, preaching party unity and party revival. "It's important to have a strong Republican party to help us win city elections and because the Democrats are so corrupt," he said as we rode from one meeting to another.

> We need to be strong enough to challenge their candidates—and at least make them put up decent candidates. . . . Besides, the Republicans are my team. They are my guys. I ran with them for district attorney in 1965 and for mayor in 1967. We would have won the mayor's race if we had had a strong Republican party. I'm running the same kind of naked reverse this time, too, without a whole lot of party support. The Republican party in the city is in bad shape and that bothers me.

His concern for "my guys" in the Philadelphia party helped reinforce his Republican party identity. But to a substantial degree, too, he was running "a naked reverse" here and elsewhere. And the recognition of his position served to buttress his individualism along with his party loyalty. It was a built-in tug-of-war.

ANTICIPATING THE SENATE

Nonincumbent candidates without legislative experience cannot be expected to be knowledgeable about or sensitive to the job of a U.S. senator. Yet it is reasonable to expect that, in moments of anticipation, they will speculate about it. And if they do, their thoughts on the subject may provide an early indication of the kind of adjustments that lie ahead for them. Arlen Specter's occasional ruminations laid heavy emphasis on the possibilities and the prospective payoffs for individual effort.

His overall view of the job was vague: "People want to share in the material benefits of society. They want to have dignity, and pride. The job of a senator is to help." Or, "People have a lot clearer idea of the DA's job: he prosecutes people. They think a senator votes on economic matters and helps get things for them." But when he focused on the representational aspects of the job, he became more specific: "Pennsylvania is a state with a great diversity. . . . The problem [of the job] is the same problem my sister faced, teaching six grades in a one-room schoolhouse in Kansas, or the problem a lawyer with a general practice has, handling many clients without a specialty. It's the problem of dealing with hundreds, even thousands of interests." This general description seemed more invigorating than daunting. Indeed, in the course of his frequent references to the subject, he outlined a strenuous program of outreach for his constituents—patterned, not surprisingly, on his experience as district attorney.

In Scranton and Wilkes-Barre, for example, he promised to set up separate district offices for the first time. As we drove away from Scranton, he explained.

> There is an enormous problem of getting out of touch in a state as large as Pennsylvania. That is something that has stood me in good stead in my campaign. In contrast to my opponent, I have campaigned all across the state; and I have talked to people about their problems—the mushroom growers, the Allegheny forest, the coal miners, the lady outside the Pittsburgh stadium . . . about to lose her house. When I was DA, I held open house every week where I was available to people who wanted to talk to me. . . . And I had people on my staff who listened to complaints and looked into problems.

Off and on, he toyed with the idea of adding a mobile office to supplement his half-dozen district offices. "People would be astounded by it, to see a senator's office in a mobile van up on Route 6," he said, caught up in the image. "People say, 'we only see you guys when you're running for reelection.' It would be refreshing for them to see someone when he was not running." He never did do that. But his discussion did reflect a concern to stay in touch, to be seen and to be available throughout the state, in campaign season and out.

In the same vein, he expressed a strong determination to hold town meetings. "They are reassuring to people in the state that you are around and not aloof. People like it when they are invited, even if they don't come. It shows them that their officials are accessible." These matters of representational style, of accessibility, were his earliest and his most clearly articulated notions about what his new job would be like. And, characteristically, his scenario prescribed for himself a good deal of personal involvement.

In pursuit of the same goal, but with a lot less thought or experience, he made a specific promise in September to represent his more than two million rural constituents by seeking membership on the Senate Agriculture Committee. The suddenness with which he made this decision was some indication that his sense for how to win the election was a lot better fleshed out than his sense for how he would govern. He described how this campaign promise came about.

> There are three and a half million people dependent on agriculture in Pennsylvania. It's our second largest industry. And if one more steel mill closes down, it will be the largest. So

> it's very important to our state. It's also a good campaign
> technique to get elected and reelected. A Pennsylvania senator
> on that committee would never have to worry about being
> reelected. If I had my druthers, I would take Foreign Relations
> and Judiciary. But I can't get Foreign Relations, and I'll be very
> involved in Judiciary's matters anyway, because of my back-
> ground. Dick Schweiker was on Appropriations. That's very
> important to our state, but I doubt if I could get that. I can't
> think of a committee that would stretch me as much as
> Agriculture. And I think a senator ought to stretch himself. I'll
> be up to my ears in urban problems no matter what committee
> I'm on.... I met with several agricultural groups one morning.
> They told me that Pennsylvania had not had a senator on the
> Agriculture Committee for seventy-six years.... That after-
> noon, I made my decision. I announced it to another farm
> group. I have a good feeling for rural people. I worked on a
> farm in Kansas.... Farmers feel like the forgotten people. I can
> reach them. And when I tell them I'm pledged to get on the
> Agriculture Committee, it helps offset my big city image.

In terms of a forward look at his governing style, his comments indicate
an intention to develop a new policy interest and, at the same time, not
to be bound in his policy-making efforts by his committee assignments.

He seemed especially cavalier about sacrificing his most appropriate
committee assignment, Judiciary, for Agriculture if necessary. For he
clearly envisioned himself as an influential person on criminal matters.
"Because of my law enforcement background," he said, "southerners
will listen to me more than to some liberal who doesn't know anything
about crime. All senators worry about crime. They will listen to someone
who has prosecuted criminals." Perhaps the ex-prosecutor believed he
would be listened to regardless of his committee base.

Indeed, whenever Specter began speculating about life inside the
Senate, about what he might accomplish there and how he might
accomplish it, he became remarkably uninformed and overly optimistic. In a September session with the editors of the *Patriot-News*, he was
asked if he thought he could bring some national prominence to
Pennsylvania. The state, they said, had not produced its share of
national leaders in the twentieth century. The candidate's answer was
positive, expansive, and naive. "Yes, I think I can be an influential
senator," he began.

> I intend to speak out, to be forceful, to use the media. A senator
> from Pennsylvania enters the Senate with more prestige than a
> senator from a small state. Last night, I went to a party at Jack
> Heinz's house for members of the Republican Trust—contribu-
> tors of $5,000 or more. Senator ——— [from a much smaller

state than Pennsylvania] ... was there, and you could tell by the way people behaved that he just wasn't at the center of things. Dick Schweiker has been a hell of a good senator, but he isn't forceful. He doesn't project.... The Northeast is losing its spokesmen and there's an opportunity for someone. [Jacob] Javits is leaving; that's the biggest loss. [Abraham] Ribicoff is leaving.... [Edmund] Muskie is gone. In Ohio, you have [Howard] Metzenbaum and [John Glenn]—they don't project. Adlai Stevenson is going, but he didn't project. You've got Chuck Percy; but now you're out in the industrial Midwest. It's an exciting opportunity to look forward to.

However much this was a seat-of-the-pants set of judgments, it was diagnostic for his future career.

Specter's statement reflected a continued faith in his prosecutorial style, a belief that industriousness, energy, and aggressiveness would pay off in the Senate as they had in the DA's office. And it indicated his continued belief in the media as the way to "project" oneself forcefully on others. Out of forcefulness and the ability to project would come national stature. These judgments made no allowance for features of the institution within which influence would be sought. Clearly, for example, Specter had much to learn about the degree to which the equality of state representation in the Senate had made that body a place of special power for the small states. And a greater predisposition to reserve judgment on potential colleagues might have helped, too. Altogether, he seemed to be overly optimistic about the spokesmanship he might achieve there, not to mention how quickly it might be achieved. But at the same time, his comments seemed to be an accurate and predictable indicator of his eagerness and of his determination to try. The gap between his ambition and his understanding presaged some problems of adjustment.

If any role model emerged from Specter's assessment of northeastern senators, it was New York Republican Jacob Javits. His affinity for Javits became even clearer to me when, as we were riding around in Philadelphia and discussing the state of the Republican party, he became equally expansive about what he might accomplish within the Senate.

I think it's part of the role of all public officials and especially of a United States senator to worry about their party and to keep it strong.... That's terribly important. I remember once in 1966 when I was having lunch with Jack Javits and he said, "We've got to put together a coalition of bright, moderate Republicans." But he never called. After this election, the balance of power is going to change drastically in this state.... I'm going to be in for six years. There are things I can do. I have energy and I have ideas and I will get attention.... Frankly, I don't think it will take all that much energy. I have a lot of energy and I'll have a lot of help. There are a lot of young Republicans ready to go. . . . Everybody knows I don't have jobs to give out. . . . But I can speak at dinners, go to rallies, support candidates, push the governor to give out jobs. It will take very little by way of rewards to do some good. The payoff for political work, for Republicans, has been so small. People don't really expect much. But everything I can do, I will do.

When candidates are at home campaigning, they seem to develop these sorts of strong, party-building aspirations. But their level of aspiration typically fades once they get elected. Specter's level of aspiration dropped even as he thought out loud about what he might accomplish.

Once again the picture of a person of ambition and independence emerges from his speculations and ruminations about the future prospects of his career. His assessment of the political world around him may not have been particularly astute. When he got to the Senate, he would find that the senator he dismissed as not "at the center of things" was, indeed, "at the center of things" within the institution. But his determination to be very active and to have influence in the world of public service was unflagging.

INTERPRETING THE ELECTION

The change from campaigning to governing does not take place instantaneously. Rather, a period of adjustment intervenes to guide the transition of the newly elected. Either prior to or concurrent with adjustment, however, each winner devises a "constructed explanation" of his or her victory.[44] How the winner thinks and acts during the adjustment period (and beyond) depends in part on how he or she interprets the results of the preceding campaign. Those results may be viewed as having constraining and empowering aspects. Arlen Specter's interpretation had elements of both. The main contours of his electoral interpretation were probably well in place before he actually took his seat as a senator, and they probably got fleshed out as his adjustment period forced further attention to them. But I was able to capture or recapture his thinking only after he reached the Senate and in increments for a year or so beyond that.

Two months into his term, he offered a traditional geographical interpretation of the electoral outcome:

It was the most regional campaign in the history of Pennsylvania. I got the biggest vote in the suburban Philadelphia area that any Republican has ever gotten. I got 51 percent statewide. Normally, in order to get that margin statewide, a Republican has to get 58 percent in suburban Philadelphia. I got 66 percent. But I got clobbered in Pittsburgh. It was a case of one especially popular candidate in the west against an especially popular candidate in the east. [What about the northeast?] I lost Luzerne [Wilkes-Barre] by 4,000 votes and Lackawanna [Scranton] by 10,000. They are heavily Democratic areas. I think the abortion issue hurt me there. It hurt me in Philadelphia, too. But there, people had other things to judge me by—and they did.[45]

He had carried the Democratic city of Philadelphia by 9,000 votes. The broad regional contours had gone as expected, with his suburban vote margin exceeding his expectations and his Philadelphia margin falling below. The corrective action he deemed most urgent was to reverse his 20-point deficit (40 percent to 60 percent) in the west. Accordingly, he soon thereafter commissioned an elaborate voting study of the area, with an eye to improving his performance in 1986. The study eventually became, in May 1982, a forty-page document, "Precinct Targeting: An Election Analysis of Allegheny County, Pennsylvania." He quickly began planning, too, for ways to demonstrate a special concern for the western part of the state.

In the absence of ideological differences, Specter's campaign had emphasized his stylistic—DA stylistic—attributes. So it is not surprising that he interpreted the electoral outcome in those terms, too. Discussing his voting record a year later, on the road in Harrisburg, he said,

That's our job—to vote. My voting record is 99.5 percent. It all ties in with, "He cares, he's energetic, he works hard." That's the issue I beat Flaherty with. It was the only issue between us. I went to all sixty-seven counties, he didn't. There was not any difference between us on other issues. I had a beautiful wife; he had a beautiful wife. I drove a foreign car; he drove a foreign car. I hadn't won anything in a thousand years; he hadn't won anything in a thousand years. We were twins. Nobody cared how we sliced up the issues—except for abortion, but it never became consequential.

Before the election, when Specter had contemplated life as a senator he had expressed strong and concrete intentions concerning representational style. His interpretation of the election—that his victory turned on matters of style—doubtless reinforced his determination to maintain that style in office. And that meant paying visible and vigorous attention to his constituents. Later in the conversation, he said, "It's like being a law student. If you aren't studying, you feel that you should be. I have an agenda. I'm going to Pittsburgh so many times this year, to Erie so many times, to Wilkes-Barre so many times. And I'll be there come hell or high water." Electoral interpretations or no, it was impossible to imagine the hard-working, hard-charging prosecutor acting any other way.

On the importance of the media to his victory, I never heard Specter himself assess it after the election. Perhaps the media factor was so dominant that it was unnecessary to mention it. But Specter's campaign manager did it for him, in our post-mortem.

> You've heard the story before, I know. We campaigned all over the state in the summer and we went down 4 points in the polls. We went to the media and we went up in the polls. We outspent Flaherty in the media and we won. If we hadn't outspent Flaherty in the media we would not have won. It's as simple as that.

Not surprisingly, that was Pete Flaherty's preferred interpretation, too—that he had been outspent.[46] In the view of the Specter camp, it was a necessary but not sufficient explanation, for it begged the question of media content. And Specter, at least, believed that his persona—the prosecutorial persona—portrayed by the campaign contributed significantly to the outcome.

Ten weeks into his term, the new senator produced a final bit of electoral interpretation, one that would help preserve his basic political stance. "I'm going to stick with this President every chance I get," he told a reporter. "But basically, we have different constituencies. I won Philadelphia while he was losing it by 172,000 votes. If it comes to a crunch, I can't be blindly loyal to the White House. The needs of the state come first. I'll be independent." [47] An important crunch came in the context of a vote on the Kemp-Roth tax cut in the summer of 1981. As a candidate, Specter had scrupulously campaigned in favor of a one-year, 10 percent tax cut but no more. And he had expressly opposed the three-year Kemp-Roth proposal. On a vote to postpone the third year of the tax cut, he found himself in opposition to his president and his party. And he was put under considerable pressure to vote to retain it. He did not.

His explanation invoked the "different constituencies" interpretation of his election. "We had quite a to-do," he said.

> [Majority Leader Howard] Baker used coercive psychology in a very subtle way. He called us in and said if you are not going to stick with us, hold up your hand. I was one of four who held up his hand and said I couldn't go along with the team. . . .
>   I didn't campaign for Kemp-Roth. I feel a lot more freedom than a lot of the guys do. I didn't come in on Ronald Reagan's

coattails. Our election patterns were completely different. I carried Philadelphia; he lost Philadelphia. He carried Pittsburgh; I lost Pittsburgh.

In the strong Republican southeastern counties, I ran ahead of Reagan. In Lancaster County—the most conservative county in the United States in 1972—I ran ahead of Reagan. I was very proud of that. Those people knew me from my days as district attorney. It's interesting how that affects your idea of the team. I don't feel I owe Reagan anything.

His interpretation—like his interpretation of his primary victory—was that he had won election on his own. Indeed, he interpreted the results as confirming his assumption, as candidate, that his special strength came from places where his record as DA was well known. In other words, the candidate had produced independently wrought patterns of electoral support, and this fact would justify, if not empower, his continued independence as a senator.

Arlen Specter's interpretations of his electoral victory were largely consistent with his performance and his expectations as a candidate. His post-mortem, therefore, did not call for an outlook or for patterns of behavior very different from those he displayed as a candidate. And since our analysis of the campaign relied heavily on the salient aspects of his precampaign career, we would expect to find the new senator thinking and acting very much as the district attorney, the perennial aspirant, and, now, the victorious candidate had thought and acted. The young prosecutor, in other words, remained very much alive inside the middle-aged senator—hard working, tenacious, media oriented, and, above all, independent. One question, however, remained unanswered: How would this persistent prosecutor adjust to the U.S. Senate?

ADJUSTMENT TO THE SENATE: EARLY STAGES

The adjustment process involves both adjustment *from* and adjustment *to*. And the two aspects are connected. What you must adjust to and how much of an adjustment is required depend partly on what you are adjusting from. Arlen Specter had to adjust from a set of experiences—both occupational and electoral—characterized by individual effort and political independence. In the Senate, he would have to adjust to life in an institution that prescribed a good deal of collective effort in pursuit of legislative goals. Further, in the context of 1981, with the small but historic Republican majority, the partisan pressure for collective effort would be abnormally strong. Precisely because Arlen Specter's prior political experience—as district attorney and as aspiring officeholder—

had tended to develop and reinforce and highlight his individualism, it should be easier to trace his adjustment to the Senate than it might be for others. I make no argument that his adjustment was typical—only an especially attractive example. I shall, then, present one pattern of adjustment and relate that pattern to the development of one senator's career.

For convenience, and somewhat arbitrarily, Senator Specter's adjustment period is divided into two stages. His early adjustment stage lasted to the end of 1981—long enough to include the customary end-of-the-freshman-year appraisals that come from inside and outside the Senate. His later adjustment stage began in October of 1981, when he introduced his career-criminal bill, and ended when that bill was sent to the president for approval in December 1982. The two stages overlap in late 1981. But the point of the division is to treat the time during which he was working to pass his first important piece of legislation separately from his time of first exposure to the institution. In the Introduction, I speculated that adjustment periods normally last about two years, since it takes that long for most newcomers to be able to claim a sustained legislative effort and a substantial legislative accomplishment. Overall, then, Arlen Specter's adjustment period lasted a normal two years—beginning in January of 1981 and ending in December of 1982.

Four months after his election he and I had our first "How's it going?" conversation. His first comment focused partly on the sheer thrill of being, at long last, a U.S. senator and partly on his attempt to figure out how the Senate worked. It was clear that he was, indeed, in a transitional adjustment period. "There are several aspects of it," he began.

> One is the unrealness of it all. It's the "Wow, I made it. Here I am in the Senate. I'm really here." Then there is the mystical part of it. Over on the floor it's hard to know what's going on. Why is it that Jesse Helms delivers a forty-minute speech against the nomination of Cap Weinberger with no one listening? I was the only person in the chamber and I listened. . . . I was presiding over the Senate that day. . . . The first time I presided over the Senate, I did so with great wonderment—not terror exactly, that doesn't make sense—but with a sense of mystery about it all. "How am I going to preside?" I thought. "I don't know the rules . . . " Actually, a little man sits in front of you and whispers in your ear, "Without objection, so ordered." And you say, "Without objection, so ordered." So it runs. But it's mystical.[48]

Clearly, he had a lot of learning to do. He concluded, "So I'm trying to learn all about the process. I'm trying to learn all about how this solar system works, how the entire galaxy works—with the 100 of us revolving around—and how the laws of gravitation work around here."

ADJUSTMENT FROM THE PRE-SENATE CAREER

In many respects, Specter was experiencing a normal set of adjustments. He was, for example, adjusting from an occupational background that was nonlegislative. Many of his early reactions centered on a nonlegislator's reaction to a lessened control over his own schedule and time—together with his continuing attempts to maintain control anyway. "A tremendous number of people want to see me, and I'm seeing too many people," he said. It was the same with his three committee assignments. "I've attended my committee meetings religiously," he said. But, in an article headlined, "Specter Races Hands on Clock," he described the time dimensions of his schedule. "The biggest surprise is the demand to be in multiple places at the same time. There will be a meeting of the Agriculture Subcommittee of Appropriations at the same time that there's a meeting of the Judiciary Committee at the same time Veterans Affairs is meeting, buzzers are ringing and you are supposed to be on the floor." [49] Trying to be in four places at once was a new experience for the former DA. "We're quadrophrenic," he exclaimed, "schizophrenic is not enough." [50] His time allocation problem was more severe than anything this nonlegislator had yet experienced.

So, too, was his information problem. Regardless of occupational background, the overwhelming need for information presents an immediate dilemma for every newcomer. In Specter's case, the problem arose over the president's early proposal for massive reductions in the budget. "I'm very concerned about the budget cuts," he said in March.

> There are some big items in there. Things are moving with exhilarating speed. We have been given materials an inch thick with no idea where the cuts are coming from. [Majority Leader Howard] Baker wants us to move ahead. I checked with [my staff]. . . . We decided to find out what other senators are doing. We found they are not responding. Maybe in general they are, but there are no piece-by-piece analyses available. I caught Baker in the steam room the other day. He's very hard to find; he's so busy. I asked him how I could get some of these programs back on track. He said, "Go see [Budget Chairman] Pete Domenici." I managed to get a half hour of his time this afternoon. Those chairmen are so busy.

A week later, at his first press conference, he prefaced his answer to questions on the budget with a typical newcomer's adjustment-time comment. "I'm swimming. I'm swimming," he said, "I'm trying to keep my head above water."[51]

He was not, of course, helpless in keeping himself afloat. He was building a staff, and he was associating himself with regional sources of information. In both cases, he was following the very lines he had anticipated in his campaign comments. Aside from his Pennsylvania connections, he recruited his largest bloc of staffers (four) from the office of the defeated Jacob Javits—one of his favorite role models. And, following up on his anticipatory focus on regional spokesmanship, he became the Republican co-chair of the bipartisan Senate Northeast-Midwest Coalition. This informal Senate organization, along with a similar House organization, works for fair taxing and spending treatment for a region concerned about being disadvantaged at the hands of the sun belt states.[52] From the ongoing research of this group, he acquired a valuable set of bearings in coping with the budget. It was Sen. John Chafee, the Rhode Island Republican, who had persuaded him to become co-chair of the regional group. And subsequently, it was within the rubric of the Chafee Amendment to restore budget cuts in areas of concern to the coalition that Specter eventually worked out his approach to the budget.[53]

Arlen Specter's natural response to these time-allocation and information-gathering pressures—not surprisingly—was to work hard, very hard. In this respect, his occupational background facilitated his adjustment. In February, a Pennsylvania journalist described him as following "the workaholic discipline he maintained as an attorney, immersing himself in the minutiae of subcommittee hearings, correspondence and managing his staff." He told her, "There's a lot of hard work to do, but I'm used to that." And she noted: "He frequently harks back to his days as DA, when he was able to hold weekly open houses, conduct his litigation and be home for dinner every night at 7."[54] To the degree that DA-style hard work would solve his adjustment problems, there was nothing to worry about. But the reporter's reaction was to wonder whether this performance could be repeated in the Senate. "Whether his religious indulgence in detail will survive the year is questionable," she wrote.

Six months later, a top staffer was still worrying. "He hasn't developed any focus yet, and I'm very concerned about that," he said. "He's trying to do everything. With a state our size, you almost have to do that. But it's his style, too. He once described himself as a swarm of locusts blanketing all subjects. That's the way he's been so far." The observers were suggesting that individual effort, however spectacular and energetic, might not be enough in the new institution.

In some important respects, however, Specter learned that individual effort would help to ease his adjustment problems. He found that his prosecutorial background and style were almost immediately and appropriately transferable to the hearing rooms of Senate committees. And to that degree, at least, the new job required little or no adjustment from or adjustment to.

In our March conversation, he conveyed, the comfort of this occupational fit—even as he was still overwhelmed by the newness of it all. "In the Appropriations Committee hearings, it was a great, thrilling experience to be in Room 318, a giant room, listening to Secretary of the Treasury [Donald] Regan, Budget Director [David] Stockman and Federal Reserve Chairman [Paul] Volcker," he recounted.

> I got my turn to ask questions and I asked a few. The next day, we had four economists. . . . We moved to a smaller room, 1114. It was really fascinating. I got to ask questions then, too. The next day we were going to hear from the GAO, the Bureau of Labor Statistics, and some others. I got to the hearing and nobody was there. . . . The staff asked me if I would be willing to preside. I said, "Of course. I came to the Senate.". . . I ran the hearing. And I asked the three witnesses what they thought the effect of decontrol would be at the pump for the consumer. I didn't say, "What, if any, effect," as a lawyer would do. Not one of those palookas would answer the question. They were afraid to admit to anything. I learned something there. . . . It's been very educational. Of course, it's easy for me because of my training as a lawyer in fact finding.

His description—the emphasis on asking questions, the reference to the lawyer's skills, the adversarial stance toward the witnesses—reflects an obvious warming to a familiar occupational routine.

The persistence of his prosecutorial demeanor was illustrated in one staff member's account of an occasion when Specter had missed a vote on the Senate floor.

> SPECTER: Did you call over to the committee?
> STAFFER: Yes, the clerk said you knew there was a vote on.
> SPECTER: Did you ask him how I knew? Did you ask him if he asked me? Did you ask him what I said to him?
> STAFFER: Arlen, I'm not trained to ask those kinds of questions. He said you knew, so I assumed you knew. When I was a teacher, one of my students came to me and said he couldn't hand in his paper. I asked him why. He said his dog swallowed it. I told him, "All right; try not to let it happen again."
> SPECTER: If I'd heard that story, I'd have gone to find the dog, opened his mouth, put my head in, and looked to see whether the paper was in there.

That attitude would serve him distinctively and well in some aspects of his new job.

On the other hand, the story also indicates that Specter's adjustment would require some recognition that individual effort had its limits. Some of those limits flowed from aspects of the Senate that were inescapably different from his DA experience. The most obvious among these, perhaps, was the reality of "the enterprise"—the necessity for working collaboratively with a large staff in order to cope with both the information and the allocation pressures of the new job. By August Specter was talking knowledgeably about the need for adjustment to staff:

> I didn't anticipate there would be so much delegation. In the district attorney's office I had 160 assistants. I was used to delegating. But ... there was a pretty clear cut distinction between what they did and what I did personally. Here, I have to vote on matters where I have to take brief summaries [prepared by my staff].[55]

It was an apt early description of the enterprise and of the reliance senators typically place on their staff. It was a relationship that would require some adjustment by the former DA.

ADJUSTMENT FROM THE CAMPAIGN

On the matter of adjusting from his election campaign, Specter was experiencing only a modest need to alter course. In terms of the substantive policy concerns he had articulated on the campaign trail, he envisioned little or no change. "It's a continuum," he said in March. "There are a lot of campaign promises to be fulfilled. We have to look after the export of coal, coal regulation, steel, pollution issues, Japanese imports, textiles ... education matters ... Jewish issues. ... I have a full plate of things." Not surprisingly, he added, "My toughest issue is abortion." But, despite the promise of continued controversy, he held to the position he had maintained throughout the campaign.

> I'm convinced I'm on the right side. But the anti-abortion people came to see me. They threatened me. I asked them why they thought their threats would make a difference to me in January, when it didn't make a difference to me in October when I was fighting a life and death election.[56]

Looking back, only one of his campaign positions continued to worry him. "I haven't said anything I can't stand behind," he began.

Of all the issues I got involved in during the campaign, only one troubles me. . . . It's aid to parochial schools. It concerns me because I was on the other side in my mayoralty election. I don't know whether my stand cost me [that election] or not. But this time I thought that because I was so opposed to the Catholics on abortion, it would not be polite or right for me to oppose them on school aid, too. You were there when I had that tough dialogue with those people.

A year and a half later, he was still telling his constituents, "I'm not sure how I'll vote on that issue." [57]

The most pressing substantive matter for all senators in the first seven months of 1981 was the budget. On this subject, the Pennsylvania newcomer had to flesh out some of his campaign ideas and alter others. He had to decide for the first time which budget cuts to fight; and he had to support in the end a three-year tax cut he had previously opposed. In working out his positions, however, he displayed a whiff of independence that was perfectly predictable on the basis of both his election campaign and his electoral interpretation.

When the president invited the freshman Republicans to the White House for a breakfast pep talk on his budget, Howard Baker (R-Tenn.) appointed Specter spokesman for the group. The distinction reaped for him a widely reprinted picture of him sitting next to the president. And it provided him with an opportunity to convey to the president the worries of his regional colleagues—worries about mass transit, urban development, and education, which eventually got rolled into the Chafee Amendment. Emerging from the meeting, Specter assumed a posture of loyalty-cum-independence:

I do not think the president would say he has to have it all his own way. He is not asking us to be rubber stamps. He is concerned about those who would chip it away and would therefore destroy its integrity. . . . Probably all of us in our own ways will want to see some modification made, but within the overall context of respecting the president's bottom line.[58]

Watching this performance, one Pennsylvania scorekeeper predicted, "In the mob of Reagan rookies, most of them Sun Belt rightwingers, Arlen Specter will be easy to watch. He's the one on the tightrope." [59] As applied to someone who had long been a Republican in a Democratic city and a moderate in a conservative party, it was hardly a startling prophecy.

When he turned from the policy promises to the representational promises of his campaign, the newcomer became enthusiastic and upbeat. "All the rest of the stuff is easy—working for Pennsylvania. The rest comes easy because it's what I'm used to, working hard and working long hours for twelve million clients." And he was full of the kinds of plans he had promised on the campaign trail. "I plan to keep in close touch with Pennsylvania," he said.

> The first week in February, we held an open house in Philly. We did that when I was DA and it was very successful. We plan to do that in the major cities. I promised the blacks a day in Pittsburgh and that's set for April. I'm going to open my district office in Wilkes-Barre and we'll go there for that. . . . We're committed to a tour of the northern tier this summer. That should be fun. We did it during the campaign. I think first impressions are important. I think the first year is important in maintaining your contacts—more important than renewing them in your fifth year. It's also instructive as to what people feel needs to be done and should be done.

It was a theme he had emphasized throughout his campaign—and his career. The tireless, ubiquitous prosecutor and candidate intended to be a tireless, ubiquitous U.S. senator.

The one representational commitment Specter had not fulfilled was his promise to seek membership on the Agriculture Committee. But he believed that circumstances had prevented him from doing so. At the point in the assignment process when he had to choose between Appropriations and Agriculture, he chose Appropriations. It was the top committee assignment of his predecessor and one he had not expected to be able to get. As he explained in March:

> Agriculture was available along with Appropriations on the first round. I took Appropriations. I had never promised to make Agriculture my first choice. On the second round, Agriculture was gone. So I took Judiciary. Appropriations is a rare opportunity for a freshman. I'm on the Agriculture Appropriations Subcommittee; and that's better, people say, than the Agriculture Committee itself. The farmers understand that and they are happy. . . . They knew I hadn't promised to make Agriculture my first choice. If Agriculture had been available on the second round and I had taken Judiciary over Agriculture, *then* I would have had some answering to do to some unhappy people.[60]

Reaction at home was mild and short-lived. Between them, the pair of committee assignments—Appropriations and Judiciary—would enable Specter to watch over the allocation of federal money to Pennsylvania and to further his most deeply held policy interests.

In their earliest stages of adjustment, Senate newcomers sort, by trial and error, the elements of their prior experience that are usable in the new environment from those that are not. Occupational background and campaign experience, we have suggested, are two elements that get tested. In Arlen Specter's case, his background as district attorney continued to hang heavily over his early days in the Senate, just as it had over his election campaign—as the measure of many things. We have noted, for example, continuing applications of individual effort, of prosecutorial skills, and of political independence in his early adjustment to the new job. On the other hand, we have found clues that this well-developed work style might not, by itself, produce a satisfactory adjustment to the Senate.

Arlen Specter understood the essentially trial-and-error nature of the early stage and recognized that additions to or subtractions from his established ways of doing things might be helpful to him. In that spirit, he deliberately acted from the very beginning of his tenure to reverse, or hold in abeyance, one essential element of his familiar political style—his devotion to the media. He decided that his adjustment to the Senate would be aided if he kept a low profile inside the Senate by shunning the media outside the Senate. It was a decision, in effect, to temper one of his most time honored, individualistic modes of behavior. It was a decision that ran counter to his naive rush to judgment on various senators when he was campaigning. It reflected a more realistic view of how favorable reputations are built inside the institution. It demonstrated, in short, an unexpected early sensitivity to the communitarian mores of the institution.

When I asked him, in March, what his goals were for the first couple of years, he answered:

> I have goals, but they don't have any particular structure to them. Earning a good reputation in the Senate comes first, as it does in anything you do as a person, as a citizen, as a lawyer. A good reputation is the pervasive goal. And that you get by being punctual, by being meticulously courteous and, it goes without saying, being honest and having integrity.

"Senatorial courtesy," he observed, "runs deep in the institution, very deep.... There is a great deal of protocol around here." His intention was to follow protocol, to do what was expected of him, to fit in and not to stick out. For an energetic, media-oriented politician, it called for a noteworthy change of styles. "I'm keeping quiet, staying in the background," he said. " I got into a fight with my staff because I have refused to issue press releases. I believe you ought to learn before you speak."

"I believe," said his press secretary, "that some of the old hands told him the first impression you make here is very important and that you want to get known as a worker and not as a publicity hound." For Arlen

Specter, the "worker" part of this prescription was second nature; but the "publicity hound" part was another matter. Still, he was following the prescription. "Nobody has said anything to me about staying in the background," claimed the senator,

> but it's not different from any other place where people are expected to learn before they start to speak up. I've had a lot of experience in the DA's office, living right in the middle of the media. I know what that's like. But I can see the value in a contrary position. I'm not interested in the media. It's a long term, and the issue of my reelection will turn on a lot of considerations other than the media attention I get right now.

His first press release was not issued until late March.[61] His March press conference on the budget, mentioned earlier, was the only one he held in the first nine months of service. This deferential, low-key, communitarian governing style dominated his early adjustment stage.

Accordingly, the low profile theme dominated media scorekeeping for a year or more. In an early article headlined "Specter Keeps a Low Profile," a Pennsylvania reporter described his senatorial style as "less the politician and more the methodical lawyer." Specter, reported the writer, has "studiously avoided publicity, eschewing headlines and early legislative initiatives." She concluded: "He will keep a low profile, at least until he can master senatorial protocol." It was a behavior pattern that the journalists accepted at face value—partly because they contrasted it with the superheated public relations activity of the other Pennsylvania senator.[62]

Still, they found it somewhat puzzling. In all of his prior political experience, Specter had sought media attention—free or paid for—and had relied heavily upon it for his success. In an article one month later, headlined "Low-Profile Specter Issues First Press Release," the same author and a colleague wrote that "reporters covering the keystone delegation are slightly bemused by Specter's reserved approach."[63] Traveling with Specter, a state capital columnist complained that "the state, with its myriad problems needs more than [Specter's] bland, playing-it-safe style representation in Washington."[64] Among the convinced, the bemused, and the complainers, there was agreement on the low-visibility style of the Pennsylvania newcomer.

A widely distributed Associated Press profile, in September, continued the low-profile description of Specter's Washington style. The article was given various headlines where it appeared:

Specter Likes to Get All of the Facts
Senator Specter Wants Facts Before Speaking

"Freshman" Specter Starting Out Cautiously
Specter Prides Himself on Being Thorough
Specter Earns Respect of Fellow Senators
Specter Approach Methodical
Specter Gets Facts Before Making Points as Freshman in U.S.
    Senate.

In the body of the article, the Senate newcomer makes an explicit contrast with his pre-Senate behavior. "My approach to the Senate has been a lot different than that of District Attorney of Philadelphia," he said. "Back then, I was always confronting people in the opposite party and generating news. I don't think a Senator should be too ambitious to generate press. I don't think it is very well received by colleagues and much of the public." [65] This was the campaigner who could hardly contain his desire to "speak out, be forceful, use the media" and "project." Now he was invoking perhaps the oldest and most basic of all the distinctions of the communitarian Senate—the preference for the work horse over the show horse.

As late as March of 1982, a Philadelphia journalist was saying privately, "The story line on Arlen back home is that he went to Washington to be a senator and disappeared." In his own profile, entitled "Cautiously, a Junior Senator Seeks His Stride in Office," this reporter adhered to the media consensus regarding stylistic change.

> In contrast to his high visibility days as district attorney when his behavior often seemed to define the words "ambitious" and "abrasive," he has taken a quiet low-key approach to the Senate, learning the job, keeping his mouth shut and evincing the respect for the institution that the institution demands. . . .
> His plan is to give up short run headlines for long term results.

He quoted the Senator to the effect that "we are still maintaining an attitude of being very circumspect . . . [as] the best way to be an effective senator," and to the effect that it is best to "be cautious, be cautious, take it slow and easy. It's a six year term and what's really important is what you can get accomplished." Inside reputation, Specter was saying, would lead to inside accomplishment. The reporter concluded, "For now, he appears to be more concerned with what his 99 Senate peers think of him than with what his 11,866,728 constituents in Pennsylvania do." [66] In terms of his expressed goals—gaining a favorable reputation, being an effective senator, and getting something accomplished—his posture exemplified institution-mindedness. At the same time his posture ran contrary to expectations generated by his behavior as DA and during the campaign. This disjunction rendered some aspects of his early adjustment anything but normal.

BECOMING A LEGISLATOR

By all accounts, the one noteworthy accomplishment of Specter's first year was his successful effort to save the Justice Department's Office of Juvenile Justice and Delinquency Prevention (OJJDP) from the extinction planned for it in the president's budget.[67] Here, his position as chairman of the Subcommittee on Juvenile Justice of the Judiciary Committee was the crucial ingredient. It was the major agency within his subcommittee's jurisdiction. Its grants to states went mostly for programs to separate juveniles from hardened criminals in detention facilities; and its budget was slated to be folded into a large block grant within the Health and Human Services Department (HHS).

By saving and protecting part of its budget, Specter saved the agency. As we shall see later, by saving the agency, he saved his subcommittee's jurisdiction; and by saving his subcommittee's jurisdiction, he saved his subcommittee—which he needed to launch his major legislative effort. The budgetary stakes were tiny: $70 million. But every fight, in 1981, to protect a categorical program against the administration's strong thrust toward block grants involved substantial political and philosophical stakes. And the test of Specter's ability to protect his subcommittee's jurisdiction placed his reputation on the table as well.

In his one-man hearings, Specter subjected administration witnesses to a hard interrogation and produced a large number of local officials to express their need for the program. From the former he wrung the admission that the OJJDP's job remained undone, that the program might be swallowed up within a huge HHS block grant, and that, as a private matter, they had mixed feelings about the proposal they were defending.[68] From the local witnesses, he drew forth praise for the program's success, declarations of continued need, and prophecies of catastrophe if the administration's plan were carried out.

Among the latter group, one witness held special interest for Specter. He was the director of public safety programs for the State of South Carolina, representing both his own state and the National Governors Association. His support for OJJDP could, in turn, be expected to be of unique interest to the chairman of the Judiciary Committee, Strom Thurmond of South Carolina. Speaking from his twin positions, the witness argued that if the OJJDP programs were placed in competition within a block grant, they would be severely disadvantaged, if not destroyed. "Welfare programs or . . . school programs," he argued, "are the ones which get first priority when it comes to getting money, as opposed to the youth who are in the justice system. . . . Why is it? I guess it is because there are stronger constituent groups for them." Specter added a suggestive concluding comment to the testimony:

> When you talk about constituency pressure, you are talking about one of the fundamentals of representative democracy. I have observed a tremendous response from people across the country to the elimination of this program. If that voice is heard in other senatorial ears ... it might have a substantial effect.[69]

Having invited the South Carolina witness to lobby his senator, full committee chairman Thurmond, the subcommittee chairman turned to some inside lobbying of his own.

Available public accounts indicate that Specter's success was the result of his individual lobbying efforts. One account emphasized his fight against the Office of Management and Budget—that he "figured out who, how and where to fight ... deciphered the procedural mechanics, did his political homework."[70] The other account emphasized his success in "persuading the obstinate Strom Thurmond." According to a Democratic Committee aide, "He was tough but tactful with Thurmond, and he wasn't afraid to work with the Democrats." As for lessons learned, said the senator, "I've found it's absolutely necessary to make the painstaking effort to talk to people.... I don't want to ... just make a momentary splash for publicity."[71]

Confirmation of Specter's individual effort—DA-style effort— is discernible in the reaction of a subcommittee aide to Specter's accomplishment.

> He won that fight against all odds. And he got noticed at the Justice Department. They found out that this guy won't give up, that he's a fighter; that he's a real bulldog. You think you can tire him out? Never. He'll never quit. And if you do him in, he'll getcha. He got a Justice Department guy over here and creamed him. "How dare you wipe out the entire program over which my subcommittee has jurisdiction.... " How Justice will react to their defeat I don't know.... I'm hoping they'll say, "this guy is a real tiger. We're going to have to deal with him for ten years. We'd rather have him with us than against us...." Arlen got a lot of credibility out of that. People know that if he goes after something, he'll be tough to beat.... As a lawyer he always took on the toughest case. I thought he was taking on Justice because it was the hardest case he could find. He loves a challenge.

It was a small-scale example of what one strongly motivated, talented person could accomplish in the Senate. It was one of those small successes that accumulate into Washington reputations. And if his staff was correct, the essence of that reputation would be his persistence—the same refusal to quit that had characterized his pre-Senate political career.

His rescue of one tiny program captured no media attention. But, from a wholly different field of endeavor, evidence of his persistence did make its way into the local papers. A nearly inviolate aspect of Specter's daily regimen—on the campaign trail as well as off—was his game of squash. And he had brought that passion with him to the Senate. "Squash is a wonderful way to make friendships," he said. "When you play squash, you talk all the way over and all the way back. I even organized a round robin . . . and that led to more friendships." He played squash like he protected his subcommittee's jurisdiction. "[Senator Robert] Packwood hit me on the [racquet] arm so hard this morning that I could hardly lift it," he said one day in January, "but I won." A week later the *Washington Post* described a match in which Senator John Warner wanted to quit after four games and in which Specter "wheedled" him to play the customary five games. When Warner insisted on a bobtailed fifth game, Specter "put him away in the tie breaker." [72]

Later in his term, Specter reached the *Post*'s "Style" section when Packwood hit him again with his racquet—this time fracturing Specter's cheekbone, sending him to Walter Reed Hospital for repairs and to the sidelines for seven weeks. [73] The next day, Specter said:

> I'll be back at it again as soon as I can. I've played a great deal of squash. I haven't been hurt too badly. I once had seven stitches over my nose. I've run into the wall several times. Once I had a lot of X-rays to make sure I didn't have a concussion. And during my gubernatorial primary I fractured my ribs playing. I couldn't get my name in the paper for my campaign, but my broken ribs were all over the papers.

In recreational as well as occupational pursuits he exhibited the same persistence.

BUILDING A REPUTATION

On the customary freshman year report cards, Arlen Specter received a lot less attention—good or bad—than some of his fifteen classmates. Indeed, he was the only freshman excluded altogether from the *Washington Post*'s scorecard. [74] When the Pennsylvanian's press secretary called the reporter to ask, "Why didn't you include Arlen Specter?" the reply was, "I couldn't place him." The *Wall Street Journal*, however, placed him and gave him good grades. In a paragraph praising the two class leaders, the reporter concluded that two others, Arlen Specter and another freshman, "have been less visible but are thought of as able and conscientious by many of their leaders." [75] The Associated Press gave him top grades, adding his name to the top two senators mentioned by the *Journal*: "Three of the new Republicans . . . have won high praise for learning quickly how to get things done in the Senate . . . [and because they] are quietly effective and are really quick studies." [76]

A Pennsylvania journalist reported to a statewide audience that Specter had "earned respect from colleagues for his legislative acumen." [77] Finally, in recapitulating the scorekeeping of others, a Philadelphia reporter passed along to his readers the summary judgment that "compared to the other members of the class of 1980, his marks are high indeed." He added, "The words most often used to describe his performance are 'thoughtful,' 'solid' and 'cautious.' " [78] It was a favorable report card. And, since local scorekeepers take their cues from Washington participants, the Pennsylvania newcomer would seem to have achieved the early, favorable reputation he most wanted.

The media's consensus, although positive in tone, was vague. But that, too, was Specter's preference. "There have been several articles written about the low profile I've maintained here," he reflected at year's end.

> That was by deliberate design. As a body, the Senate hates aggressiveness. People here say there are two things you can legitimately talk about—matters affecting your home state and issues on which you are an expert. When I was district attorney, I adopted an aggressive, high-level profile. I thought that as a Republican officeholder in a Democratic city, I had to do that. As one of a hundred senators, I'm in a different situation . . . I haven't wanted a high profile here. You've seen the *Wall Street Journal* article on the freshman class, blasting away. Or the *Washington Post* article, blasting away at so many of them. People are just waiting for you to make some mistake.

Unlike many of his classmates, he had made neither mistakes nor headlines. However imprecise it might be, therefore, his report card was all pluses and no minuses.

One partial exception, perhaps, was Congressional Quarterly's set of presidential support scores, printed locally, showing him to be "the sixth most rebellious Republican senator" in terms of his support for the president.[79] In the minds of people highly supportive of the president, this element of the score card would contain minuses as well as pluses. But Specter had worked sensitively to cushion the impact and the visibility of his independence. "I'll tell you what I've done quite a bit of," he explained in January:

voting but not speaking. The guys at the White House get livid when you speak out against them. If you vote against them and they win, they forget it. If they lose, and it's not by one vote, they don't care. They don't want you to make yourself the focus. They understand why you have to vote; but they don't understand if you become a cheerleader. Again, it's that feeling against self-aggrandizement.

But a Gannett News Service scorecard had nonetheless singled him out as "one freshman who did break ranks" on a particular committee vote. And it recorded Specter's observation that, on that occasion, "[I] stuck out like a sore thumb." [80]

The political independence that had characterized his career had kept him—and would continue to keep him—despite his best efforts, "easy to watch . . . the one on the tightrope." This position was a fact of life for him. But it did not overshadow or alter the favorable judgments on his reputation or his adjustment. Not, at least, during the first half of his adjustment period. It remains to follow the Pennsylvania freshman into the second half.

NOTES

1. Philip Lentz, "A Seat in the U.S. Senate: It's What He Really Wants," *Philadelphia Bulletin,* October 27, 1980.
2. Stuart Brown, *Pittsburgh Post-Gazette,* November 6, 1980.
3. See, for example, Michael Levin, "The Washington Senator Who Doesn't Always Play Ball," *Pennsylvania Gazette,* October 1984.
4. A reporter traveling with him called him "very much the attorney at law: urbane and intense, pompous and verbose, ambitious and smart." Lentz, "A Seat in the U.S. Senate."
5. Lucille Craft, "Specter Keeps a Low Profile," *Scranton Times,* February 10, 1981.
6. "For the U.S. Senate: Arlen Specter," *Philadelphia Inquirer,* October 13, 1980.
7. Kit Konolige, "Specter Seeks Image: Old Problem Bedevils Senate Hopeful," *Philadelphia News,* October 24, 1980.
8. Lentz, "A Seat in the U.S. Senate."
9. Ibid.
10. "Excerpts from the Specter-Flaherty Debate," *Pittsburgh Post-Gazette,* October 28, 1980.
11. Lentz, "A Seat in the U.S. Senate"; Levin, "The Washington Senator."
12. See also *Congressional Record,* February 23, 1982, S970.
13. See also Chuck Stone, "Specter Needed in U.S. Senate," *Philadelphia Daily News,* October 24, 1980.
14. Paul Taylor, "A Difference in Techniques," *Philadelphia Inquirer,* September 9, 1980; see also Russell Cooke, "Specter Favored by Polls, Persists with 'Urgency,'" *Philadelphia Inquirer,* October 30, 1980.

15. Associated Press, "Specter Simply Can't Get Enough Debates," *Record* (Coatsville), October 16, 1980.
16. Ron Goldwyn, "Flaherty, Specter Debate in Phila., but Longstreth Emerges as the Star," *Philadelphia Bulletin*, September 16, 1980.
17. Janet Novack, "Dispelling Image of a Loser: 'I Won More . . . Than I Lost," *Philadelphia Bulletin*, October 28, 1980; Taylor, "A Difference in Techniques."
18. Ashley Halsey III, "Now, a Loser . . .," *Philadelphia Inquirer*, October 28, 1980; Stuart Ditzen, "Pa. Senate Campaign: It's Silent Running," *Philadelphia Bulletin*, ca. September 1, 1980; Konolige, "Specter Seeks Image"; Novack, "Dispelling Image of a Loser."
19. Doug Harbrecht, "Specter Hopes Philly Edge Puts Him over the Top," *Pittsburgh Press*, October 26, 1980; Kit Konolige, "Tight Senate Race Hinges on Western Pa.," *Philadelphia Daily News*, October 28, 1980; Carmen Brutto, "Specter Aiming for High Visibility," *Patriot-News* (Harrisburg), October 28, 1980; Carmen Brutto, "The 'All New' Pete Flaherty," *Patriot-News* (Harrisburg), October 26, 1980; Richard Fontana, "The New Pete," *Pittsburgh Post-Gazette*, October 22, 1980; Hedrick Smith, "Pennsylvania Results Give Kennedy 9,800 Vote Edge," *New York Times*, April 24, 1980.
20. Ditzen, "Pa. Senate Campaign."
21. Taylor, "A Difference in Techniques."
22. Kit Konolige, " 'Fighter' vs. a 'Producer,' " *Philadelphia Daily News*, September 25, 1980.
23. Halsey, "Now, a Loser."
24. "For U.S. Senate," *Philadelphia Daily News*, October 7, 1980.
25. Scott Macleod, "Specter, Flaherty Race Middle-of-Road Track," *Pittsburgh Post-Gazette*, October 27, 1980.
26. "Excerpts from the Specter-Flaherty Debate."
27. *Philadelphia Bulletin*, October 26, 1980.
28. *Philadelphia Daily News*, October 7, 1980.
29. *Philadelphia Inquirer*, October 13, 1980.
30. *Sunday Patriot-News* (Harrisburg), October 26, 1980.
31. Ditzen, "Pa. Senate Campaign."
32. "Our Poll Shows Pete Ahead for Senate," *Philadelphia Daily News*, October 26, 1980.
33. Philip Contz in *Philadelphia Bulletin*, October 26, 1980.
34. Ditzen, "Pa. Senate Campaign"; Ron Goldwyn, *Philadelphia Bulletin*, September 16, 1980.
35. Macleod, "Specter, Flaherty Race."
36. Lentz, "A Seat in the U.S. Senate."
37. Konolige, "Specter Seeks Image."
38. Associated Press, "Specter Simply Can't Get Enough Debates."
39. Doug Harbrecht, "Specter Outspends Flaherty 6 to 1 in Senate Bid," *Pittsburgh Press*, October 21, 1980.
40. Part of the story of his relationship with the party is told in Ron Javers, "Is There Life After Reagan?" *Philadelphia Magazine*, September 1980.
41. Russell Cooke, "Heinz Shares His Clout with Specter," *Philadelphia Inquirer*, October 31, 1980.
42. Lentz, "A Seat in the U.S. Senate."
43. Flaherty used a similar picture against him later in the campaign. See Charles Fancher, "Specter, Flaherty Trade Accusations," *Philadelphia Inquirer*, October 28, 1980.

44. The term is that of Marjorie Hershey, *Running for Office* (New York: Random House, 1984).
45. For a similar post-mortem, see Kit Konolige, "Pete Loss an Eerie Deja Vu," *Philadelphia Daily News*, November 6, 1980.
46. Frank Matthews, "Pete Flaherty: Still a Bit 'Smitten' By Politics," *Pittsburgh Post-Gazette*, August 25, 1981.
47. Sandy Grady, "Like a Gypsy, Specter Eludes Reagan's Long Arm," *Philadelphia Bulletin*, March 19, 1981.
48. Five months later, he was still talking about this experience. Chris Collins, "Specter Races Hands on Clock," *Valley News Dispatch* (Tarentum), August 15, 1981.
49. Ibid.
50. Chris Collins, "Senate Class of '81," *Evening Press* (Binghamton, N.Y.), August 16, 1981.
51. "Specter Struggling with Reagan's Budget Cuts," *Valley Independent* (Monessen), March 25, 1981.
52. See Michael McManus, "Northeast Anger at Budget Cuts: Too Little Too Late?" *Rochester Democrat and Chronicle* (N.Y.), March 27, 1981.
53. Gail Gregg, "Senate Orders $36.9 Billion in Budget Cuts," *Congressional Quarterly Weekly Report*, April 4, 1981, 602-603, 612.
54. Lucille Craft, "Specter Keeps Low Profile."
55. Collins, "Specter Races Hands on Clock."
56. See Craft, "Specter Keeps Low Profile."
57. *Oil City Derrick*, August 11, 1982.
58. Associated Press, "Senators Criticize Budget Opponents," *Somerset Daily American*, March 19, 1981.
59. Grady, "Like a Gypsy, Specter Eludes Reagan's Long Arm."
60. See Terry Dalton, "Specter Ducks Agricultural Panel," *Centre Daily Times*, December 6, 1980; Chriss Swaney, *Greensburg Tribune-Review*, January 11, 1980.
61. Craft, "Specter Keeps Low Profile."
62. Ibid.
63. Mick Rood and Lucille Craft, "Low-Profile Specter Issues First Press Release," *Sunday Patriot-News* (Harrisburg), March 23, 1981.
64. Harry Stoffer, "Specter's Playing it Too Safe," *Bucks County Courier Times*, August 23, 1981.
65. Associated Press, "Specter Likes to Get All of the Facts," *Titusville Herald*, September 30, 1981.
66. Larry Eichel, "Cautiously, a Junior Senator Seeks His Stride," *Philadelphia Inquirer*, April 6, 1982.
67. See Senate Committee on the Budget, Transcript of Procedures, "Senate Concurrent Resolution 9, Revising the Second Budget Resolution for FY 1981 to Include Reconciliation," March 17, 1981, 135-157; Eichel, "Cautiously, A Junior Senator Seeks His Stride"; Associated Press, "Specter Likes to Get All of the Facts."
68. Senate Hearings, Subcommittee on Juvenile Justice of the Committee on the Judiciary, "Abolition of the Office of Juvenile Justice and Delinquency Prevention," Washington, D.C., April 1, 1981.
69. Ibid., 61-63.
70. Eichel, "Cautiously, a Junior Senator Seeks His Stride."
71. Associated Press, "Specter Likes to Get All of the Facts."

72. "Weekend," *Washington Post*, February 5, 1982, 26.
73. Chuck Conconi, "Personalities," *Washington Post*, March 10, 1983, March 24, 1983.
74. Bill Peterson, "The Senate's Thunder on the Right Was a Contralto Overture," *Washington Post*, January 17, 1982.
75. Albert Hunt, "'Popsicle Brigade': New GOP Senators Impress Their Seniors, Though Not Favorably," *Wall Street Journal*, December 14, 1981.
76. Mike Shanahan (AP), "Popsicle Brigade: Most Freshman Senators out of Rhythm," in *Daily Herald* (Monongahela), December 18, 1981.
77. Gene Grabowski (AP), "Congressmen Leave Abscam Behind Them," *Lock Haven Express*, December 1981.
78. Eichel, "Cautiously, a Junior Senator Seeks His Stride."
79. Larry Eichel, "Survey: Heinz, Specter Among Most Rebellious in GOP," *Philadelphia Inquirer*, January 9, 1982.
80. Collins, "Senate Class of '81." See also "Specter Saves Tobacco Supports," *Erie Times*, October 6, 1981.

2

Learning to Govern

AGENDA SETTING AND ENTREPRENEURSHIP IN CONGRESS

The business of Congress is lawmaking. Senators spend much of their time turning ideas into bills and bills into laws. It is a large part of what we mean by governing. Political scientists have recognized the centrality of this activity in their studies of agenda setting and of bill passing. Most of these studies portray individuals seeking to achieve policy goals amid a complexity of players, opportunities, and constraints. Generalized studies tend to emphasize the complexity; particularized studies tend to emphasize the individuals. The perspectives differ, but the activities and the constraints described are very much the same.

In that sense, there is nothing new about one more study of a legislator's effort to achieve a policy goal. Perhaps, however, a career-oriented perspective will add another layer of understanding to a common body of knowledge. It may teach us that part of policy making is *learning* how to make policy and that what a policy maker needs to learn depends a lot on what he or she knew before starting.

Agenda setting is the process by which decision makers came to pay attention to, and work on, some problems and not others. Studies by Jack Walker and John Kingdon describe that process in and around the legislature.[1] Walker helps us to differentiate among types of legislative agendas, or types of problems to which legislators pay attention. There is, he says, a "recurring agenda," which consists of subjects to which legislators must pay regular attention—such as annual budgets, authorizations, and appropriations. There is also an "occasional agenda," consisting of problems to which legislators must pay intermittent attention—such as reauthorization of expiring legislation and problems that arise out of domestic and international events.[2]

In Walker's typology, there is a third, "discretionary" agenda, which consists of problems to which legislators choose to pay attention, but with which they are not required to deal.[3] Items on the first two agendas take precedence over, and tend to squeeze out, items on the third. The discretionary agenda is, therefore, the most difficult for outside groups or inside legislators to crack. A legislator whose policy goal does not fall within the bounds of the first two agenda types and whose policy cannot, somehow, be displaced upon them, faces an initial, built-in agenda-setting difficulty. Arlen Specter's first major governing effort began in the context of that institutional difficulty.

A second perspective on Specter's agenda-setting activity is presented in Kingdon's treatment of policy entrepreneurs.[4] Agenda setting, he tells us, is a process in which problems get recognized, solutions get proposed, and political conditions get created without much relation to one another until some temporary set of circumstances brings the elements together in such a way as to focus the attention of decision makers. It is a complex process filled with uncertainties. The people who commit resources to the business of specifying problems, advocating solutions, and seizing favorable opportunities and who, therefore, act to bring problems, policies, and politics into alignment, are "policy entrepreneurs." They are found in and out of government.

Entrepreneurs within the legislature, Kingdon says, are positioned to operate in more "streams" of the agenda-setting process than are outside entrepreneurs. Legislators can "soften up" other decision makers' receptivity to a problem, can specify the alternatives for dealing with that problem, can recombine problem and solution in exchange for the support of other decision makers, and can take advantage of favorable opportunities to push other ideas from their personal agendas to the decision agendas of their colleagues. Policy entrepreneurs typically display expertise and political skill, says Kingdon; and "probably most important, successful entrepreneurs are *persistent*" (italics added).[5] Arlen Specter's efforts on his career-criminal bill can be seen as an instructive example of the activity—and the education—of a policy entrepreneur.

Ideas about good public policy, says Kingdon, do not originate in any one place or belong to any one individual. Consequently, I will not try to establish a genealogy for the career-criminal concept or for the idea of legislation tied to that concept. Since forty-one states already had laws dealing with habitual criminals, the origins of the concept lie outside of Congress.[6]

As closely as a legislative idea can be attached to a single legislator, however, the career-criminal bill introduced on October 1, 1981, by

Arlen Specter belongs to him. It grew out of his own experience as the district attorney of Philadelphia. Its provisions were crafted by his own staff. No outside agency or group contributed to it. No constituency—in Pennsylvania or elsewhere—pressed for it. Viewed in terms of its congressional origins, it was one man's home-grown, pet policy initiative. The resources he expended on it were spent in the pursuit of two intertwining goals—good public policy and a reputation for accomplishment among his colleagues. The saga of the bill is the story of the individual effort of a person who believed above all—and was experienced above all—in the exercise of individual effort.

GETTING STARTED: FALL 1981

The problem attacked by the bill was longstanding and well documented. Violent street crime was on the increase, and a sizable proportion of such crimes were being committed by repeat offenders. The premise of Specter's bill was equally straightforward: if these "career criminals" could be kept behind bars, violent street crime would be significantly reduced.[7] The new senator from Pennsylvania was steeped in this problem. What he had felt most acutely as district attorney of Philadelphia was the frequent failure of state criminal justice systems to mete out swift and severe sentences to habitual offenders. His bill was the direct result of that experience.

When he first began to broach his ideas publicly, during his August tour of the state, he commented often along these lines: "There has been an unwillingness of state judges to impose necessary sentencing. The state courts do not tackle the crime problem."[8] Similarly, he stated, "I believe state law enforcement across this country has failed to deal adequately with the problem of career criminals." Reporting on Specter's speech to a group of Pennsylvanians concerned about juvenile offenders, one reporter wrote: "Recalling his days as a Philadelphia district attorney, Specter said he was constantly frustrated by state judges' refusal to impose lengthy prison terms against convicts who had committed '20 armed robberies or 30 burglaries.' "[9] It was this special angle of vision, born of indelible experience, that led directly to the solution proposed by the Specter enterprise. A top staffer said: "It was his idea. It was not the case of some smart young staff person coming up with something. He came to us and said, 'How can we make state judges give stiffer sentences?' "

The novel solution devised by the senator and staff was to target a certain group of "career criminals," to make a particular offense of theirs into a federal crime, and to mandate a sentence of life imprisonment upon conviction for that crime. The targeted offenders were to be people who committed a robbery or a burglary with a gun after already having been convicted of at least two robberies or burglaries (with or without a gun).[10] "Robberies and burglaries are the most vicious forms of street crime in this country," he told the Senate, "[and] a high percentage of robberies and burglaries are committed by a limited number of repeat offenders." [11] A rule of thumb often used by Specter was that 10 percent of the criminal population committed about 70 percent of such crimes.

The novelty of the idea lay in the proposal to put the federal criminal justice system to work in a class of cases heretofore thought to be under the exclusive jurisdiction of local law enforcement officials—to create a federal crime where none had previously existed. Indeed, the idea behind the stipulation of *armed* robbery or burglary was to make the connection with interstate commerce thought necessary to create a federal jurisdiction. "[Specter] knew just what he wanted," said one aide. "The staff's problem was how to do it in a manner that was constitutional." They attached an intent of Congress section at the end of the bill, providing that "the United States should ordinarily defer to state prosecution," but allowing for exceptions "in consultation with appropriate state or local officials." Whether the final draft was constitutionally—not to mention politically—acceptable would become the subject of later concern and debate.

A week before he introduced his bill, Specter summarized his thinking in a letter of September 25 to President Reagan, which read, in part:

> From my experience as District Attorney of Philadelphia, I have found that a relatively small number of career criminals commit a large percentage of the robberies and burglaries, constituting the most troublesome aspect of street crime in the United States.
>
> These career criminals are able to commit numerous crimes because of lengthy delays in state court trial systems and lenient sentences by state court judges . . . .
>
> My proposal is to establish a new federal crime, punishable by life imprisonment, for anyone who commits a robbery or burglary with the use of a gun after having been previously convicted of two or more robberies or burglaries. Robbery and burglary have been selected because these are the most prevalent street crimes and are most easily identifiable . . . as having interstate implications.
>
> The nexus for federal jurisdiction would be present with the use of a gun and by the congressional conclusion . . . that such career criminals operate in interstate commerce.[12]

In anticipation of a presidential speech to the International Chiefs of Police on September 28, Specter had already floated his ideas with the associate attorney general in the Justice Department and with the White House counsel. And in his letter to the president, he wrote, "I have discussed this proposal with Justice Department personnel and have gotten a favorable preliminary response." At the most, he was hoping for a similar signal from the president; at the least he was pursuing the entrepreneurial task of softening up the administration for the reception of a new idea. His ideas received no mention in the president's speech, which was limited to support for the recommendations of the Attorney General's Task Force on Violent Crime. "He was vibrant," said Specter of the president, "[but he proposed] no major initiatives to deal with violent crime in a new way." When he introduced his bill, therefore, the senator was temporarily disappointed but nonetheless hopeful of administration support.

What the senator from Pennsylvania formally introduced on October 1 was a package of three bills: his career-criminal bill plus two others (see Appendix). One of the others provided for the incarceration of career criminals in federal prisons. It sought to encourage state judges to hand out stiff sentences in the face of objections concerning the overcrowding of state prisons by making space available in the federal prison system. It was mentioned in Specter's letter to the president. And Specter said that he had gotten "a favorable preliminary response" on this idea, too. It was carried along for a while as a useful adjunct to the main bill.

The third bill provided for the teaching of "a marketable job skill and basic literacy" to long-term prisoners before their release from prison. It languished almost from the beginning. Specter's press release, for example, mentioned only the first two bills.[13] By the end of the month, he was saying privately, "The only part of the package that has any chance of passing is the first part."

On October 1, 1981, in a small room on the first floor of the Capitol, Senator Arlen Specter held the second press conference of his term, for the purpose of announcing the introduction of his Career Criminal Life Sentence Act of 1981. Its forty-four lines represented his first major legislative initiative. And he had high hopes. "I think this is going to pass," he told reporters beforehand. "This may be the most significant criminal law in years."[14] Fourteen reporters—three from television, six from newspapers, and five from radio—came to the press conference to question and to kibitz ("I guess Arlen's taking this one seriously." "If I were the bottom person on Judiciary, I'd take it seriously."), and to ask questions of the bill's author.

In his opening comments, the senator reminded them, "I've been in the area of crime fighting for a long time," and spoke of his DA experience. He outlined his argument that "the American people are sick and tired of street crime" and that "the states are incapable of making significant efforts" to reduce it. He introduced the bill as the natural extension of a career-long substantive interest and an expression of his expertise in criminal matters. And reporters saw it exactly that way. In anticipation of the press conference, one Pennsylvania account began: "Arlen Specter appears to be pursuing a reputation as the Senate's specialist in criminal justice legislation."[15]

Journalists' questions anticipated some of the reservations Specter would encounter later. He answered all of them with vigor and confidence. One questioner observed that the bill's expanded federal role ran totally counter to the mood of the Reagan administration and asked what response he had encountered thus far on Capitol Hill. Specter replied:

> There has been a favorable response. . . . There's great concern about crime. Next to economic recovery, it's the second issue. It may be more important than national defense, inflation and interest rates. . . . There's really been no major initiative to deal with violent crime in a new way. . . . The state courts customarily give a slap on the wrist. . . . There's a lot more toughness in the federal courts. . . . It's time for the federal government to get into the problem of street crime, robberies, and burglaries.

He was asked how much it would cost to build the prisons necessary to house the career criminals. He answered that "if the plan has a realistic likelihood of dealing with crime, people are ready to pay for it." He estimated that as many as two thousand career criminals might be sentenced to life imprisonment in the first year alone. And he added, as he had written to the president, that the Justice Department and the Bureau of Prisons had given "favorable preliminary responses" to questions about prosecutorial capacity and prison capacity.

Specter was asked what impact the bill would have on the states. "The states are given deference," he answered. "There is protective language to give the states authority in the first instance." And, by waiting until two or more crimes have been committed under state law, he pointed out, "We give the state two bites of the apple ... two chances" before the federal government steps in. He emphasized, again, his difficulty as DA in getting state judges to hand down tough sentences.

Once more, he was asked what kind of support he expected in Congress. "There's a lot of support," he repeated. "[Strom] Thurmond and [Edward M.] Kennedy were prime sponsors of the mandatory sentencing bill. I've been talking to a number of colleagues, and I've found a good deal of support." He answered several other questions—some about the criminal justice situation in Pennsylvania—and concluded the press conference with this observation: "It is a problem that has been too big for the states. The states have not been able to deal with the problem." In view of Specter's adjustment-period decision to keep a low media profile, the press conference send-off represented a noteworthy departure.

The reaction of Specter's public relations staffers centered on their inability to attract national attention despite a determined effort to do so. The day before the press conference, for example, they had scheduled a background session for the media. Specter's press secretary was disappointed.

> Only one person came—a guy from the *Baltimore Sun*. The staff had hoped there would be more. We had contacted *Newsweek*, the *New York Times*, the *Washington Post*, and so forth. But nobody seemed to be interested. Some of them said they would come, but they didn't. It was pretty thin.... We are trying to crack the national media, but so far we haven't been successful.

As for the press conference itself, aides had a mixed reaction—statewide success, national failure. As one staffer said:

> We didn't get any of the major TV networks. But we had a couple of TV stations and some less known national radio networks. We had a good representation of the Pennsylvania press. And we've gotten a good play in the state.... We plastered the Senate TV, radio, press, and periodical galleries with announcements of the press conference. And we personally called all the major TV networks and national newspapers. All we got out of that was the *Toledo Blade*.... We haven't been able to get any national publicity yet. With a freshman senator you have to be awfully lucky to get any publicity. There has to be almost nothing [else] going on.

Media reaction to the press conference indicated clearly that Specter's career-criminal bill would not be an attention-getting legislative venture. Whatever he accomplished would have to be done without benefit of national publicity.

The reactions of the Specter staff, however, suggested a changing attitude toward national publicity on their part—namely, a blossoming desire to get some. Reflecting on the press conference, one top staffer said, "We started slow, but we've gained momentum since summer. We haven't made the national networks yet. Arlen wanted to start slowly, almost casually—as if he didn't care about press. He wants the media. But he doesn't want to appear to be a hustler."

At lunch, after the press conference, Specter gave similar signals of a changing direction. He told a visitor from home:

> It was a conscious decision on our part to keep quiet during our early period here. I didn't say a word in public for two months. I've just started to speak out now. . . . Today's press conference was the second time I've called the press for a formal conference. I'll be saying more. I want to talk about immigration. . . .

Quite apart from its effect on his legislation, the press conference could be seen as a minor milestone in the evolution of Specter's senatorial career.

By the very act of introducing his bill, now numbered S 1688, in the Senate, Specter had secured a bit of official attention for it. Acting as both expert and entrepreneur, he had placed a problem on the Senate's agenda. At one level, he had also engaged in the specification and consideration of alternative solutions to the problem. As he told the press conference, "This is the end of a very long thought process." And as a staffer put it, "We must have written seventeen drafts." It had been a prototypical entrepreneurial performance. Still, the bulk of his work lay ahead.

The next step was to move the subject from his personal agenda to what Kingdon calls the decision agenda of the institution.[16] That meant getting the official attention, first, of the relevant subcommittee, second, of the full Judiciary Committee, and, finally, of the full Senate. The difficulty of the task was magnified by two conditions: the idea behind the bill would be a novel one for each committee, and the type of agenda involved in each case would be the discretionary one.

As we follow Arlen Specter through these further agenda-setting activities, we shall need to think of him as acting in concert with his staff—that is, as part of a larger collective enterprise.[17] For our purposes, the Specter enterprise consisted mainly of the group of four lawyers who worked with him on the bill. The point man within this group was legislative staffer Paul Michel (pronounced "Mishel"), who had worked with Specter for seven years in the DA's office and who had since risen to the post of deputy associate attorney general ("the number five spot") in the Justice Department. In Specter's view, "Paul knows more about criminal procedure than anyone in the United States." Michel explained his decision to join the staff.

> I'm here because I thought the best way to launch Arlen's Senate career was in the area of crime. It was the one area where his expertise was unequaled. In the Republican party,

there isn't anyone in the same ballpark. I also thought it was the area in which he had great credibility. I still believe that it's the best place for Arlen to make his mark—the only place in the hot sun.

Working with Michel on the bill were Bruce Cohen and Jonathan Levin, two promising young associates Specter had plucked from his own law firm. Cohen became chief counsel for Specter's Subcommittee on Juvenile Justice, the top staff position there. Levin had been the issues coordinator in the election campaign, and he worked with Michel on the personal staff. These three early staffers were joined in the summer by Kevin Mills, a young Washington lawyer who became Cohen's assistant on Specter's subcommittee. The four were known to the senator as "the justice gang." They were totally without experience on Capitol Hill; S 1688 became, in Michel's words, "our maiden voyage."

More interestingly, the group was described by Michel as a miniature law firm. A couple of days before the press conference, he explained that

> Specter's experience is complemented by mine and by the others. We are not dependent on outsiders. We can be creative and do better work than, say, the CRS [Congressional Research Service]. We consult them, but we don't need them. In that way our office is different from other Senate offices. And we hope to be able to make a difference. Crime is the one area where other senators will take Arlen's word. He knows more about robbers and burglars than anyone in the United States.

What makes this comment interesting is the strong sense of expertise-based self-sufficiency and independence it expresses. It strikes a posture for the miniature law firm that mirrors the posture struck throughout his career by its senior partner. And it hints that the Specter-plus-staff enterprise might place the same heavy reliance on *its* effort that the new senator had long placed on *his*. The staffers placed overwhelming stock in the authority of Specter's expertise. These characteristics increase our interest in questions about the viability or the consequences of extreme individualism as a governing style.

In the days before and after the press conference, his top aides painted a picture of their boss's individualistic style after nearly a year in the Senate. "I think the part Arlen likes best is the hearings," one said.

> He likes to cut through [the prepared questions] and ask questions that reveal something. That's the part of the process he is most comfortable with, the part that fits with his experience as prosecutor. . . . What he doesn't like is the clubby side of the Senate. Oh, it's "hi, Arlen" in the hall, and there's a

lot of this handshaking and shoulder hugging. But he's not a hail-fellow-well-met type. . . . He's very direct. If he likes you, he likes you. If he doesn't, he doesn't. He won't get into a room with someone he doesn't like. That's fine. But it's not the clubby, "old boy" style that predominates. . . . I'm worried about that because I think you have to be that kind of person to succeed around here.

The comment calls to mind Specter's assertion on the campaign trail that "I don't join clubs. I don't belong to any clubs." Reflecting on Specter's difficulty with his party at home, the aide said, "He carries a lot of political scars. He's always looking over his shoulder. His problem is he just doesn't know who he can trust." With regard to this go-it-alone preference, a second staffer noted that "he likes to fly alone. He won't even let the staff fly with him. That's just the way he is. He's a loner. . . . He's very self-sufficient. He doesn't like people to wait on him. And he relishes his privacy."

In their view, the individualistic prosecutor had not yet adjusted to the communitarian aspects of the Senate. He remained, at bottom, a loner. The individualistic Senate holds plenty of rewards for such people—many of whom choose to make little by way of further adjustment. But would a loner's strategy be sufficient to pass the career-criminal bill? Alternatively, would the senator from Pennsylvania come to value and to learn the collegial arts of consultation, negotiation, and coalition building?

Specter's comments in the October press conference indicate that he had engaged in some entrepreneurial softening up of colleagues and administration officials. When a policy entrepreneur is also a legislator, softening up and coalition building proceed simultaneously. Both are directed at securing support from colleagues and other decision makers. At the time of his press conference, however, Specter had made very little headway—less even than he thought he had. His declaration of "a favorable response" and "a lot of support" from Congress and of "favorable preliminary responses" from the executive branch were expressions of hope rather than evidence of support. And this pattern would become a familiar one.

A week earlier, he had sent several pages of his thoughts to members of the Judiciary Committee with a closing sentence that said: "I am preparing such legislation and seek your support and cosponsorship." [18] But, admitted a staffer, "we didn't lobby anyone for support." Thus, the team did not secure any co-sponsors until March of 1982, five months after Specter introduced the bill. On the first of October he had not yet secured the support of any of his subcommittee members—nor of any of the full committee members.

His conclusion, that the committee chairman, Strom Thurmond (R-S.C.), and key committee and subcommittee Democrat Ted Kennedy (Mass.) were supportive was an unwarranted inference drawn from their known views that might be considered tough on crime. And he had obtained no indication from Thurmond concerning the subcommittee to which his bill would be referred. He had not arranged for anyone to introduce a companion bill in the House. Nor had he consulted with the chairman of the relevant House Subcommittee on Crime, who declared his opposition to the bill the moment it was introduced.[19] It would be a long time, too, before the "favorable preliminary responses" he reported from the executive branch could be turned into anything resembling a commitment.

Specter's preliminary consultations and negotiations had been largely pro forma. His softening up activity had left him, therefore, without any solid support and without any notion of what a supportive coalition might look like. For that matter, he did not know what might come next. As one staffer put it the day after the press conference, "We are dead in the water. We have launched a sailboat, but there is no wind." The evidence strongly suggests that Specter's deepest political instinct was not to secure legislative allies but to go it alone—that the independent Philadelphia prosecutor was alive and well inside the Senate sponsor of S 1688.

The obvious first step was to get a hearing for the bill. "Hearings are the only bridge from where we are now to wherever we want to go," said a staffer. "Unless we get hearings, we will have died on first base." In the absence of any other negotiated arrangement—and there had been none—Specter's entire package would be referred routinely and properly to the Subcommittee on Criminal Law. In the immediate aftermath of the press conference, Specter's staff accepted that scenario. The prospect was met with pessimism, for the Subcommittee on Criminal Law was found to have a discretionary agenda already "choked up" with "a big backlog" of legislative proposals. Besides, the enterprise believed that "neither [Subcommittee Chairman Charles 'Mac'] Mathias nor his staff have the slightest interest in crime." An aide said later, "Our fear was that our bills would be sent to that subcommittee and die there."

Under Judiciary Committee rules, Chairman Thurmond had a good deal of discretion in the matter of referral to subcommittees. But, early on, that avenue of escape seemed unlikely. As Michel saw it:

We're trapped. The jurisdiction of Arlen's subcommittee, taking the broadest view, is extremely narrow. So the bill won't go there. And that's the only subcommittee over which he has any control. So he has no tool, no forum, no platform for his ideas.

You can't do anything without a platform.... There's a wall in front of him, and there's no crack in that wall he can move through.

For the next two weeks, the staff worked to find "the wind," "the bridge," "the platform," "the crack" it needed to start the career-criminal bill on its way.

They succeeded. The tactic that worked was an appeal to Chairman Thurmond for a joint referral of Specter's package to the Subcommittee on Criminal Law and to his own Subcommittee on Juvenile Justice. The explanation, as volunteered by one staff negotiator, was that

> we got lucky—well, not just lucky. Arlen had put his two bills together—one of them defining the career criminal and the other providing that career criminals held by the states would be put in federal prisons. Taken together, then, the two bills gave assistance to the states, and "assistance to the states" lies at the heart of our subcommittee jurisdiction, even though it is entitled "juvenile jurisdiction." So we could argue to Thurmond's legal counsel for a joint referral. Also, Mathias' subcommittee is already stacked up with bills that aren't moving.... And some of those bills belong to Thurmond. So he was willing to go for joint referral. So there were two reasons: Thurmond was pissed off at the Criminal Law Subcommittee, and we had enough of a jurisdictional hook to make our case. Besides, Thurmond likes Specter.

"Specter was very happy," said one aide. "He said it was the best news he'd had all year. His pet bill will be in the subcommittee he controls."

There is no evidence that Specter spoke to Thurmond on the matter. But Specter did believe that he had been a good committee member. "I have made it a point to get to every committee meeting on time," he had said earlier. "In fact, Strom Thurmond has complimented me several times: 'If everyone on the committee were as punctual as Senator Specter, we could get these hearings started.'" In that sense, his early adjustment strategy may have paid off. And there was the contribution of Thurmond's longstanding differences with Maryland Republican Mathias.[20] In any case, Thurmond's decision gave Specter the initial traction he needed.

But Thurmond's decision gave no grant of autonomy to Specter's subcommittee—whose activities still remained subject to the chairman's control. And Thurmond's staff quickly reminded the Specter enterprise of that fact. "We had to raise hell," said one staffer, "about the use of rooms and about scheduling in order to get ourselves a hearing." Not long afterward, two Specter staffers mused about their relationship to Chairman Thurmond.

> STAFFER A: I think his staff is terrified of Thurmond.
>
> STAFFER B: He really runs that committee.
>
> STAFFER A: I know, that's what scares me.
>
> STAFFER B: Arlen has been reading history, about what senators wore and how they acted. He thinks Thurmond is a throwback.
>
> STAFFER A: It's different. Under Eastland, [former committee chairman James Eastland, Democrat of Mississippi] there were no subcommittees. He decided what happened. Thurmond has subcommittees. But he tries to control the subcommittees by using hearing dates and witness expenses and things like that—all negative things.
>
> STAFFER B: Everything in the committee goes through him. And he treats subcommittees differently.
>
> STAFFER A: I know. What bothers me is that we're on the wrong end of the scale. We're on the shortest leash of all.

Despite the chairman's favorable decision, therefore, the underlying relationship between the Specter enterprise and the chairman seemed a good deal more problematic than supportive.

WINNING ADMINISTRATION SUPPORT: WINTER 1981-1982

To the observer of the Senate at work in the early 1980s, nothing seemed more important to the governing goals of individual senators than the preferences and attitudes of the Reagan administration. Above all else, Republican senators needed the support or the acquiescence of the Republican administration if their ideas were to have any chance of becoming law. Ideological constraints, budgetary constraints, and partisan ties conspired to elevate the administration's views to an unusually strong position, against which no contrary legislative preferences could stand. And this was doubly true for new items, such as the career-criminal bill, for which a place was being sought on the Senate's discretionary agenda. The operating premise of the Specter enterprise became, as one staffer put it: "Until we get the administration's approval, there isn't much sense in lining up other support."

In their thinking about the substance of their October hearing, Specter's staff focused mainly on the posture of the administration. They wanted to follow the practice of inviting an executive branch official to be their lead witness—the higher up and the more favorable, the better. "We're trying to get to the attorney general," said one.

If he comes, it doesn't matter who else comes. We'll get good national press coverage. But he probably won't come. The chief of the Criminal Division of the Justice Department will come. We're trying to get the administration to come out in favor of our bills, but we're afraid they are going to be noncommittal. They haven't taken the time to study them yet.

At this point, the lawyers were upset at the administration's "weak, hesitant, and slow" attitude toward crime legislation. They remained disappointed that only the specific recommendations of the attorney general's task force—"ideas they have been stuck on for years"—seemed to be under consideration. A top staffer complained:

There's no one to talk to. It's like playing tennis, hitting the ball and having nothing come back. When we talk with them, they make generally favorable noises. But they don't decide anything or criticize anything. We sent our proposal to the Justice Department six weeks ago and not one word has come back. The attorney general doesn't know as much about crime as my wife, and cares less.

On October 26, the chief of the Criminal Division, Assistant Attorney General Lowell Jensen—a former district attorney with an interest in repeat offenders[21]—did come to the opening hearing. The attorney general did not, and for good reason.

The words and the circumstances of Jensen's testimony revealed that what Specter had optimistically called "favorable preliminary responses" at his press conference had not yet hardened into support. Jensen's prepared testimony, stating flatly that "we support the enactment of this legislation," had been suddenly *disapproved* in the higher reaches of the administration.[22] Jensen had been sent to the subcommittee to be encouraging in general but nonsupportive in particular. The essence of Jensen's oral testimony was that

the Department of Justice supports your aim to deal more effectively with career criminals; however, time has not allowed the Office of Management and Budget to analyze all of the implications of this alteration of federal jurisdiction. . . . As a general matter, the administration opposes expansion of federal jurisdiction. This area, however, is one where an exception may be made to that rule. Also a thorough analysis of the budgetary impact of this bill has not been completed. . . . As a result of those considerations . . . I am not in a position to offer direct support of the bill from the Department.[23]

Administration doubts apparently centered on matters of budget and federal jurisdiction. Jensen's testimony cast a long shadow over the remainder of the hearing.

He was followed to the witness table by law enforcement officials from New York City and Detroit, who stressed the need for career-criminal legislation. Their testimony was eased and fortified by the collegial atmosphere prevailing among professionals with the same career backgrounds, as the following exchange demonstrates.

> *Specter:* Our next witness is going to be the honorable William Cahalan who, like Lowell Jensen and Arlen Specter, has spent much of his adult life as a prosecuting attorney. I have known Bill Cahalan for the better part of two decades . . . as prosecuting attorney of Wayne County, Michigan. . . . [W]elcome to these hearings. It is a delight to see you again.
>
> *Cahalan:* It's good to see you here. It's good to have a voice in the Senate.
>
> *Specter:* A voice which you have helped influence through a number of seminars, meetings and other contacts over the course of many years.[24]

The two local officials were followed, in turn, by four scholars, each of whom had worked to identify and predict criminal careers. From them, Specter won a consensus that he was "heading in the right direction" in his career-criminal conceptualization. He concluded with the observation that "we are trying to fast-track this thing."[25] Specter's total immersion in the issue area was made amply clear in his close and friendly questioning of the witnesses. "I know an awful lot about this subject," he said afterward. "But I learned some things today. I learned from the experts that we're on the right track."

At lunch afterward, discussions between the senator and his four staffers centered on whether to devote the next two assigned subcommittee hearing dates to S 1688 or to something else.

> SENATOR: We've got a little momentum this morning. We've got to keep it up.
>
> STAFFER: If we don't keep it up, no one else will. *(They decide to devote one hearing to S 1688, and they discuss possible witnesses.)*
>
> SENATOR: We've got to have some people who will talk about the costs. If that's what's bothering Meese's office, we'll have to address it; maybe some people who can talk about the prisons or the use of alternative facilities.
>
> STAFFER: We may have to admit it will cost money because it's right.
>
> SENATOR: I want a memo on the whole problem of costs. I think that's where we've got to go from here.
>
> STAFFER: But we still should have [Manhattan District Attorney Robert] Morgenthau in to talk about the need. We've got to keep

the heat on concerning the need for the bill.
SENATOR: I agree.

Walking back to his office, Specter returned to the problem of the administration—especially top White House domestic policy adviser Edwin Meese, reported to be among the doubters:

We're trying to light a fire under the administration. They haven't thought it through. They aren't moving. I don't think it's correct to say they are doing it deliberately. I just don't think they have focused on it. Meese is shuffling so many papers back and forth. This bill is not high on his list of priorities. I understand that. We have to make them think about it.... We'll have more facts to lay before the administration when the time comes. We'll be better able to address Meese's concerns. Maybe we'll go to the president.

The entrepreneur had begun to contemplate even greater momentum on an even faster track.

If, as the first hearing had revealed, some people in the administration were not yet convinced, the question in Specter's mind had quickly become whether a second hearing would be sufficient to "light a fire" under them. To put it more positively, the question was whether there was some quicker, more certain way to bring about administration support. To someone with a strong belief in individual effort, the obvious answer was to try some personal diplomacy. To someone who was already committed to an executive-branch-first strategy of coalition building, the obvious locus was the upper reaches of the administration. To an aggressive prosecutor, the obvious target was the president.

Knowing as much as he did about the subject and believing as much as he did in the bill, Specter was supremely confident of his ability to persuade others. And his preferred method of persuasion was a direct, one-on-one encounter. He was, therefore, following both habit and preference when he decided to postpone a second subcommittee hearing and ask, instead, for a private meeting with the president. It was his first such request as a senator. That fact was a measure of the significance he attached to his legislation.

The meeting between Senator Specter, accompanied by staffer Paul Michel, and President Reagan took place on November 13. Accompanying the president were Attorney General William French Smith, Counsellor to the President Edwin Meese, Legal Counsel to the President Fred Fielding, and White House Congressional Liaison Chief Max Friedersdorf. A week later, Specter exclaimed: "I had a terrific meeting with Reagan. Ask Paul Michel for the details. I had a great meeting; Reagan's for it. I think we can get it passed—if we can solve the prisons problem." He believed he had achieved the breakthrough he needed. He issued an instant press release with the heading, "Specter Says President Reagan Supports His Career Criminal Bill." In it, the Senator wrote, "I am greatly heartened by the President's support of this legislation. His encouragement will make it possible for us to get this law enacted." [26]

By Michel's account, the meeting lasted about thirty minutes. "Specter talked for about ten minutes, without interruption, explaining the ideas behind the bill and what it would do." Then, "the attorney general agreed that it was a good idea, that it followed up the recommendations of his Task Force on Violent Crime and that it would have a practical, not just a symbolic, impact." But then Smith expressed two reservations. First, he said that he had heard there was overcrowding in the prisons. Fielding agreed with him. Specter said, "I have heard there is not." A discussion ensued. Smith's second reservation was that "OMB would object to the cost of the bill." But, concluded Michel, "It was pretty clear to me that the attorney general was in favor of it. . . . Then Meese spoke up forcefully and said he liked the bill, that he was quite favorably inclined." (Specter and Michel had met with Meese the day before to explain their case.) "Meese has been mostly critical of the bill. Now he is strongly supportive of it." Then, continued Michel, "the president made comments indicating that he was quite favorably inclined." After a somewhat "repetitious discussion," Meese weighed in again, saying, "This bill more than anything else would give us something concrete to carry out the work of the Task Force on Violent Crime—to implement our whole approach . . . This bill will actually prevent crime."

After Meese's comment, the president concluded matters. As Michel interpreted the president's comments,

> The essence of it was, "I'd like to do it." He said to Meese and to Smith, "Can't you go back and double check on the matter of room in the federal prisons?" He also seemed to say, "Can't you convince OMB that it won't break the bank?" The implication was that if OMB doesn't protest violently, that the president will probably endorse it.

The staffer's interpretation of the president's posture was far more cautious than that of the senator. It would not be the last time that Arlen Specter's estimation of his support would test the bounds of optimism.

Michel's caution came with good reason, for he had been left with the follow-up work on the matters of prison capacity and program cost. This work took him down the hierarchy from the White House summit and into the maw of the hydra-headed administration—into places where the president's writ, however strongly asserted, became attenuated and subject to the diverse perspectives of his subordinates. The OMB was concerned about costs. The Domestic Policy Council wanted to be consulted. The Justice Department was worried about prison space. And all of them, as Michel saw it, would be considering "the subtlest issue, [of] whether the bill was in the spirit of Reaganism, since it increased federal government involvement." Because he knew the Justice Department in a way that his boss did not, Michel was especially cautious about assuming their acquiescence. "There is a group inside the Justice Department—the career guys, not the political appointees—who say it's not the proper field for the federal government to get involved with little robbers and burglars." He worried that they might go to "war" through "back channels" and force the attorney general to "start backsliding."

A month of fact finding and negotiation ensued. It was highlighted by two events. The first was a four-page letter from Specter to Attorney General William French Smith on November 24 in which the senator scaled back his idea to a pilot program—one involving five hundred career criminals a year rather than the two thousand he had assumed until then:

> The President seemed to favor initially implementing the bill on only a pilot program basis.... If the pilot program is accorded the priority it warrants, all issues of space and cost can be resolved satisfactorily.... I hope that you will agree with my view that initiating the pilot program of prosecutions under the bill is entirely feasible.[27]

The second event occurred a couple of weeks after the letter. On the basis of favorable signs from both Justice and OMB, a second subcommittee hearing was scheduled for December 10, at which Assistant Attorney General Lowell Jensen was expected to deliver the endorsement he had canceled in November. Again Jensen had prepared a "strongly supportive" statement from the Justice Department. But again, on the day before the hearing, his testimony was blocked by others in the administration. This time, the objection came out of the blue—from the director of the Domestic Policy Council in the White House, Martin Anderson, who "had not been involved before.... [He] expressed objections based on the idea that state jurisdiction was being invaded by the federal government and the overcrowding of the prisons."

Despite the "fire" lit by the meeting with the president, a declaration of administration support seemed as far away as ever. Afterward, a member of the enterprise summed up.

> Our toughest task is still to convince the administration that they've got a big problem, one they haven't done beans about.

All they have done so far is mouth off. People are getting impatient and a little bitter about crime control. Our bill is the most hard hitting, cost-free approach there is. You can have all the task forces and all the dream bills you want, but they aren't going anywhere. Our bill will really accomplish something. But we have to convince the administration of that.

That is where Arlen Specter's top-down coalition-building endeavor rested at year's end.

Four months of softening up and soliciting support from administration officials had revealed something important about the policy content of the career-criminal bill. Not only was it competing for space on a crowded discretionary agenda; it was a new and different kind of issue—one that did not fit easily into established categories or precommitted positions. It was not easy to get people to focus on it, and it was not easy to sell. Each administration official had to be educated before he would take a position, but an educated official by no means meant a committed official.

The ongoing task of education was often frustrating for the Specter enterprise. "I'm trying to educate them by giving them the documents to read," explained a staffer. "The trouble is, you don't know whether they ever read them—thoroughly or even the first two pages." Few officials seemed to have an incentive to work at it. "You've got to come to it with a completely fresh mind," said another staffer. "It's not like other bills you're used to seeing. It's subtle. The first reaction of most people is to be against it. But if you walk it through with them, they usually think it's a good idea." Because it was Specter's strategy to win administration support first and to win it from the top down, a huge proportion of the education of senior officials had to be done by the senator himself—one by one. It had always been expected by his staffers that he would have to carry the day. But the newness of the issue helped to underscore the need for a strong individual effort.

Beyond the novelty of Specter's particular approach to the career-criminal problem, there exists a characteristic of the larger policy area that also encouraged his entrepreneurship. Violent street crime is a highly dispersed activity, a trait that discourages the organization of public support for fighting crime. In the words of one staffer:

Crime is a million little incidents, not a few big ones. It's not like foreign affairs. Crime is chronic, a million incidents spread out over . . . a zillion street corners. The victims are atomized; the perpetrators are atomized. The problem only gets the president's attention at the rhetorical level, not at a functional level. It's everybody's problem and nobody's problem.

There is no broad, organized constituency for anticrime legislation. For example, "The NAM [National Association of Manufacturers] and the Chamber of Commerce ought to be lobbying against crime. . . . They lose $50-80 billion due to excess crime, crime for profit. But it's not their issue." Groups with an interest in the problem have no incentive to organize. As a result, said one staffer, "there is no momentum coming down the stream to force the president's attention."

The picture is that of a policy area with a narrow "throat," one in which only a very few "experts" will have an incentive to organize and will be able to exercise inordinate control over legislative solutions. As the Specter group saw it, one expert group with both the incentive to organize and the ability to operate in the narrow throat was the National District Attorneys Association (NDAA). "While they claim to represent the public," said an aide, "they only represent themselves. In November the group had endorsed S 1688 "in principle" but had "urged" Specter to "revise the Bill to provide that referral of cases for prosecution in the federal courts shall be by *mutual consent* of the local prosecutor and the United States Attorney." [28] And in their testimony before the sub-committee on December 10 they had reinforced their "guarded opinion" about S 1688. [29]

In mid-December, a staff member emphasized both the nature of the issue and the importance of the senator's individual effort. Jensen's testimony was withdrawn, he explained, because

> Martin Anderson was taken aback by the newness of the idea. He came to the problem fresh and without any background in it. So Specter is writing him a letter about it now. Stockman's Deputy at OMB was worried about the prisons. So we have talked with him. . . . Our problem is at the OMB, White House level. We have to educate a wholly new group now. I've been meeting with some of them and Specter has met with some of them. A lot of paper is being passed to them. We think they will come along when they understand the bill.

In late January, Specter looked back on the last months of educational effort. "You know about our meeting of November thirteenth with the president, where he said at the end, 'Let's go with it; I'll leave it to you to work it out,'" he began.

> The attorney general said he was for it; Ed Meese was for it. And they told me to work it out with OMB. I had a long battle with Ed Harper, the number two man behind Stockman there. They don't want to spend one extra nickel. He kept asking me, "What will it cost in 1985?" And I kept saying that I didn't know what it would cost in 1985, but that prosecutors

can exercise discretion and prosecutions can be controlled. I said that they should go with it now, that it will be a showcase for the administration in a very important area. We had a long wrangle and at 6:30 [on December 9] he said OK and signed off on it.

I thought everything was set and then I got a call from the Justice Department saying that they could not testify in favor because it had been held up at the White House. I said the president, the attorney general, and Ed Meese had agreed to it and I didn't understand how there could be any problem. But I traced it in the White House to Martin Anderson, the domestic policy adviser. He said it was the first he heard of it and that he had not had a chance to study it. Yesterday I had a meeting with the Justice Department and with Anderson's subordinate.... I think we're back on track as a result of that meeting.... I think Anderson will support it now. And I think OMB is still agreed.

The meeting at the Justice Department to which Specter referred helped precipitate some changes in the bill. Both the Justice Department and the Domestic Policy Council wanted an elaboration of the federal-local jurisdictional relationship in order to ensure a *federal* role. As we noted earlier, the NDAA, too, wanted an elaboration, but in order to ensure a *local* role. In an effort to accommodate the sensitivities of these several groups, Specter's staff members added two pages of intentions and procedural guidelines, giving local prosecutors the major role but leaving a last-ditch capacity in the hands of the federal authorities.

"Isn't it fascinating," Specter said one day, rolling his eyes skyward, "these meetings with the bureaucrats may be more important than the meeting of November thirteenth with the president, the attorney general, Ed Meese, and Max Friedersdorf." He was learning something about the scope and the byways of his coalition-building task. Commitments did not come easily. Even summitry was not enough.

Shortly thereafter, the revised draft of the bill went to all parties, with the implicit message, as one aide put it: "This is it. Say yes." The bill was now renamed The Armed Career Criminal Act of 1982. It now prescribed a mandatory prison sentence of from fifteen years to life, with no parole. Michel said:

Once the White House and Justice sign off on this draft, our impression is that we've got a deal from top to bottom. The next step will be for a high Justice Department official, probably Jensen, to come before the committee and announce the administration's support—in emphatic terms, we hope.

Specter was optimistic. "We're going to get it. We'll get it," he exclaimed.

> If we get it through it will be really big—a really big piece of legislation. It's not just what it will do for Arlen Specter. It will revolutionize criminal prosecutions in this country. State judges will impose heavier sentences, and if defense lawyers complain, the judge can threaten to send the case to federal court. Once they get to federal court, they'll have to face one judge. There won't be any more dancing around.

His pursuit of S 1688 was still driven by the twin goals of good public policy and a good reputation in the Senate.

On March 18, Lowell Jensen came to Specter's subcommittee to announce, at last, "I am pleased to advise you that the Department of Justice supports S 1688 in its form now." [30] As a public performance, it was an anticlimax after two false alarms. Specter acknowledged these words with a barely perceptible nod. And in his press release, he simply dusted off his premature comment of four months earlier. "I am greatly heartened by the Reagan administration's support for this legislation. I believe it greatly enhances our chances of getting it enacted into law."

Yet it was a major victory. Privately, Specter expressed a heady optimism.

> I thought it went very well today. We got Lowell Jensen and the administration to approve it. That was a great step forward. Now we can go ahead and talk to the guys about it. [Jeremiah] Denton's for it; [Orrin] Hatch is for it; Mathias is for it; I'm softening up [Alan] Simpson. I've given the order to have the markup soon. And I've talked to Baker. He says he'll move it out. I think we're going to get it passed. I think [House Subcommittee Chairman] Bill Hughes will go along. We could have a nice bill signing ceremony—say, in October. That wouldn't hurt a bit, would it?

Arlen Specter's upbeat assertions of support had never been predictive of his political success, nor were they now.

As it turned out, his bill would not even be taken up by the Judiciary Committee until the last week in September. A bill-signing ceremony was much further away than that. His optimism about the outcome, however, was characteristic. And it was a distinctive variety of optimism—born of his confidence that by his individual effort, he could generate the support and do whatever else was necessary to bring about the desired outcome.

Thus, the more reliable predictor of his success would be his own persistence. And nothing less could explain his success so far in winning administration support. If anyone was paying any attention to S 1688, it was because Arlen Specter made them do so. Everyone he encountered in the executive branch had had to be persuaded. And no one he encountered had yet expressed enthusiasm for the bill to match his own. He and his staff had had to push the bill up to and over every administration hurdle—supplying expertise, direction, intensity, and determination.

John Kingdon has called persistence the most important entrepreneurial skill in the business of moving ideas onto agendas. The Pennsylvania senator can surely serve as Exhibit A in support of that generalization. Sheer persistence had always been his stylistic trademark—as district attorney, as candidate, as senator, and even, we have noted, as an amateur athlete. Now, as his comments of March 18 indicate, he would have to take that quality into the legislative arena—to the Senate Judiciary Committee and to its counterpart in the House.

WINNING SUBCOMMITTEE SUPPORT: SPRING 1982

The first legislative hurdle for Specter and his staff was to win approval within his own five-member subcommittee. As they contemplated that task, the essential amateurishness of the enterprise became obvious. Not one of them had ever faced the vote-gathering task before. Nor did any of them warm to the job. The result was an early tendency to underestimate the difficulties of majority building and to be less effective at it than those experienced on the Hill might have been. Assessing their prospects within the subcommittee in mid-December, for example, one aide predicted: "We could get the bill through the subcommittee *now*, probably. But in the full committee, it won't go anywhere until the administration gives its approval. Once it does, the committee Republicans will fall into line." In February, another staffer made a similar prediction. "We can draw together some documentation . . . and report the bill out of subcommittee whenever Arlen says so. When he turns us loose, we can start talking to members of the subcommittee and try to line up four or five votes." After Jensen's endorsement in March, a staffer said, "We've decided to vote the bill out of subcommittee . . . [and] that shouldn't be hard, now that we have administration support and the support of the DA's association."

Each of these predictions was too sanguine. Even after administration approval, it was six months before committee Republicans fell into line. The staffers never could produce four or five subcommittee votes. And the DA's association turned out to be opposed to the bill, not for it. In short, the votes came a lot harder than the inexperienced Specter enterprise had imagined in December or February or March.

Partly, of course, wishful thinking within the enterprise stemmed from their neglect of serious legislative work while they sought administration support. Not having talked around, the staffers did not know what was out there. Lacking information, they could only speculate. Specter claimed that before he had approached the White House, "I touched all the bases with my colleagues in the Senate on this matter."[31] But these were, again, pro forma contacts at best, and they yielded little by way of useful information on support patterns. But the problem also resulted from a reluctance within the enterprise to plunge into the serious business of coalition building.

In deciding how to get the bill through the subcommittee, for example, Specter's aides held back from collective action. They decided not to have the markup Specter had ordered earlier. They decided, instead, to poll the bill out of subcommittee. That is, they sent a paper ballot to the five members separately, asking them to vote for or against the statement: "I cast my vote to report favorably S 1688 as amended."

Perhaps they did this because they felt certain of a favorable vote, or, alternatively, because they wanted to postpone a full discussion. Perhaps they did it to save themselves time or to lighten the burden of their colleagues. Whatever the reason, the avoidance of a subcommittee meeting meant that they would forgo the opportunity to build a core of allies and that the task of educating and coalition building would continue to be done by the senator and his staff one on one. Specter would talk to his colleagues; his staffers would talk to other staffers. The polling decision was, in effect, a decision by the Specter enterprise to continue to go it alone.

As they began the business of vote gathering, a division of labor was created within the enterprise. Michel's main job became to write a lengthy report to accompany the bill on its prospective journey. "I have dropped everything and I'm devoting all my attention to writing a report," he said in late March.

> I'm trying to make it as powerful as I can. It is filled with facts and figures, testimony from the hearings, statements by everyone from the president on down. It will help when we take the bill to the full committee. . . . It will help the others make their arguments with staff. Whether or not we need a hundred-page document I don't know. But we might. And on that chance, I'm spending all my time on it.

Kevin Mills was put in charge of circulating "the polling agreement" to each subcommittee member—in effect, to the key staff person for each member. And as part of that mission, it was his task to persuade each staffer. To Bruce Cohen was left the job of preparing the way for the bill in full committee.

But the engine and the throttle of the enterprise remained the senator himself. And the division of labor prescribed the largest task of all for him. As one of the staffers put it:

> In the end, two things will decide the issue. Is the bill considered good politics? I think that it is and [that] it will be considered to be so. And more important than that will be Arlen Specter's reputation as a man who knows this field up and down, backwards and forwards. That will be the decisive thing.

The miniature law firm was banking most heavily on the effort of its founding partner.

When they turned to the actual business of head counting in the subcommittee, the group found a good deal of uncertainty. The four subcommittee members, in addition to Chairman Specter, were Republicans Jeremiah Denton (Ala.) and Charles Mathias plus Democrats Howard Metzenbaum (Ohio) and Edward Kennedy. To a large degree, the problem for the enterprise was the same as it had been in dealing with the executive branch. "The bill is so subtle, so different," sighed a top staffer in mid-April. "How do you sell it to people? How do you get their attention? I'm getting a little weary." The bill embodied a novel approach; it did not command enthusiasm or attention; and, upon examination, it raised sensitive questions of federal encroachment into local jurisdictions.

The distinctively congressional ingredient in this mix was the depth of concern for the encroachment problem. In their April 29 progress report to Specter, the staffers who had talked to subcommittee members or their staffs wrote, "The exercise of federal jurisdiction in this area of traditionally local police powers is a major stumbling block to the favorable reporting of S 1688."[32] And one of them said privately, "It's not seen as a tough-on-crime bill. It's seen as a federal-intrusion-into-state-jurisdiction bill." That view, moreover, was a view held widely within the legislature but not to the same degree in the executive branch.

In the executive branch, the values of localism had been expressed by a career group in the Justice Department. They had conducted a "back channel" opposition—and lost. In Congress, however, the values of localism are carried in the bones of every legislator and in the representational mission of the institution itself. Since law enforcement had always been the province of local government, any idea that seemed to diminish that control would have to overcome an up-front, built-in skepticism among legislators. That skepticism could be heated up and strengthened when and if local groups became sufficiently exercised to make an argument out of it.

That is exactly what the National District Attorneys Association had decided to do. Having endorsed S 1688 in principle in November, but having failed to get the "mutual consent" language the organization sought in the bill supported by the administration in March, the group withdrew its support in April. In noting this development, the staff progress report said, "They want to possess the power to veto the authority of the federal government to initiate prosecutions under S 1688. This change *cannot be accepted,* but we are hopeful that some agreement can be reached." [33] A staffer elaborated.

> They object to the provision that gives a Department of Justice official the opportunity, in rare cases, to override the local district attorney in initiating a prosecution. We think that is an essential provision of the bill. It is *nonnegotiable.* I think they'll go along in the end. Even if they don't, it's not disastrous. But it is serious. They are among the people who have to implement the legislation. And when one of the groups that has to carry out the legislation is opposed to it, that can be trouble. The problem is that the opposition of the DAs could produce serious and active opposition in the Congress. . . . It is not the group that is so important, but . . . the DA is a very significant political figure. They have very close ties to senators and congressmen.

If forced to decide between supporting an unfamiliar legislative idea and yielding to the opposition of familiar local figures, the natural inclination of most legislators would not be difficult to figure out.

Among subcommittee members, there was as much uncertainty as there was support. Senator Denton—who, in Specter's March 18th assessment was "for it," and who moved quickly to become the bill's first co-sponsor—began to have second thoughts. Well into May, he refused to poll the bill out favorably because of "questions on the exercise of federal jurisdiction." [34] Eventually, he resolved his doubts in favor of the administration's position. Senator Mathias, who had been regarded from the outset as "favorably inclined," took a different path. He withheld his vote until the enterprise agreed to add to the bill a couple of pages of "findings" to explain why the federal government was needed in this area of crime control. The cumbersome addition more than doubled the size of the bill. [35] Howard Metzenbaum was skeptical of the bill from the outset, and remained so.

Ted Kennedy, the only member of the subcommittee to attend a subcommittee hearing or to praise its efforts publicly, withheld his support for S 1688 because of the opposition of Boston's district attorney, the president of NDAA.[36] A Specter staffer explained:

> The Boston DA [Newman Flanagan] is taking the most extreme position against the bill: that no prosecution can be initiated except on the signature of the local DA. I don't know if he's pushing Senator Kennedy or Senator Kennedy is pushing him, but the active opposition of Kennedy could make things very difficult. If one or two senators get interested in stopping this bill, they can probably do it.

Reflecting on the opposition of the NDAA, a Specter aide said,

> Like all bureaucrats, they want to control their turf. That control is more important to them than effective penalizing of violent criminals. What really bothers them about any language that allows the federal government to step in is that the local press will interpret that as a finding by the federal government that local law enforcement has failed. Don't forget, these are all elected officials, for two or four years. It's the stigma they fear. . . . It's not a matter of principle with them. It's a matter of politics.

Furthermore, the district attorneys would be advocating the principle of local jurisdiction to legislators whose orientation, too, was strongly local.

In mid-May Specter spoke to the National Legislative Conference of the NDAA in Washington.[37] Curiously—given the looming importance of the group—his staffers seriously discussed among themselves whether he should leave a debate on the Senate floor to visit the group. Specter quickly settled it. "I think we ought to show the flag," he said. "We made a commitment and we should keep it." In his talk he invoked a lot of fellow feeling. "I have many fond recollections of NDAA sessions over the years. . . . I dug down into the box of my experiences in the association and it helped me in my tight Senate race. . . . It's nice to have an old friend like Lowell Jensen around. We get more business done than anyone when we can talk prosecutor talk."

He gave the group a roundabout but unyielding pitch. He told them that "anything with a price tag" was difficult to sell, that "when the subject of cost came up [in his meeting with Reagan] a pallor came over the group," and that any federal help for law enforcement would face "a long and difficult road." He urged the prosecutors, nonetheless, to work for prison construction; and he argued that if S 1688 passed, prison construction would be more likely. On the bottom line, however, he stood firm—and at one point almost defiant. With regard to S 1688, he said:

The federal government is putting its toe in the water. I can understand the sentiment of the DA who wants to have final recall on it. But it's hard to structure a federal act without giving federal jurisdiction. . . . I don't know whether we can get Career Criminal passed with the attitude of the District Attorneys Association. We're going to try to steamroller you anyway.

He closed, however, on a collegial note. "Whatever you do on 1688, I have a guidebook—'from DA to the United States Senate'—which some of you may be interested in." The president of the NDAA gave Specter a plaque; and he reiterated that his organization did not yet support S 1688. Then the senator left. No negotiation had taken place or been suggested; a lot of uncertainty remained.

One week later, S 1688 was polled out of the Subcommittee on Juvenile Justice. The three Republicans voted in favor; the two Democrats abstained. There was no reason to think of it yet as a partisan issue. Specter had prospected among Democrats as well as Republicans—he had always worked easily across the aisle. But his Republican colleagues had been willing to accommodate him, while the Democrats simply held their fire. There had been no chance to negotiate. S 1688 had, however, arrived on the agenda of the full committee; there it would face its major legislative test. Strom Thurmond would assume the pivotal position once occupied by Ronald Reagan—except that the chairman exercised greater control over his small legislative domain than the president did over his vast executive territory.

As they moved S 1688 along in the executive branch and in the Senate, the Specter enterprise had paid little heed to what might lie ahead in the House. Their strategy was to worry about the House after they had succeeded in the Senate. When, in December, the senior Republican on the House Judiciary Committee, Robert McClory (Ill.), offered to introduce Specter's bill in that chamber, they asked him not to. "We told him that some glitches had occurred with the administration and we'd rather wait till those get ironed out. He agreed." The idea seemed to be that others should follow their lead.

In midsummer, however, they learned that a Judiciary Committee Democrat had introduced the bill. Again, Specter's staff had tried to stop it. "He stole it from us," complained an aide. "They were very open about it. We told them we'd rather they didn't introduce it. They said they were going to do it anyway. They said, 'It's a free country.' We said, 'We could never ask you not to introduce it, but if you asked us, we'd say we'd rather you didn't.' "

The senator took no interest in the event. When I first asked him which House member had introduced his bill, he answered flatly, "I don't know." The enterprise had its own timetable and plan for broaching the issue in the House, and they did not wish to be disrupted. Their desire to go it alone was intercameral as well as intracameral.

Insofar as they had developed a strategy for the House, it centered on winning over the member of the House Judiciary Committee whom they considered the key to success there. He was Rep. William Hughes, chairman of the committee's Subcommittee on Crime, to which S 1688 would eventually be sent. The Democrat Hughes was a former prosecutor, and his New Jersey district was near Philadelphia. Specter felt that his bonds with Hughes augured well for their relationship. Occasionally, he would estimate the likelihood of Hughes support. In December he said, "The bill is so narrowly drawn that I believe [Committee Chairman Peter] Rodino and Hughes will go along." In January he was still optimistic: "I've got a problem over in the House. They are not likely to be impressed with the administration's endorsement—tonight I'll get a chance to talk to Rodino and Hughes and those people on an informal basis."

For his part, Hughes was preoccupied with a piece of legislation of his own. It was a bill providing federal assistance, both monetary and organizational, to states and localities for an array of law enforcement purposes. The bill (HR 4481) passed the House overwhelmingly in early February. It was a bill in the spirit of the former Law Enforcement Assistance Administration (LEAA). Up to that point, Hughes had not been interested in career-criminal legislation and Arlen Specter had shown no interest in supplying federal money for local law enforcement needs. But when the time came for him to face seriously the matter of House support for S 1688, Specter would be forced to take a substantial interest in the Hughes bill.

The public debut of the Specter-Hughes relationship took place, at Specter's initiative, in hearings before Specter's subcommittee on the same day, March 18, that the administration agreed to support S 1688. Chairman Hughes came—as Specter knew he would—to lobby for his own bill, HR 4481. Hughes's prepared opening statement contained no mention of S 1688. The senator raised the career-criminal issue, however, during questioning. Hughes answered somewhat gingerly, "I think your legislation S 1688 is a very serious initiative and I must confess it has a lot of aspects that I like. . . . One of my concerns . . . is over the role of the local prosecutor. . . . I think the [new] language you just read tightens it up considerably. . . . I commend you for S 1688. I am happy to see you moving forward with it." There was encouragement but no commitment. Specter concluded by telling Hughes (and McClory) that "the subcommittee is going to move ahead with HR 4481. . . . I have concerns as to the reactions of my colleagues as to cost. . . . [But] I share your evaluation of a high priority for this kind of legislation." [38] There was encouragement there, too, without commitment. Taken together, the affair had all the earmarks of a mating dance.

Specter's assessment afterward was that "I think Bill Hughes will go along." I pressed the obvious question. I asked him whether Hughes wasn't holding back on S 1688 because he was trying to trade HR 4481 for S 1688. "He'd like that," Specter replied. "I don't think I can deliver for him on HR 4481. . . . It's in the wind." He was not embracing the idea of a quid pro quo. And his slowness in doing so can be attributed to his longstanding desire to remain independent and not to entrust his fate to others. "It's hard for him to realize that you need to engage in a quid pro quo," a top staffer generalized. "He doesn't want to owe anybody anything." Specter's restraint in the Hughes relationship was embedded in his loner's style. But he was clearly being put under pressure to embrace HR 4481.

Two local prosecutors followed Hughes to the witness stand on March 18; they, too, plumped hard and enthusiastically for HR 4481 and the LEAA model. When coaxed by the chairman, they spoke favorably about S 1688. But their obvious concern lay elsewhere. Privately, one of them—Philadelphia's own district attorney—told an attending local reporter afterward that "the DAs respect Arlen, are glad he's there and are glad he's taken criminal justice as his area of interest; but they consider his support of HR 4481 as the test of whether Arlen Specter matters to them in the Senate." On April 21, the senator from Pennsylvania—with bipartisan support from within the Judiciary Committee—introduced a companion to the Hughes bill. It was called the Justice Assistance Act of 1982, and it became S 2411.[39]

Specter's March view that "I think Bill Hughes will go along" was not based on hard evidence. From the beginning of his effort, the Pennsylvanian's predisposition had been to interpret sympathetic interest as an expression of solid support. He had not yet learned to distinguish between positive general statements and commitment. His own devotion to the bill was so aggressively positive that he easily misread the posture of others. Although his misreading did not make him any the less persistent in his efforts, it slowed and obstructed his coalition-building activity. For he often failed to grasp the limits of his own personal abilities. And he often overestimated his existing base of support. With Representative Hughes, it gradually became apparent that Specter's early estimate contained a large, and familiar, dosage of wishful thinking.

Staff-to-staff consultations made it clear that Hughes and fellow members of the House committee were having the same initial difficulties coping with the idea that everyone else had. "We've had the same experience with every person or group we've presented it to," said a staffer in April.

> At first, they are skeptical, dubious and confused. Crime control people are influenced by the last fight they had. . . . When they hear that our bill is about crime control, they go check and say "Oh, yes, the issue there is gun control" or "the issue is putting more money in the hands of local authorities." They aren't willing to see that neither of those approaches are the answer. It's almost an ideology we're running into. If they take the time to look at our bill, they say, "Oh, that's just a piddling little bill. The real problem is gun control." They don't see that this bill actually does something. It doesn't tinker with language. It takes some very evil people off the streets and puts them away.
>
> Our only hope is Bill Hughes. But he's gone from noncommittal to mildly opposed. . . . Arlen has introduced a bill that's very compatible with Hughes' bill, on legal assistance. We'll try to get it passed in the Senate. That's all we can do. People say, "go back and talk to Hughes again." What good would that do? We've shot all our ammunition.

By June Specter had become more realistic in his estimate of Hughes's support; but he remained upbeat about what he could accomplish by way of his personal effort in the long run. "I'm working on him and making progress," he said. "I've worked out a relationship with him. I'm helping him with his bill over here. He's mildly negative, but not immovable."

A month later, Specter and Michel had a luncheon meeting with the House subcommittee chairman. Specter was pleased. "Bill Hughes and I have struck up a more expansive relationship," he reported. "He laid out a whole group of bills and asked me to support them. I found that I could vote for every one of them. He has not supported 1688 flat out, and I haven't asked him to do that. Maybe that's a mistake. But I think he will support it when the time comes."

Paul Michel's reading of the luncheon concurred in the details, but not in the deeper reading of Hughes's posture. "Arlen did not mention 1688. As he said, 'I don't believe in doing business that way; I don't think it works; and besides, I agreed with him on all his bills anyway.'" But Michel believed that Hughes was still far from supportive.

> Hughes has the belief that any crime bill that passes, other than his LEAA bill, will detract from the chances of that bill. He also has a very strong but illogical feeling about gun control. He's a nice guy. But he believes so strongly in gun control legislation that he thinks somehow or other our bill

will harm gun control.... So on the merits, he doesn't much like our bill. Maybe it's a tribute to our efforts with him that he hasn't come out against it.

In truth, it *was* the efforts of the enterprise that had kept hope alive.

On December 7, with S 1688 still sitting on the agenda of Hughes's Subcommittee on Crime, the contrast between the attitudes of point man Michel and the senator himself over Bill Hughes remained. They exchanged views on the subject.

> MICHEL: Hughes appears to be still very ambiguous about your bill.
> SPECTER: He told me he was for it.
> MICHEL: I know that's what he says to you. But when he talks to others, what he conveys is his ambiguity.
> SPECTER: His exact words to me were, "I'll do everything I can to get your bill through my committee." *(Picking up his phone)* Get me Bill Hughes.

Afterward, Specter mused, "That's another fascinating thing: staff-to-staff communication is not the same thing as member-to-member communication."

Clearly, the persistent prosecutor relied heavily on the latter. And he remained optimistic about his relationship with Hughes. "I think Bill Hughes will push my bill through his committee because he knows how hard I'm working on his bill over here.... There is no deal involved. But he will naturally help me if I am helping him." Specter's early prediction that Hughes would go along might yet prove accurate. But six months afterward, the best Specter could realistically conclude was that "we are getting close; but we are still far away."

By jumping ahead with a commentary about the Specter-Hughes relationship, I have bypassed the further adventures of S 1688 in the Senate, and we shall return to those events shortly. This chapter ends with the career-criminal bill safely on the agenda of the Senate Judiciary Committee and with its author beginning to worry about placing it on the agenda of the Subcommittee on Crime in the House. The theme of the story so far has been the remarkable entrepreneurship of the freshman senator from Pennsylvania. From the idea of the bill, to the introduction of the bill, to the winning of administration support, to subcommittee passage and beyond, the entire operation had been a one-man show—at least one man and the enterprise he led.

The same reliance on aggressive, independent, individual effort that had marked his pre-Senate career was being brought to bear in the legislative process. Specter was advantaged somewhat by characteristics of the issue and of the larger policy area. But he was disadvantaged somewhat by the exaggerated individualism of his effort. No other senator, no other Senate staffer, no research organization lent resources to his coalition-building effort. It is hard to build and hold legislative majorities without allies and supporters, as Specter would eventually learn. Still, he had strong policy preferences, he knew his subject, and he persisted in his fashion. And it was, above all, this determination, the refusal to quit, that had carried his bill to the full committee. It would carry the bill a good deal farther before he was through.

NOTES

1. Jack Walker, "Setting the Agenda in the U.S. Senate," *British Journal of Political Science* 7 (October 1977): 423-445; John Kingdon, *Agendas, Alternatives, and Public Policies* (Boston: Little, Brown, 1984).
2. An example of policy making on the recurring agenda is Richard F. Fenno, Jr., *The Emergence of a Senate Leader: Pete Domenici and the Reagan Budget* (Washington, D.C.: CQ Press, 1991). An example of policy making on the occasional agenda is Richard F. Fenno, Jr., *The Making of a Senator: Dan Quayle* (Washington, D.C.: CQ Press, 1988).
3. Walker, "Setting the Agenda," 424-427.
4. Kingdon, *Agendas, Alternatives, and Public Policies*, 38-47, 130-137, 184ff.
5. Ibid., 190.
6. For the prevalence of habitual criminal statutes in the states, see U.S. Senate, Subcommittee on Juvenile Justice of the Committee on the Judiciary, Hearings on the Career Criminal Life Sentence Act, October 26, 1981, 31ff. An early study by the Institute for Law and Social Research is reported in David Weimer, *Improving Prosecution?* (Westport, Conn.: Greenwood). Kingdon's discussion is found in *Agendas, Alternatives, and Public Policies*, chap. 4.
7. *Congressional Record*, October 1, 1981, S10937-S10940.
8. United Press International, "Specter Proposes Life Term," *Lebanon Daily News*, August 12, 1981. See also Associated Press, "Specter Seeks Tough Penalty," *North Penn Reporter* (Lansdale), August 15, 1981.
9. Kathy Kelly, " 'Career Criminals' Should Get Life, Specter Contends," *Pittsburgh Press*, August 11, 1981.
10. His original idea was life imprisonment for "a fourth major crime." See Associated Press, "Sen. Specter: 4-Time Losers Must Get Life," *Express* (Easton), August 15, 1981.
11. *Congressional Record*, October 1, 1981, S10937.
12. Letter from Arlen Specter to President Reagan, September 25, 1981.
13. Press Release, "Specter Wants Life Sentences for Career Criminals," October 1, 1981. The three bills are printed in *Congressional Record*, October 1, 1981, S10938-S10939.
14. Mick Rood, "Specter Bill Would Jail Career Crooks," *Harrisburg Evening News*, October 1, 1981.
15. Mick Rood, "Specter Spurs Criminal Justice Image," *Sunday Patriot-News* (Harrisburg), September 27, 1981.
16. Kingdon, *Agendas, Alternatives, and Public Policies*, 3-4.
17. The seminal work on congressional staffs as enterprise is Robert Salisbury and Kenneth Shepsle, "U.S. Congressmen as Enterprise," *Legislative Studies*

Quarterly 6 (November 1981): 559-576.

18. Memorandum, "Federal Enforcement Against Career Criminals," September 24, 1981. Also sent to Committee members, "Constitutionality of a Federal Career Criminal Life Sentence Act," September 25, 1981.

19. Mick Rood, " 'Career Criminals' Target of Specter," *Patriot-News*, (October 2, 1981. Representative William Hughes "said Thursday he opposed the Specter life sentence bill. Hughes said it wasn't necessary for the federal government to handle what have been traditionally matters of state jurisdiction."

20. See Donald Baker, "A Democrat's Republican Joins the List of Non-Candidates," *Washington Post Weekly*, October 14, 1985; Meg Greenfield, "A Republican Outsider," *Newsweek*, October 7, 1985.

21. An account of Jensen's work in the area will be found in Weimer, *Improving Prosecution?*

22. U.S. Senate, Subcommittee on Juvenile Justice of the Committee on the Judiciary, Hearings on the Career Criminal Life Sentence Act, October 26, 1981, 23, 14-15.

23. Ibid., 14, 15.

24. Ibid., 24. See also p. 14.

25. Ibid., 133.

26. Bill Sternberg, "Reagan Backs Specter Crime Crack-Down Bill," *Lock Haven Express*, November 16, 1981; Associated Press, "Specter Says Reagan Likes Jail Proposal," *Warren Times-Observer*, November 14, 1981.

27. Letter from Arlen Specter to Attorney General William French Smith, November 24, 1981.

28. Resolution of the Board of Directors of the National District Attorneys Association, Reno, Nevada, November 10, 1981.

29. Hearings on the Career Criminal Life Sentence Act, December 10, 1981, 139-140.

30. U.S. Senate, Subcommittee on Juvenile Justice of the Committee on the Judiciary, Hearings on Federal Financial Assistance to State and Local Law Enforcement, March 18, 1982, 103.

31. Larry Eichel, "Cautiously, a Junior Senator Seeks His Stride," *Philadelphia Inquirer*, April 6, 1982.

32. "Progress Report: S 1688, the Armed Career Criminal Act of 1981," April 29, 1982, 2.

33. Ibid.

34. Memorandum to Karl Moor and Senator Denton from Kevin Mills and Senator Specter, "S 1688 Polling Agreement," May 6, 1982.

35. "Amendment in the Nature of a Substitute for 1688," March 17, 1982.

36. See Statement of Senator Kennedy and Statement of Honorable Newman Flanagan, District Attorney, Suffolk County, Mass., President-Elect of National District Attorneys Association, Hearings on the Career Criminal Life Sentence Act, December 10, 1981, 138-148.

37. Agenda, National District Attorneys Association, National Legislative Conference, Hyatt, Arlington, May 16-19, 1982, 3.

38. Memorandum, "Statement of the Honorable William J. Hughes, Chairman, Subcommittee on Crime of the House Judiciary Committee, before the Juvenile Justice Subcommittee, Senate Judiciary Committee," March 18, 1982; Hearings on Federal Financial Assistance, 91-94, 101-102.

39. *Congressional Record*, April 21, 1982, S3776-S3783.

3

Governing Accomplishments

THE ENTREPRENEUR

In May of 1982, S 1688 had come to rest on the decision agenda of the Senate Committee on the Judiciary. The bill's sponsor had pushed it to that point by himself. The task of building committee support for it lay ahead. But Arlen Specter had not yet faced—indeed, he had avoided—negotiation inside the legislature; his ability to build and sustain a supportive legislative coalition had not been tested. It was not yet clear, therefore, how far his prowess as an entrepreneur would carry him along the road to success. Policy interest, expertise, and energy would be guaranteed. But the senator from Pennsylvania still had things to learn about collective action in the Senate, about some of the keys to effectiveness in the body—the how and the when of anticipating procedural problems, gauging opposition strength, negotiating for support, and strengthening personal ties.

To that point, at least, Specter had displayed a marked tendency to overestimate what he could accomplish singlehandedly; he exaggerated the readiness of others to accept his personal persuasions, and he underestimated the time he would need to engineer agreement among numerous participants. He lacked the ability to gauge intensity of opinion—to differentiate between a sympathetic comment and a solid commitment. And he tended not to pick staffers and not to cultivate colleagues who might help him learn about such matters. Often, therefore, he misunderstood the strength of support for S 1688. And he found himself again arguing cases he thought he had won.

The problem was not entirely his. The issue was by nature difficult to sell to others. Still, Arlen Specter seemed not to be a natural coalition builder. He did not approach the legislative business, instinctively, as a matter of collective action. He did not think first in terms of allies or in terms of what it might take to win support from whom and at what cost. His natural inclination was to drive straight ahead, alone, taking each hurdle as it came and relying on his ability to persuade the necessary people as he went. He had made one important strategic decision: to begin by securing formal administration approval. Once he had settled that, his strategy was to apply his persistent prosecutor's style to whatever support problems lay ahead.

These stylistic preferences were derived, we have argued, from a time-tested nonlegislative pattern of behavior. The pattern could, of course, be modified; that, after all, is what adjustment is all about. Indeed, Specter had already demonstrated an adaptive capacity—with his early, self-conscious decision to submerge his previous preoccupation as DA and as candidate with media attention. At the beginning of the summer of 1982, however, there was evidence that further adjustments might be needed in order to pass S 1688—that a highly individualistic style might have to be accommodated still further to the constraints of the collectivity. And it remained to be seen whether or how or to what degree such adjustments would be made.

In midsummer, three-quarters of the way through the normal two-year adjustment period, I asked the freshman senator directly what he had learned thus far. "It's been a lesson in the intricacies of the legislative process," he replied.

> There are so many currents. There are the main currents that flow from the administration. There are the main currents that flow from the committees—Pete Domenici and the budget, for example. And there are so many tributaries off that mainstream—amendments to the budget. Then you have smaller streams—and S 1688 is one of those. Then you have lots of trickles, bills that aren't serious and aren't going anyplace. . . . It has been a fascinating experience to watch individual performances. Some—Domenici on the budget and [Robert] Dole on the tax bill—have been extraordinary. Some have been very weak. . . . It's a complex process, which makes it very difficult to get anything passed. That's particularly true in this Congress because spending is so tight. But maybe that's always been the case.

It was the comment of someone who was still learning—someone who was still part spectator, part doer—and learning from both angles. He had developed a realistic sense for the place of his career-criminal bill in the larger scheme of things, as a serious piece of legislation, on the highly constrained discretionary agenda of the institution. He also showed a lively, and very senatorial, interest in the ability of individual senators to make the intricacies of the process work for them and, in so doing, to acquire good reputations for themselves.

Later in the same interview, Specter provided a further perspective on S 1688, factoring it into his broader legislative agenda. He was, after all, a man who prided himself on his ubiquitous election campaign, who looked forward afterward to working on "a full plate of things" and who later likened himself to "a swarm of locusts blanketing all subjects." So we should not assume that his pet project was his only involvement—far from it. In midsummer, he divided his legislative interests into three categories—crime and judiciary committee matters, state-oriented issues, and foreign policy. The last he described as "almost a must category for all of us . . . a big part of every guy's job." Like many legislators with a special taste for foreign affairs, his interest took root in his undergraduate days. And it was a matter of foreign policy, not a matter of criminal justice, that provided his first opportunity for coalition building beyond the boundaries of his committee. The opportunity arose in the broadest of community settings, on the floor of the Senate—a place where every newcomer gets tested before his or her adjustment period can be said to be over. Specter's action was, therefore, an essential part of his education. And it affected his activity on S 1688.

THE SUMMIT RESOLUTION: SPRING 1982

On April 14, at a time of public concern over the U.S.-U.S.S.R. nuclear arms build-up and a time of public speculation about the possibility of a summit meeting between the leaders of the two countries, the senator from Pennsylvania wrote to the president urging him to "act now" to initiate such a meeting—"in order to reduce the risk of nuclear war and stop the escalation of the arms race." [1] He did so, he said, in a context in which "there is an intention to move forward with summit talks, but [in which] there is some possibility that it may not happen or there is some possibility they will be delayed." [2] "There's a battle going on for the president's mind," said Specter privately. "The goal of the resolution," said an aide, "is to keep the president from sliding backwards toward the farthest right-wing group, to keep him from moving away from negotiations."

Specter's interest grew directly out of his service on the Appropriations Subcommittee on Foreign Operations, out of the dominance of defense issues in the work of the parent Appropriations Committee, and out of several trips he had recently taken to major defense installations in the United States. This experience, he believed, gave him sufficient standing in the policy area. On April 15, he addressed a "Dear Colleague" letter to each senator asking for co-sponsorship of a "Sense of the Congress Concurrent Resolution" calling upon the president to convene a summit meeting "at the earliest possible date." [3]

This kind of nonbinding resolution is a favorite of individual senators who want to convert a personal opinion of some sort into an opinion of a Senate majority, hoping to focus interest, attract publicity, and, if possible, influence behavior. The resolution is merely an expression of opinion; it requires no action by any committee; it cuts across the normal flow of legislative business; its passage forces no implementation; and no other official need act on it. Because it is an opinion, however, and because it often disrupts normal procedures, it may stir controversy.

When, on May 4, Specter offered an amendment "to express the sense of the Congress recommending a summit meeting on reducing the risk of the occurrence of nuclear war," controversy emerged. [4] It was a narrowly confined controversy, involving very few senators. But it pitted the Pennsylvania freshman against the established defense and foreign policy leaders in the Senate. Therefore, it exemplified the contrast between individualistic and communitarian modes of decisionmaking. In Specter's eyes, the contest took on David-and-Goliath dimensions, since he was virtually alone in prosecuting his case. His call for co-sponsors attracted only one other senator; eventually a second senator signed on. Both were Democrats. Only the first one entered the fray on the floor.

There was a demonstrable lack of interest in the resolution. That did not necessarily mean a lack of support for it; it meant only that most senators probably believed the resolution to be inconsequential. The exceptions were the official guardians of senatorial policy making in the area—the senior members of the Armed Services Committee and the Foreign Relations Committee. For them, the resolution posed an invasion of their turf and a pretension to their policy expertise. Because the resolution was proposed as an amendment to the defense authorization bill, the leading opponent became Armed Services Committee Chairman John Tower (R-Texas). But, with arms control issues falling at the intersection of defense and foreign policy, Foreign Relations Committee Chairman Charles Percy (R-Ill.) was close behind.

These opponents began with the restrained argument that the resolution failed to follow normal legislative procedure and added that, as a consequence, it would be harmful to the timing and substance of the president's own efforts to work for a summit. Tower interrupted Specter's initial presentation to ask: "Have there been any hearings on the senator's amendment?" ("No.") and "Does the administration support the amendment?" ("I have had no response.") [5]

The fact is that the administration opposes this amendment and opposes it strongly. Is it the suggestion of the Senator from Pennsylvania that, regardless of what the administration position is, he intends to press on with it, even if the administration opposes it for reasons that it might undermine the bargaining position the administration has? Is he prepared to press on with it even in the absence of hearings, even in the absence of giving the administration an opportunity to present its case to the appropriate committee, the Foreign Relations Committee? [6]

Chairman Percy argued that Specter's was one of ten arms control resolutions scheduled for hearings before his committee. "They do not belong on this [defense authorization] bill," he said. "This is not the right bill to put them on. [They] are properly referred to the Senate Foreign Relations Committee and a resolution will come out of [that] committee." [7] He and Tower urged Specter to withdraw his amendment and to route it through committee hearings instead, but to no avail.

Specter did not quit. He argued that it was appropriate for the Senate to make such a "suggestion" to the president, that it was appropriate for him to author such a suggestion, that the defense bill was an appropriate vehicle to carry the suggestion, and that "the Senate can move forward to a judgment without hearings." [8]

Given the lack of interest in the resolution, Tower's escalation of the debate from procedural to substantive arguments is noteworthy. When he realized that Specter intended to persist, he came out with guns blazing and tried to overwhelm and undermine the freshman. He said that the resolution was "naive and dangerously misleading," that it implicitly embraced a discredited strategic doctrine, that it placed more blame on the United States than the Soviet Union for the arms race, that it would lead to decreased U.S. military strength, and that its author did not have enough facts at his disposal (on such matters as the details of "mutual assured destruction," "sufficient and urgent hard target kill capability," "the flying time of B-52 bombers from the U.S. to the U.S.S.R.," and "submarine communication systems") to make credible judgments. [9]

Specter stuck closely to the wording of his resolution. It was, he reiterated,

being offered in the context of a most respectful suggestion to President Reagan. It is not being offered precipitously ... [but] after a great deal of thought. . . . I believe it is appropriate for the Senate to say to the executive branch: "Start talks. It is not inconsistent with acquiring strength. We agree that the United States should agree to acquire strength, but start to talk." I think it is directly relevant, directly germane and should be considered at this time. [10]

His co-sponsor rose to help him on a couple of occasions. No one else spoke for the resolution. Several senior members of the Armed Services Committee—Senators John Stennis (D-Miss.), Strom Thurmond, Barry Goldwater (R-Ariz.), and John Warner (R-Va.)—spoke against it. They called upon their colleagues "to place a measure of trust in those of us who work in this area." [11] Therefore, Arlen Specter's initial effort to gather votes on the Senate floor became one more test of his individualistic style.

When Specter reviewed the debate afterward, he emphasized his head-to-head confrontation with Tower.

> We debated it for two days and Tower became very opposed to it. He didn't think it should be on his bill. He didn't think we should tell the president what to do. He thought it should go to committee first. And he didn't think a freshman should propose such a resolution. He didn't say that, but he felt it.

Specter also emphasized the care and the preparation that lay behind his debate performance. And he talked a lot like a prosecutor arguing before a jury.

> Tower was trying to browbeat me, but I knew what I was talking about. I had gone to Grand Forks, North Dakota, to see the Minuteman. I had gone to Edwards Air Force Base in California to see the B-1 bomber. I had been to Charleston, South Carolina, to see the submarines. I told Tower that you could communicate with a submarine that was submerged. He said you couldn't. I topped him on that one. I was enjoying it. It was a situation that was very familiar to me from my courtroom experience. Tower was tough, but I've seen a lot tougher. And I can be tougher than Tower once I get going. But I knew I had to be very serious and very calm.

His performance "won me points," he believed, particularly within the enterprise. "It was good for the staff," he exclaimed. "They hung on every episode—like a baseball game, inning by inning. They all listened to it over the squawk box. It was 'our' gladiator against 'their' gladiator."

As it turned out, however, the Tower-Specter conflict took more forms than a floor debate. In the middle of the debate, Tower and his committee ally John Warner asked Specter to meet with officials of the National Security Council and the State Department to hear their views—which he did. "I'll go" Specter told his colleagues, "but I won't back off. They [the officials] told me that summits require preparation and they raise expectations. I told them, 'That's just why I think we need the resolution. The American people have a right to expect that we are preparing to talk.' . . . They said nothing to convince me I wasn't right. I told them I wasn't going to withdraw it."

Hearing this, Tower aimed an even bigger gun at the freshman. "I was on the floor debating," Specter recalled,

> and I got a note the secretary of state was on the phone. I said, "I can't talk to him now. I've got to stay here on the floor." I wasn't being disrespectful; I just didn't feel I could leave the debate. John Tower came over and said he thought I should take the call and that he would ask for a quorum call. Haig said the president was going to make a [foreign policy] speech on Saturday in Eureka [Ill.]; and he said it would be catastrophic if we voted on my resolution before the president's speech. He used heavy words—*catastrophic, overwhelming*—the way Haig does. He asked me to postpone the vote. I asked him if the president was going to propose a summit in his Eureka speech. He said he couldn't say that he would. I said, "If you ask me to postpone a vote, I'll have to do it. But I won't back off. And I'm going to put it in the [*Congressional*] *Record* that I'm putting it off because you asked me to.

Specter's determination to "press on" and not to "back off" are fully consistent with an individualistic senatorial style in general and with the predilections of a persistent prosecutor in particular.

The conflict over the resolution was an intraparty affair. The vast majority of Senate Democrats, already pushing the president hard on arms control via nuclear freeze proposals, supported the resolution. Specter's problem lay within the ranks of his majority party. In the Republican Policy Committee meeting the following week, Specter argued his case before his colleagues. In addition to his straightforward policy theme, he played a subtle institutional theme—that serious policy initiatives taken by Senate newcomers beyond the jurisdictions of their own committees deserved the serious consideration of the Senate. It was an appeal to individualistic norms. But he cast it shrewdly in a nonaggressive, self-deprecating form. Specter recounted:

> I got up to speak and got off on the right foot. I said, "This should be a very easy speech to make. I'm only opposed by the Chairman of the Armed Services Committee and the Chairman of the Foreign Relations Committee." Everyone laughed. It broke the ice.

Tower and Percy did oppose the resolution, on procedural and jurisdictional grounds. The others simply listened to these expressions of opinion; no conclusion was reached.

The first and crucial vote on the Specter resolution occurred the following day. Both sides actively solicited support during the vote. The opponents tried one last vote-gathering tactic that upset the freshman senator. As Specter recalled this "little bit of by-play":

> When the vote came, Tower placed a sheet of paper beside the text down on the front table saying that the Armed Services Committee and the Foreign Relations Committee were opposed to the resolution. I had never seen that done before, and I asked the secretary of the Senate what the precedents were. He went to find Howard Baker. I asked Tower if the Armed Services Committee opposed it or if he did. He said he did. I said, "Why didn't you say that?" Then I asked Chuck Percy. He said he had taken a kind of a poll. I said, "All right, if you took a poll. . . . But I still don't believe that is a fair procedure."

Nonetheless, Specter had his own vote-getting technique. That was, simply, to press the individualistic institutional norm—in its David-and-Goliath form—one on one with the other Senate newcomers.

> All during the debate, I was going around proselytizing the [Republican] members of the class. I didn't say Tower was being a bully, but they all knew it. Senators A and B were outraged. Senator C came up to me and said, "Specter, I don't know what you're doing, but if Tower and Percy are against you then I'm for you." [Specter cited other examples of Republicans who voted his way.]
> Tower said to Senator D, "You can't vote for that. Specter's telling the president what to do." But Senator D said, "Everyone else is, why shouldn't he?" . . . When Tower asked Senator E, "You aren't going to vote for that resolution, are you?" Senator E said, "I am. What do you think my constituents would say if I didn't?" . . . Senator F said he wanted to vote for it, but that he wouldn't be in town for the vote. When we postponed the vote, I went to him and said, "We held it over just so you could vote for it." He really didn't want to, but he had to.

The vote, on a motion to table the resolution, went 32-60 in Specter's favor. Republicans split down the middle 25-25; Democrats supported the freshman 35-7. Republicans on the Armed Services Committee, by 7-1, and the Foreign Relations Committee, by 6-1, opposed the resolution. The two committees voted 11-5 and 9-5, respectively, against it. With Specter's subsequent acceptance of some language by Tower asking the Soviets to respond quickly to any American proposal, the resolution passed 92-6.[12]

The freshman had fought for votes, and he had won a personal victory on the Senate floor. From the gallery, several colleagues could be seen clapping him on the back. "It felt great," he said afterward, "It felt especially great because I took on big bad John Tower, or bad big John Tower, and beat him. . . . The pleasure of it was that it was the first time any member of the freshman class of '80 had taken on and beaten the leadership on an issue that was tough and tenacious." Whatever the truth of that claim, Specter's own view of his performance was that he had been "tough and tenacious." That view was, of course, in keeping with his career-long self-image and with our description of his governing style.

According to Fenno's champagne test of governing accomplishment—that is, the occasion on which a new senator's staff first breaks out a little champagne to celebrate a legislative accomplishment—Specter's summit resolution was his sweetest legislative accomplishment to date. On May 12, champagne flowed for the first time in room 342 of the Russell Office Building.

As a policy matter, Specter understood that his victory would have almost no substantive impact. He admitted: "The resolution added that much (*spreading his thumb and forefinger the slightest bit*) to the movement for arms control. And it gave that much (*barely touching my shoulder*) push to a summit. But it was right to do it." The national media reception confirmed this judgment. "We got a nice story in the *Philadelphia Inquirer*," he said. "Surprisingly, neither the *New York Times* or the *Washington Post* picked it up at all." The accomplishment the Specter enterprise celebrated was indeed not a substantive policy accomplishment. It was a personal accomplishment, a floor-based accomplishment of the sort that is necessary before a newcomer's adjustment to the Senate is complete.

The experience was not like anything he had undergone before. "When you put in a bill," he said afterward, "it's like spitting in the ocean. When you hold a hearing, it's like wetting your finger and holding it to the wind. When you make people *vote*, then they pay attention. They really pay attention." Furthermore, the experience had taught him how to make people vote.

"I've learned how to do it," he exclaimed several times. By this he meant: when you have a fairly narrow bill or a resolution to introduce, do it when no one is around and then attach it later on as a nongermane matter to some reasonably uncontroversial legislative vehicle. He had learned, in short, what an individual senator might accomplish outside the committee system with the help of the Senate's germaneness rule. The experience had bolstered his confidence and broadened his legislative horizons. He could not wait to employ the same tactic again. He had prepared a resolution on the Falkland Islands dispute, which he was about to enter in competition with a similar resolution by another senator. "He's trying to add his resolution to a controversial bill, and

Baker has threatened to take the whole bill down if he succeeds. I'll put mine in like I did with the summit resolution. I've learned how to do it. The way he did his is not accepted form. I'll do mine the right way." The Philadelphia newcomer displayed an eagerness to learn coupled with an eagerness to participate.

The importance of his summit resolution, then, lay mostly in providing a quantum jump in his adjustment to the Senate. He seemed measurably more comfortable there than when he began. He had enjoyed a floor success; and he believed that his colleagues recognized it. Specter summarized his progress.

> It was a learning experience. It was the first thing I have pushed on the floor since I've been here. I have moved very slowly. Some of my colleagues have taken flyers and have come back with egg on their faces. I have spoken very little—only when I knew a lot about the subject, like crime, or on matters of interest to my state. I have felt that when I did move, I would want to be sure I knew what I was talking about. It has helped my rapport with my colleagues that when I did move [on the summit resolution] I was serious, had studied, and was success-ful—and was successful.

Moments later, he talked about the Senate as if he felt more a part of it than before. "It's a great job," he exulted. "I love it. It's still exhilarating just to be a United States Senator. It's educational. You learn not only that you can't do everything but how hard it is to do anything. . . . But if anybody can do anything, the Senate can."

WINNING FULL COMMITTEE SUPPORT FOR S 1688: SUMMER 1982

TIMING AND PROCEDURE

The effort to pass Specter's summit resolution slowed the progress of his career-criminal bill, for it diverted the attention of the senator and the energy of his staff. At the time S 1688 was being polled out of subcommittee, few, if any, Judiciary Committee members were firmly committed to it. And no concentrated effort was being made to secure their commitment. The plan was to launch a serious selling job by means of a detailed, explanatory committee report, written by top staffer Paul Michel. Michel's "original timetable" called for the report to be com-pleted "around May first." But no sooner had he begun work on it than Specter directed him to do the staff work on the summit resolution.

From time to time, Specter would bring up the subject of S 1688. "Arlen is determined to get it passed," said Michel in late April. "He told me so this morning with great vehemence. Four different times in a meeting he said 1688 was the highest priority." But, in fact, he was giving top priority to the summit resolution. And it was six to eight weeks before Michel could return to the preparation of the career-criminal report. When he did pick it up again, in late May, the bill had reached the full committee agenda. But the members of the miniature law firm were worried about time lost and time remaining.

"We're doing too much," one member lamented. "You heard Arlen ask Paul yesterday how the report [on 1688] was coming. Do you know the last time Paul even *thought* about that report? Two months ago!" A second member commented: "I've been going around trying to get people interested in the bill, but nobody's interested. . . . It's so far down on the committee agenda that they can't get interested in it. It's tenth or twelfth. They think it's come along too late." A third said:

> Specter's counting on a spellbinding report to carry the day in the committee. The problem is that no matter how brilliant the report, the first reaction of everybody we have talked to about the bill has been negative. Not that they are immediately against it, but that they are immediately hesitant. . . . Senators will not read it, so everything depends on . . . eighteen staff assistants. They will most likely read it and hesitate. They won't say to their senators, "This looks fine, everybody's for it, let's go." And the bill will bog down in committee. . . . If it doesn't get out of committee by the end of June and on the floor by July, its chances will drop from poor to nil. There will be a mad legislative scramble, with all sorts of important bills competing.

In the late May-early June opinions of the staff, time was no longer in their favor.

They entertained no doubts, however, about the persistent prosecutor's expressed desire. "Arlen wants us to finish the report above all else," said one.

> He is completely determined to go ahead. You've heard of Pickett's charge. After being decimated for two days, the southerners rallied and made a third charge. Lee told them to go back again. They did, without knowing what they were doing or why, and were wiped out. I think we're on a Pickett's charge. But Arlen is determined to keep going. He won't engage in any face-saving maneuvers off to the side. He wants to go straight ahead and all the way.

By late June, after four weeks of intensive effort, Michel had produced a 192-page draft report. And the senator was talking optimistically about moving the bill out of committee and passing it on the Senate floor.

On a visit to Pennsylvania on June 21, I inquired about the status of 1688. "It's all going well," Specter said. "It's been on the committee docket for two weeks. We've finished the [draft] report, and it's being circulated. It's two hundred pages. I think we'll get it out of committee, and Howard Baker has promised to schedule it." With respect to his committee colleagues, he admitted: "It's been hard going. I've had to convince guys like [Paul] Laxalt and [Orrin] Hatch. . . . And on the other side Metzenbaum . . . and Kennedy are opposed to it. . . . But I think I can do it. The report is very impressive. I want them all to see it, to pick it up, to feel it so they will know how much we have studied it and how serious it is." Expertise, he believed, would carry the day in committee. And he seemed less worried about time constraints than his staff.

Most of his strategizing pertained not to the committee but to the floor stage. He had, he said, persuaded Howard Baker to schedule the bill. "I personalized it, presidentialized it, partyized it, and countryized it—in that order," he explained.

> I told Baker it was something I had been working on for a long time. I told him the president was in favor of it. I told him it would be good for the party and good for the country. I told him it was a narrow issue. He said that it sounded like something that should be scheduled and that he'd find a window for it.

Looking ahead, Specter was eagerly preparing to apply the strategic lessons he had learned from his summit experience. He outlined the plan: "We'll bring it up on a Monday . . . when no one is there and no one is interested; debate the issue on Monday and vote on Tuesday." As a kind of an afterthought he noted, "Of course, anything Baker can do is limited by the fact that you need clearance from both sides of the committee. I'll need that from Thurmond and Kennedy." Characteristically, he underestimated the problems that might arise from those quarters.

On a talk show in Harrisburg, he answered a query about S 1688. "It's making good progress. I'm optimistic that it will be passed in the course of the next three weeks." As we drove away from the interview, he expressed his confidence again. "There's a lot of interest in 1688. If I can get that bill passed, it will be a hell of a deal. That's the first time I've put a definite time limit on its passage—three weeks. I did it deliberately. People are tired of vagaries." On that prediction, his staffers were more accurate than he. His deadline could not be met.

It was four weeks—July 22—before the revised draft report could be sent with Specter's cover letter to each member of the Judiciary Committee. On July 20, S 1688 occupied the same priority position on the Committee's formal agenda as it had occupied on June 15—twelfth in line. [13] In that interval, the full committee had held but one meeting to conduct business. The problem: no quorum. "Week after week, we haven't been able to get a quorum," complained Michel when he heard that the committee's executive session scheduled for July 20 had just been canceled.

> Specter's jumping up and down like a mad man. He's adamant about it and very frustrated that the committee can't get a quorum. No quorum, no meeting; no meeting, no chance for him to get the other members to focus on the bill. He goes to all the nonmeetings to try to make a quorum. He thinks that if he gets them to focus on the bill, they will pass it out of committee.

A bill's presence on the committee's decision agenda was no guarantee that it would be moved upward and onward. The process of clearing the agenda represented yet another distinct step on the road to passage. And it forced members of the enterprise to think about the internal procedures and influence patterns of the full committee.

Normally, the full committee met each Tuesday in executive session to process, in order, the items on its agenda. On Monday the top staffers from each subcommittee, majority and minority, met with the full committee staff chief to prepare the agenda for the weekly executive session. On Tuesday a printed tentative agenda would be circulated to all members. The Monday meeting, however, was strictly pro forma—at least, from the perspective of the Specter enterprise. "Nobody says anything. If you spoke up, it would be resented," explained one aide. "It's a complete waste of time. . . . We are supposed to discuss an agenda. We don't. We just accept the agenda set by the chairman." To have one's bill on the committee agenda, therefore, was to be heavily subject to the influence of Chairman Strom Thurmond.

As the difficulty in making a quorum became increasingly salient, the thoughts of the Specter enterprise turned to influencing Thurmond. "Our best bet is to have the administration call Thurmond and urge him to get a quorum," said a staff member. "If they would call Thurmond and Baker, I think we could get this bill moved ahead of some of those other bills that are more complicated and more controversial. Ours is a pretty simple bill. Once people see that, they will be in favor of it." And, if that didn't pan out, "our fallback strategy is for Arlen to use his influence with the other members, to talk to them individually, to try to get them to think about it for a minute or two and get them to come to a meeting." In either case, the burden would fall on Specter. It remained the first instinct of the enterprise, at every stage, to ask what individual action Specter might take to help pass his bill. They did not think instinctively in terms of alliances and coalitions.

Yet coalition-building possibilities existed. Other members had their bills stalled on the agenda, too. And the chairman had to be responsive to pressures from them to move their bills through the committee. In late July, having failed to get a quorum on the twentieth, and with the August recess fast approaching, the chairman did move to increase the chances of a quorum for July 27. He requested that the Republican subcommittee counsels meet separately, remove from the agenda any pending measures that might cause a member to boycott the executive session and, thus, prepare a noncontroversial agenda that would attract the ten-member majority (including one Democrat) needed for a quorum. In the all-Republican forum of counsels, Specter's representative was able to bargain. And by the processes of elimination and bargaining, S 1688 got moved up to fifth place on the tentative agenda for the next executive session. [14] Specter's staffers set about lobbying their fellow staffers to deliver their principals to the meeting. They believed that there was now a good chance that the bill would get acted upon and that if it were taken up it would be passed. His staffers reiterated, "Arlen thinks that he can persuade the others in committee." But he did not get the chance. On July 27, only five Republicans and one Democrat joined Specter at the committee meeting. For lack of a quorum, it was once again canceled.

ENTREPRENEUR AND COMMITTEE

In the wake of this major disappointment, and as the members of the enterprise girded for one last quorum effort before the recess, I talked with several of them about the committee context in which they operated and about the effectiveness of Arlen Specter in that context.

Their relationship with Chairman Thurmond and his staff, they reflected, had not been easy. For starters, there was the chairman's tight control over subcommittee budgets. "We have no discretionary funds," said a Juvenile Justice staffer. "We can't bring witnesses in without getting money from the full committee. We can't buy paper clips without going through the full committee." And there was also, in the eyes of Specter's subcommittee personnel, Thurmond's desire to keep them on "the shortest leash of all." They attributed much of this to Specter's governing style. "Party labels don't matter much to him. He's independent. And Thurmond just doesn't think a young senator should be so independent." Several of them recalled an incident, from early in the life of S 1688, when Specter had planned a hearing on the bill to coincide with the day of a widely publicized "walk against crime" in the District of Columbia. Thurmond deliberately scheduled the markup of another bill in the time slot scheduled for Specter's hearings—and then never held the meeting. They took it as a not very subtle early warning to the newcomer to be less aggressive in enhancing his reputation for fighting crime.

Day to day, of course, the Specter-Thurmond relationship meant the staff-to-staff relationship. But that relationship left much to be desired. A top aide explained:

> Arlen will talk to Strom and Strom will say "OK, I'll tell my staff to do it." Then we'll call the [committee] staff and say "My senator talked to your senator and they decided thus and so." The staff says, "OK." Then nothing happens. Or the thing grinds along slowly. If you want to move things, you have to spend time with the staff, become friendly with the staff.... [But] we are alien to the staff.... [We] don't have a cigar and a drink with them. We're too busy.... We worked for five weeks—the entire office—on the insanity hearings. Five days before the hearings, we called up our witnesses. Not one of them had heard from the committee staff since the original call asking them to testify—"Will you testify?" "Yes." That's all they had discussed—not when to come, where to park, where to stay, nothing. The committee did not want us to hold hearings. They can make things difficult or easy.

For the Specter subcommittee, "on the shortest leash of all," internal relationships tended to be difficult.

In the late spring, Specter ran into opposition again, this time on hearings he planned into the abuse of juveniles in the Oklahoma prison system. "We put in a request for money for an investigation," recalled one staffer, "and the request came back [marked] 'no.' We chose to construe the answer as denying us the money but not as a refusal to allow the investigation. And we sent our investigator out there. That was a hard decision." While their investigator was in Oklahoma, a member of the subcommittee staff weighed the possible consequences of that decision for Specter. "It may sour his relations with Thurmond. And that may affect everything else. But he's going ahead. You can't stop him. You're going to have to shoot him off his horse." The aide was right on both counts. The hard-charging prosecutor did not desist, and his relations with the chairman suffered.

Looking back on it, the same staffer recalled:

> Once [our investigator] came back with the facts, it was clear
> that a hearing was warranted. We set up the hearing quickly. I
> told a member of the committee staff at 11:30 that we were
> going ahead with a hearing at noon. I knew it would take them
> a while to get their act together to try to stop it. I also knew that
> if we didn't go ahead with it immediately, the hearing would
> never be held. Strom was very upset that we had sent out our
> investigator and held the hearing without his explicit permis-
> sion. . . . His reaction was partly financial. He's a tightwad. . . .
> Part of it was the speed with which it was done, without
> notifying people. And part of it was pure power: "I told you
> not to do it and you did it."

From the viewpoint of Thurmond's staff, Specter's actions were a
provocation. Afterward, when Specter requested hearings, full committee staff members would inquire, "What is this, another Oklahoma?"

There were provocations from the chairman's side, too. For example, on July 20, after one of the canceled committee meetings, the
committee staff circulated a ballot for the purpose of polling out of
committee two bills—one of which had come from Specter's subcommittee. It was done without consulting Specter's staff; the effect was to
deprive Specter of the leadership role on that particular bill. Coming as
it did on the heels of the canceled meeting, the move added insult to
injury. An aide exclaimed:

> I called them and said, "What the hell are you guys doing
> polling out one of our bills without consulting us? I wanted
> two chances for my guy to beat his chest, and you've robbed me
> of one." . . . . They apologized. But I was mad that we hadn't
> been consulted. That night I thought for a long time about
> whether to advise Arlen to object to the poll. One objection
> would sink it. But I decided instead that we couldn't do
> anything that would give Thurmond the faintest excuse to feel
> slighted. Our first job is to get it out of Strom's shop. We can't
> get the bill out without Strom. And Baker won't bring it to the
> floor without Strom's OK. So we cannot offend Strom in any
> way.

The provocation had come from the staff. But Specter's people believed
that the chairman's staffers "won't go to the bathroom without consulting Strom." Ultimately, it was the relationship with Strom Thurmond
that mattered. And in that relationship, they walked on eggshells.

To some staffers, the delicacy of it all was just plain frustrating.
"Arlen is a person of very great energy, willfulness, and force," reflected
one. "When he was district attorney of Philadelphia, he could dominate
almost any situation by virtue of those qualities. But those same qualities

count for very little here in the Senate. That infuriates me. . . . There is so much wheel spinning here." It was an expression, from the staff's perspective, of the limits of the style of the independent prosecutor in an institution that has collective dimensions—and of the continuing adjustment problems involved. It is not sufficient, in a collegial body, to be a policy expert. In order to sell your policy, it is necessary to sell yourself as someone to be trusted. Building trust requires having a record in the body; and establishing that record takes time.

The neophyte staff had to learn these things as well as the Senate newcomer. Yet for the frustrated staffer, the only answer was to apply still more energy to the task.

> I'm very pessimistic. I don't think we'll get a quorum. I don't think Thurmond will try hard enough. I told Arlen that I think the only way we will get a quorum is for the administration to call Strom Thurmond and say "We want this bill. You must get a quorum." The person we . . . [should] turn to is Ed Meese. He and Arlen get along well and respect each other. We met with Meese before; he liked our bill; crime is clearly within his bailiwick; and he understands the bill because of his background as a Los Angeles County prosecutor. He's our ace in the hole.

It was yet another one-on-one assignment for his boss. But it was also a nonsenatorial solution to a senatorial problem.

A second staffer viewed the problem, similarly, as one involving Chairman Thurmond. But his solution prescribed action within the Senate rather than a call for outside help.

> Two of our bills are most important—the trade bill and career-criminal. Right now neither one seems to be going anywhere fast. I'm not sure why. Arlen gets mad if you say "it's just the legislative process." He doesn't believe you have to wait till you've been here forever to move your bills through commit-tee. But I don't think he's willing to do the amount of quid pro quo that you need to move these bills along. He thinks they ought to carry on their merits. . . . I think that if he wants the career-criminal bill, he's got to swallow his pride, go to Strom Thurmond and say, "Strom, I want this bill more than anything else. . . ."

Like the first staffer, this person was posing the same problem of adjustment faced by an inveterately independent operator when placed in a collegial setting. His advice called for accommodation to the chairman's concerns. But he did not expect his senator to reach for the telephone anytime soon.

Partly, the staffer explained, he did not expect his boss to take a supplicant's approach to Thurmond because he did not believe Specter really thought of S 1688 as the one bill he had to have. And that was the case because the senator's work habits made it impossible for him to set or communicate priorities. As his aide described it:

> He doesn't delegate well. He likes to manage everything himself. When he wants something done, he will tell whichever staff person is with him at the time. He may tell several people.... Then we have mixups in signals and we lose memos. His attitude when he wants something done is "Do it." He doesn't want to go into details.... There is no chain of command in the office, just an inner circle of four or five people.... No one knows what he's thinking or what his priorities are. When he says "Do it" to someone, that means that priorities will have to shift. Other things won't get done. But he doesn't realize that.... He sees the problem intellectually, but he's so used to that style of doing things he can't change. His problem is how to channel that very powerful intellect ... I've said to him, "Arlen, you have got to put down on paper your agenda for the next few years—what you want to accomplish, what your goals are." ... He needs a better sense of direction. He doesn't know where he's going.

According to this staff member, Specter had not yet solved an adjustment problem he had faced from the very beginning—the increased need to delegate.

A third staff member applied a similar diagnosis to their dilemma with the career-criminal bill:

> I think it's his first priority. At least when he thinks about it, it is. When he gets through thinking about Lebanon, grain sales, and summits, it is. The question is: how much time has he spent personally talking with [Sen.] Chuck Grassley about it? How many people on the committee has he spent time with? Has he gone up to [Sen.] Max Baucus and said, "Max, this is my bill and I want to move it?" Max would say, "I don't know what it's about." And Arlen could give him a quick capsule.... I can write a fifty-page memo and it won't have any effect compared to thirty seconds on the floor between Arlen and another senator. That's the way the Senate works. If Arlen asks, they'll say, "Sure, Arlen." He knows that we're working on the staff level. The question is: What has he been doing? I wish you'd ask him the next time you see him. I should know what he's doing, but I don't. He says it's his top priority. But I don't know that he acts as if it is.

There was no doubt about Specter's expressed determination. But there was doubt about whether he was conveying that determination clearly to others. In this case, a lack of coordination with his staffers seemed evident. Still, the staff counted most on the abilities of their senator. And their prescription, as always, called for even more individual effort on his part. "Let Arlen do it" remained the operating premise of the Specter enterprise.

In the light of these expressed doubts about whether Specter had yet done all he could—and about what, in fact, he had done—I asked the senator and two of his aides separately for their head counts on committee support for S 1688. The request revealed two interesting facts. First, none of them had yet recorded such a vote count. Second, they had not yet shared even their preliminary assessments with one another. Their neglect of this elementary step in coalition building was wholly in keeping with a similar neglect during the subcommittee stage. And it confirmed my sense, from the staff interviews, that the main focus of their attention lay elsewhere—in the relations between Specter and Thurmond and in the governing style of their leader. They tended to treat the committee members by assumption, the assumption being that Specter's expertise and persuasiveness would win the members over when and if the time came. Faced with my request, however, they produced their vote counts.

A comparison of the three estimates showed, not surprisingly, great uncertainty about who would and who would not support the bill; not surprisingly, that is, in light of their lack of effort, their lack of coordination, and the diversity of their sources of information. Not surprisingly, too, the exercise showed Specter to be both the most certain and the most optimistic. Table 3-1 presents their overall estimates in four categories: yes, maybe, no, and don't know. In the aggregate, these on the spot vote counts seemed to predict ultimate success— especially if "maybe" was translated, reasonably, as "leaning yes." But looking at the list of senators, it is the uncertainty—the intercoder unreliability—that is most striking.

The three vote counters agreed on only four of the nineteen Judiciary Committee members—all were predicted "yes" votes—one of them was Specter's. Twelve members had at least one "maybe" or "don't know" next to his name. As for the five "no" votes, each was associated with a different senator—two Republicans and three Democrats. Uncertainty tended to be greatest, naturally, for the committee Democrats. But six of the ten committee Republicans were regarded as other than "yes" votes by at least one of the judges. And three of the "don't know" votes on Specter's list were Republicans.

The judgments of the staff members derived, of course, from their

TABLE 3-1 Estimated Full Committee Support for S 1688

	Specter (7/29/82)	Staffer A (8/2/82)	Staffer B (7/30/82)	Complete Agreement?
Republicans				
Thurmond	DK	N	M	N
Mathias	Y	Y	N	N
Laxalt	Y	Y	Y	Y
Hatch	Y	Y	Y	Y
Dole	Y	Y	M	N
Simpson	Y	Y	DK	N
East	DK	M	Y	N
Grassley	DK	Y	M	N
Denton	Y	Y	Y	Y
Specter	Y	Y	Y	Y
Democrats				
Biden	Y	M	N	N
Kennedy	Y	M	N	N
Byrd	DK	Y	M	N
Metzenbaum	Y	N	Y	N
DeConcini	Y	Y	DK	N
Leahy	Y	M	M	N
Baucus	Y	M	M	N
Heflin	Y	M	Y	N

Code: Y = yes; N = no; M = maybe; DK = don't know.

staff contacts. These were most extensive for staffer A. Specter's judgments, on the other hand, were derived from his one-on-one conversations with his colleagues. In view of the enterprise's heavy reliance on those contacts, it was instructive to listen to the senator's running commentary as he produced his head count. It is clear that he perceived his main obstacle to be the reluctance to expand federal jurisdiction. But he did not see that as a partisan matter. He believed that he could overcome that obstacle by a combination of policy and personal argumentation. That is, he would combine three arguments: that crime was a big problem, that he was a credible crime fighter, and that he had been a cooperative colleague. Consider the following (randomly ordered) ruminations about individual senators.

Senator A ("yes"): "He'll say, 'I don't know about federal jurisdiction. But crime is a problem. The states haven't done all that good a job. The administration does support it. Arlen Specter is no flaming liberal. He's a team player. He understands crime. Besides, we've got to give these younger guys a chance to make a contribution, too.' "

Senator B ("don't know"): "He could be a problem. He won't like federal jurisdiction. It's a matter of states' rights with him."

Senator C ("yes"): "He may be a problem, but I think he'll go for it. I've helped him on a couple of things. He's been pressing me hard to co-sponsor his . . . bill. But I tell him I can't and he understands. On one of the amendments the other day, I voted against him. He asked if I would wait around in case he needed my vote. I said I would. I hung around. When the vote got to be 66-30, I asked him, 'Can I go to lunch now?' He said, 'OK.' Those kinds of things help you around here. If you extend yourself a little for others, they will do the same for you. In a close call, that counts."

Senator D ("yes"): "He's OK. He looks upon the two of us as the swing men in the committee. The other day he said to me, 'You and I are the only two people on the committee who listen to the arguments and make up our minds. No one can figure out how we will vote.' "

Senator E ("don't know"): "He's a funny guy. A little while ago, he was trying to pass [a certain] bill out of his subcommittee. He was having trouble getting a quorum, so I went. As it turned out, I made a series of objections that torpedoed the bill. He got flustered and adjourned the meeting. I went to him and said, 'I think we can work this thing out. I think we can compromise. I want to help you out.' . . . We met in my office with staff and worked it out. I went three-quarters of the way with him. That sort of thing will help a great deal on the bill."

Senator F ("yes"): "He has complete confidence in anything I say in the criminal area. He'll sign off on everything I say. No problem."

Senator G ("yes"): (I asked, "Will he go as far as F?" Specter replied,) "He wouldn't go that far for his mother! He'll say, 'This crime-control stuff is just a code word for antiblack. But Specter isn't antiblack. Specter is a pretty liberal fellow. Crime is a real problem.' He'll be convinced on the merits."

Senator H ("yes"): "I hate to say this, but he's all over the place on this bill. He has absolutely no confidence in his own judgment on this matter. I don't understand it."

Senator I ("yes"): "He's an anticrime person and he's not a states' rights person. He likes the idea. He'll make up his mind quickly—not like Senator H—and that will be that."

Senator J ("yes"): "He has given me a flat commitment in support of it. But he may go south on me despite that commitment, once he hears all the arguments. I have told everyone why it's a good bill. But I haven't given them the opposing arguments."

Senator K ("don't know"): "He hasn't focused on it; but he'll be troubled by states' rights . . . whereas Senator A will say, 'Specter needs the bill,' with K it may work in reverse—sibling rivalry. But I've established a relationship with K. He lobbied me on [a] vote this year. 'We've got to have you,' I told him. 'I'm going to vote against the bill. But on the amendments, I'll hold off and let you make me an argument.'. . . I said, 'I won't vote until you've had a chance to talk to me.'. . . K appreciated that."

Senator L ("yes"): "He's hard to figure out. He was a former prosecutor and he's quite conservative. He's worried about jurisdictional problems. I think he'll come around. If he does, he'll be a good person to have on our side. So will [Senator M, another projected "yes" vote] if he comes along."

Senator N ("don't know"): "I've talked to every member of the committee but him."

Clearly, the Pennsylvania newcomer had done a lot of what he and his staff believed he should do. He had contacted the membership of the committee personally. On the other hand, he had obtained few, if any, reliable commitments. A good number of his projected "yes" votes turned out to be, on closer inspection, much closer to "maybe." The more complete his reported judgments, the more cautious they were. As his staffers had suspected, therefore, a lot of one-on-one work remained to be done.

In this regard, it is important to note Specter's obvious sensitivity to his community relationships. His staffers, we have noted, worried about his effectiveness with his colleagues—that his aggressive prosecutorial abilities were inappropriate to the Senate. But Specter obviously understood the importance of good personal relationships and of the procedural favor trading that underlay those relationships. "Personal relationships are very important around here," he generalized. "Do people like you? Do they trust you? Are they envious of you? Do they think you are trying to push too many bills?" At least, these matters figured prominently in his support calculations. Just how much his longstanding stylistic preferences would be attenuated by these demands of collegiality might remain in doubt; but his intellectual recognition of their importance in Senate life would not. Collegiality was a factor that could not help but impress any newcomer when he or she had to seek support from another senator for something of unique importance to him or to her. The career-criminal bill was just such a matter for the newcomer from Pennsylvania.

In the same conversation with the senator, I found no disagreement with the idea that he would have to carry the load himself. But I found a good deal less anxiety and frustration than I had expected. He accepted his current difficulties, was willing to adopt a longer time horizon, and seemed optimistic about the eventual outcome. Underlying it all was the sense that he had, indeed, learned from what had happened. "The bill is going fine," he began.

I'm distressed that I'm having so much trouble getting it up for a vote. We can't get a quorum. It took time to get the report written and time to get it polled out. . . . It's been quite an experience to talk and negotiate with everyone—to talk to all those characters in OMB whose names I have completely forgotten now. I don't have a position of strength. I don't have the right subcommittee chairmanship to move it through the committee. It really belongs to the subcommittee on criminal law. And the administration isn't going to do anything special for me. I'm too independent in their eyes. . . . It's been a good learning experience. I've kept the bill separate from the big crime bill. I have taken it carefully every step of the way.

He believed, he said again, "If I can get it up [in committee] next week, I can pass it out of committee. Baker says he'll put it on the calendar. The problem is, can we get a quorum next week?" He seemed prepared for the worst. As our conversation ended, he commented: "It won't be the worst thing that could happen if the bill doesn't pass this year. I have time . . . I still think I can get it passed in the Senate. I don't know about the House. There may not be enough time. But getting it passed in the Senate will count." That is, "count" toward the kind of reputation he wanted to achieve. And "count" toward a sense of adjustment to the Senate. Psychologically, if not substantively, the success of his bill remained a matter of the highest priority for him.

REVISION AND PASSAGE

On August 4, the committee finally succeeded in getting a quorum; but Specter's scenario did not work out. Trouble came not from any direction he had anticipated, but rather from a direction that had long concerned his staff. In the Monday agenda-setting session of top subcommittee staffers—this time attended by Democrats as well as Republicans—the committee staff again tried to produce a noncontroversial agenda. And they announced that, in private conversation, some staffers for Democratic senators had objected to S 1688. With no discussion of specifics, the career-criminal bill was removed entirely from the committee's August 4 agenda. Specter's people did not know, at first, where the objections had come from and whether they had come from senators or from their staffs. Their longtime fear had been that their problems would come from a hesitant staff. "Staff people don't know how to treat the bill. It confuses them," said one aide. Another asserted, "It's different from anything most people are used to. That's particularly true of staff." They suspected staff problems now. "If it's at the staff level," said one staffer about the objection,

that presents all kinds of roadblocks for us. It means we may
have the votes, but we'll never get it to a vote. . . . I've asked
Arlen to talk to Kennedy and Biden to see what the problem is.
My guess is that they won't know what he's talking about. No
senator has focused on it. Senators may go along with other
senators. . . . "It's a tough crime bill. OK. I'll go with you, Arlen,
on a tough crime bill." If that works, we can circumvent the
staff. Can you imagine having the votes of senators and being
held up by staff?

One objection, as they suspected, came from the enterprise of
Democrat Ted Kennedy. He, they believed, had been strongly influenced by Boston's district attorney, Newman Flanagan. "He [Flanagan]
got the DAs' association to withdraw their support [for S 1688] and now
the DAs are killing us." Nor had they made headway with the Kennedy
staff. "I spent an hour talking to Senator Kennedy's staff person the
other day," said one Specter aide, several days before the objection was
registered.

[She's] a twenty-six-year-old woman who worked in the Justice
Department. She is typical of the staff people we have to deal
with—young, bright, law clerk type, never tried a case, never
practiced law, never prosecuted a criminal, and doesn't understand the prosecutorial experience. I'm afraid that some senators will be captured by their staffs. At least they'll be convinced the bill is controversial. And that's enough.

The objection from Kennedy's staff was not the only one. But the others
remained unidentified. At the executive session, Specter spoke up on
behalf of his bill, working to keep it alive and trying to smoke out
objections. But it was not acted on—which meant it would not have
another chance until after the August recess.

In the aftermath of this setback, Specter's aides were pessimistic but
persevering. One reflected:

There are some bills which people feel just ought not to be
passed. They are just too new or too complicated or too poorly
understood. Maybe this is one of them. But if you work for
Arlen Specter, you don't stop. You keep right on working. The
problem is, will we ever get another quorum? Maybe on the
twelfth—the twelfth of never.

Another one imputed his own pessimism to Specter. "I have the
sense," he said,

that for the first time Arlen thinks the bill may not go
anywhere. Up to now, he's always been optimistic—"I've
talked to the members, we'll get it done." I've always been

more pessimistic. I've told him he needed a push from the administration, that he couldn't do it all by himself. I think he sees that now. I say all this because of the instructions he's given me now, to think more broadly and more long run about a crime-control package. With 1688, the idea always was, "get it done this year, show what a newcomer can do, get on the scoreboard." Now he seems to be talking more about the long run.

This staffer added, "Strom is upset at Arlen, but Arlen doesn't see it at all." And another chimed in, "It's ironic that we should have to plead with the Democrats now, but Specter has cut all his bridges with Thurmond."

But Specter, leaving for the August recess, was less pessimistic than they and was still pushing.

I don't think Kennedy has focused on it yet. He and I are going to sit down and talk about it. I think it will be focused on one day soon. It depends when we meet, whether we get a quorum, what place it is on the agenda. . . . Thurmond is noncommittal. But Hatch is for it; Laxalt is for it; Denton is for it; Biden is strongly for it; Metzenbaum is OK. I've done a lot of lobbying. And the process goes on.

The persistent prosecutor was neither downhearted nor defeated. He was the same man who had told his constituents during the campaign, "I don't discourage easily. In fact, I don't discourage at all."

I left Washington at the August recess, too, and returned only briefly in December. But in late September, Arlen Specter's entrepreneurial persistence paid off. S 1688 was taken up and passed by the Judiciary Committee on September 21. [15] It passed the full Senate just nine days later. But the price of support in both arenas was his acceptance of the position of the National District Attorneys Association (NDAA). In full committee, it was Chairman Thurmond who insisted. On the Senate floor, it was Edward Kennedy who did so. The senator from Pennsylvania yielded the "nonnegotiable" ground he had held from the beginning by agreeing to two changes: first, to allow no federal prosecution under the law without the consent of the state prosecutor, that is, to adopt the original "mutual consent" stipulation of the NDAA resolution; and second, to place this stipulation among the substantive provisions in the main section of the legislation instead of in a separate "intent of Congress" section at the end of the legislation. With those changes, S 1688 passed the Senate 93-1 on September 30, 1982. [16]

In a letter, Specter described briefly what had happened in the committee:

As I'm sure you will recall, we had enormous difficulty getting a quorum.... There were a number of objections from Senators Baucus, DeConcini, Kennedy, Leahy, Metzenbaum, East and perhaps others. We finally got it up for consideration ... late in the afternoon on Tuesday, September 21.... I had spoken individually to Senators East, Baucus, Kennedy and DeConcini concerning their objections and ... I had discussed it with Senators Thurmond, Hatch, Dole, Simpson, Mathias and Grassley.

At the hearing ... there were only ten Senators present and Senators DeConcini and Mathias were edging out the door. After I had explained the bill, Senator Thurmond was handed a letter from his aide from the National District Attorneys Association objecting to the bill on the ground that it took authority away from the state prosecutor. At that juncture, Senator Thurmond announced that he was opposed to the bill because it was an intrusion on states' rights and he always had fought against intrusion on states' rights, including running for President in 1948.

Senator Biden, who had been very helpful, then proposed a compromise which would require acquiescence of a state prosecutor. While I would have preferred not to make that compromise, I was prepared to do so. When I agreed, Senator Thurmond said he would support the bill. [17]

As Specter's bill had been written from the outset, the *federal* crime occurred whenever someone was indicted for a robbery or burglary after having been convicted twice previously under *state* law. And although prosecution by the federal authorities was "ordinarily" to be subject to agreement with the local prosecutor, some latitude was left for the federal prosecutor to initiate, on his own, the proceedings in federal court. In the Judiciary Committee meeting, Chairman Thurmond's original position undercut both of these provisions. He first argued that the federal crime occurred only if all three robberies or burglaries were *federal* offenses; state offenses would not count. That would have limited the application of the bill to a tiny number of federal offenses (against post offices, military bases, and so on), since most convictions for robbery and burglary involved state law. Second, Thurmond argued—as a fallback position—that the federal prosecutor could get involved only when requested to do so by the local prosecutor. Thus, he would have taken away from the federal authorities all their remaining capacity to initiate proceedings on their own.

To Specter, this meant giving an absolute veto power to the local authorities in determining a federal crime. He had resisted strenuously up to this point, both for his own reasons and for fear of losing the support of the Justice Department. It was Sen. Joseph Biden (Del.), the ranking committee Democrat—not Specter—who carried the rebuttal against both of Thurmond's arguments in the committee. Biden was able to negate the first argument entirely and to save a requesting, though not determining, role for the federal authorities in the second argument. That is, the federal authorities could decide on their own to make the case for federal prosecution. But the local people could reject, that is, veto, the request.

An excerpt from the transcript of the meeting (with italics added) follows.

> *The Chairman.* Now, if he [Specter] wants to introduce a bill here, the *third federal offense,* where they violated the *federal law,* I will go with him. But I do not want to say to take over from the state because there have been two crimes committed there and say the third one will be a federal offense. I am just opposed to mixing up the jurisdictions. I am opposed to expansion of federal power. I will have to vote against it, Senator, as I told you before. I am not convinced.
>
> *Senator Biden.* Mr. Chairman, may I suggest something that maybe would allow you to vote for it, if Senator Specter would consider it?
>
> In section 4(a) of Senator Specter's bill, it says:
>
>> It is the intent of the Congress regarding the exercise of jurisdiction under this Act that ordinarily the United States should defer to State and local prosecutors of armed robbery and armed burglary offenses. However, if, after full consultation between the local prosecuting attorney and the appropriate federal prosecuting authority, *either* the local attorney requests or concurs in the federal prosecution and the Attorney General finds such a prosecution practicable, *or* the Attorney General, Deputy Attorney General, Associate Attorney General, or designated Assistant Attorney General, *determine that a federal prosecution is necessary* to vindicate a significant federal interest, et cetera.
>
> Is the Senator from Pennsylvania willing to drop the portion of the language that begins with "or" and just leave it to the consultation between . . . the local prosecutor and the Attorney General, if they both agree that it should be prosecuted. It would seem to me it would solve the Senator from South Carolina's problem. . . .
>
> I would respectfully suggest that the Senator from South Carolina should consider federal jurisdiction if, in fact, the local authorities are willing to have that extended, and that the

Senator from Pennsylvania should consider dropping that section from the bill. It would make everybody happy, and a practicable solution.

Senator Specter. Well, Senator Biden, the District Attorneys Association was willing to support the bill, as the testimony from its National President, Newman Flanagan, said, if there was concurrence on both sides. Frankly, the concern that I have had is on a federal bill to give, in effect, the *veto* power to the District Attorney. But I am not cast in concrete on the issue.

Senator Biden. Well, if you are not, I would move to amend the Senator from Pennsylvania's bill to strike everything after the word "practicable" in section 4(a) of the bill, so the last sentence ends at "either the local prosecuting authority requests or concurs in federal prosecution and the Attorney General finds such prosecution practicable."

I would so move that amendment, Mr. Chairman. I would beg the Chairman to take a good look at that, because I think that may solve his problem and give us what Senator Specter is absolutely accurate in attempting to achieve. . . .

The Chairman. Senator Biden has made a suggestion that you take out from "or the Attorney General" on down to the end of that paragraph. Now, if you want to take out three words above there, so it will read this way: "However, if, after full consultation between the local prosecuting authority and the appropriate federal prosecuting authority" and take out *"either"* and say *"the local prosecuting authority requests federal prosecution,* and the Attorney General finds such prosecution practicable."

Senator Biden. Mr. Chairman, the reason why I would not want to amend it that way would be that I think that the purpose here is to be able to provide some leverage on the State courts in terms of moral suasion here. *I want the federal prosecutor to be able to make a request of the local jurisdiction,* to be able to prosecute in federal court. But I *also want to give the local jurisdiction the right to say "No, we don't want you to do that."*

Otherwise, what we will have if we leave it up to merely the local prosecutor making the request, we are essentially—although technically we have changed the law—right where we are now. Local prosecutors are overburdened as it is now.

The Chairman. Well, under your position, would the local prosecutor request it?

Senator Biden. He could request it.

The Chairman. Well, suppose he does not request it or does not concur in it?

Senator Biden. If he does not concur, it does not go forward, under my proposition.

The Chairman. I will go with it if you can get the proper wording on that.

Senator Specter. I would accept the language which Senator Biden has proposed, if that would be agreeable to you, Mr. Chairman.

Senator Biden. I would suggest we move the bill with that amendment, Mr. Chairman, subject to your staff having the right to—

The Chairman. That the government will not have jurisdiction unless the local people—

Senator Biden. Concur.

The Chairman. —request or concur—

Senator Biden. No. Concur. *The federal officials can request, but if the local officials do not concur, federal jurisdiction does not lie.* ...

The Chairman. If you want to leave it up to Senator Specter and see if we can get together, all right. Otherwise, I cannot go along with it.

Senator Specter. I will agree to that, Mr. Chairman.

The Chairman. That you and I can get together.

Senator Specter. With the substitute, I move its adoption, subject to the amendments which we have discussed here.

The Chairman. Well, subject to the verbiage that you and I- -

Senator Specter. Will work out. I agree.

The Chairman. If we can agree.

Senator Specter. Fine.

The Chairman. Is that agreeable, then? All right, all in favor say "aye."

[Chorus of "ayes."]

The Chairman. All opposed, "no." "Ayes" have it. [18]

Senators Thurmond and Specter did meet and they worked out language agreeable to both, along the "request or concur" lines suggested by Biden. The bill was delayed temporarily on its trip to the Senate floor, when Senators Kennedy and Leahy placed holds on it. They did so at the behest of the NDAA, which was arguing that the new jurisdictional language was fine, but that it belonged in the operative section of the bill (sec. 2) and not in the intent of Congress section (sec. 4). It was the view of Specter's staff that this represented a wholly new demand by the NDAA. "Even though it was blackmail" said one, "we had to agree to move the language up. Time was running out and we were getting too much flak." They agreed to a Kennedy amendment moving the language (see Appendix). With that change, the bill was brought up in the Senate by unanimous consent on September 30. It passed the Senate after a brief speech by Specter and the amendment by Kennedy—in about twelve minutes.

There was no champagne in the office. "We sat around talking about it for half an hour and then went on to other things," recalled an aide. Had they talked about their ability to predict the behavior of individual committee members, they would have noted that the person with the most accurate midsummer assessment of objections and probable votes was not the senator, whose contacts were with his colleagues, but staffer A, who had the closest contacts with each senator's staff. On a matter where expertise is thought to be controlling, a staff member's antennae may be more sensitive to argumentation than his or her senators'. As a result of staff-to-staff consultation, staff members may know how senators will eventually respond before the senators know themselves.

Doubtless, the Specter staffers did talk about the accomplishment. "People who have been around here for years," said one afterward,

> couldn't think of a time when a freshman senator introduced a
> bill that was totally his own work and got it passed so quickly.
> It took exactly one year minus a day. People say that the life
> cycle from mental conception to passage in the senate is in the
> three-to-five-year time frame, regardless of the seniority of the
> senator.

Specter himself wrote in the October 8 letter cited earlier, "We have been working on the concept and the drafting since the start of 1981, so I consider it a two-full-year venture." Doubtless there was much pleasure taken in the accomplishment.

My own distance from the denouement precludes any satisfactory explanation for Biden's crucial contribution to the success of the bill. I can say only that Specter had, from the very beginning, assumed that Biden—the leader of committee Democrats on crime issues—was totally supportive of his effort on its merits and that Biden respected his experience and judgment in criminal matters. Specter's willingness to vote with the Democrats in committee enhanced this relationship. But I never heard Specter say anything to indicate any sense of reliance on Biden—far from it. Everything that I had heard from beginning to end had emphasized and assumed the total self-reliance of the persistent prosecutor. Evidently, it became obvious to Biden, and perhaps to Specter too, that the newcomer could not go head to head with the chairman when the crunch came; that Thurmond could be persuaded to modify his views only by a more important, more senior figure; and that Biden as the ranking committee Democrat was someone with whom Thurmond was accustomed to negotiating regularly on the full range of committee business.

An added factor, of course, may have been the strained relationship between Thurmond and Specter, as it was frequently articulated by Specter's staff—but, it should be noted, never by Specter himself. Indeed, when I asked him later why Chairman Thurmond agreed at all to negotiate some new language with him, Specter answered:

> Because I have worked out a very good personal relationship with him. All my showing up to make a quorum and attending the meetings—all that counts, now, at the end. Howard Baker asked me if I would nominate Strom Thurmond for Senate President Pro Tem. I said I would do so with great enthusiasm, wrote to Baker, and sent a copy to Thurmond. I don't think he gets many letters like that, do you?

"Personal relationships are important around here," he added. And he remained optimistic, as always, about his. Whatever the case, the intervention of the most senior committee Democrat to save the pet bill of the most junior committee Republican illustrates both the nonhierarchical and the bipartisan components of the contemporary Senate.

WINNING SUPPORT IN THE HOUSE: FALL AND WINTER 1982

With the Senate passage of S 1688, the thoughts of the Specter enterprise turned in earnest to the prospects for the bill's passage in the House. That meant focusing on the activity of Rep. William Hughes, chairman of the subcommittee to which the career-criminal bill had been sent and out of whose subcommittee the bill had yet to emerge. Neither the chairman nor the Democratic majority of his subcommittee would be moved by administration support.

Hughes's main legislative interest, as noted earlier, lay in an omnibus, LEAA-style justice assistance bill providing direct aid to states and localities. It had passed the House but not the Senate. The Hughes bill was not incompatible with S 1688, but its emphasis on strengthening state and local crime-fighting efforts was contrary to the increased federal intervention contemplated in Specter's legislation. Hughes's attitude toward S 1688 was thought to run from strongly skeptical on the merits to mildly favorable on the politics. Action at the "mildly favorable" end of the scale was thought to depend on Specter's support for Hughes's bill. While denying any sort of quid pro quo, Specter had introduced a bill similar to Hughes's bill, S 2411, and was shepherding it through the Senate. Thinking seriously about the prospects of S 1688 in the House, therefore, involved a very different cast of characters and a changed strategic situation.

When I returned to Washington for a few days in early December, the Specter enterprise was pursuing two courses of action—selling S 1688 to Hughes and his subcommittee and pushing S 2411 through the Senate. "We're trying to move on two tracks," said one staffer. "There has been no deal, no quid pro quo arrangement. But there is a sense in which the two are linked. Arlen has done a lot of work on both." The comment was in keeping with the senator's innate aversion to quid pro quo arrangements. But a second staffer spoke less cautiously about the reality of the "two tracks."

> It's fascinating, 1688 is the engine that is driving 2411. The only reason Arlen is interested in 2411 is because he knows the success of 1688 is tied to the success of 2411. Implicitly and inexorably, it is becoming clear that the fate of one is linked to the fate of the other. Arlen hasn't come right out and said it yet; but I think he might if you asked him. When I talk to Hughes' guy, I'll say to him, "You and I know what forces are at work here." And he'll say to me, "Don't worry, we're moving your bill."

In spite of his preference for unencumbered individual activity, Specter was being forced into an intercameral logroll. And he was being forced to expend his energies on two bills at once.

As it turned out, the career-criminal track required more of his energies, at least in terms of persuasion. The all purpose justice assistance legislation began with bipartisan support in the Senate and remained highly popular throughout its legislative travels. [19] The only difficulty associated with it sprang from the eagerness of senators to attach all sorts of favorite legislative ideas to a vehicle that seemed assured of passage. Specter's negotiating efforts were aimed at keeping the bill free from amendments that might sink it. His negotiating efforts on behalf of S 1688, on the other hand, centered on keeping it alive.

The problem was a familiar one. One of his staffers reported:

> There is a lot of resistance on the House side—vague, philo-sophical objections about federal jurisdiction. Why should the federal government get into this? Why not just give the local law enforcement agencies what they need? They are the same arguments we got in the Senate. They just feel uncomfortable with it. . . . I'm afraid what will happen is that they will say, "Let's not rush this through. It doesn't feel right. Why don't we have another hearing?"

The Hughes subcommittee had had a hearing, on September 23, at which Senator Specter had testified. [20] But then "they went home for the [congressional] election; they forgot what it was about, and they haven't focused on it since." A Specter aide put "our chances right now [at] no better than 50-50." He continued:

> We have four problems. First, the unfamiliarity of the [House] subcommittee members with the bill; second, four out of four of the subcommittee staff members are opposed to the bill; third, the continued opposition of the National District Attorneys Association; fourth, Hughes' leadership is uncertain.

On top of those problems, the end of the session was approaching. "Even if we get it out of subcommittee," he added, "we have to get it out of the full [Judiciary] Committee, and then we have to get a rule. And there are only so many days for the [House] Rules Committee to meet. We may run out of time."

What to do about this bundle of problems? Put the persistent prosecutor to work on them, of course. "Arlen has to do a personal selling job. And that's what he's doing. . . . He's calling the members of the House subcommittee personally . . . trying to get them to think about it, doing an educational job and a selling job." The battle plan had a familiar ring to it. So did the pattern of pessimism from the staff members of the enterprise and optimism from the senator. One staffer admitted:

> Arlen is a lot more optimistic than I am. He's been talking to the members of the subcommittee. He wants to go to their subcommittee markup. He thinks he can make the argument: "We've got to do it. Trust me on the substantive details. Let's all get behind this bill." He thinks he can carry them along. I think that's more likely to work in the Senate than in the House.

One fear he expressed was that the NDAA would be even more effective in the House than in the Senate, since "the organization is dominated by the small towns. There are three thousand counties and each one has a district attorney." Whereas big city DAs tended to favor the bill, small town DAs did not. Specter was learning this, too:

> I had lunch with [ranking Republican subcommittee member] Hal Sawyer yesterday. He has a very different perspective from western Michigan, than I do. He's from a small town, rural district. So is Hughes from a small town, rural district. They don't see the need for it that I do. So it's a selling job that I have to do.

But he remained optimistic. As we conversed, he was calling Representative Hughes.

> Bill, I hear they had to get you out of the steambath. I want to talk to you about your bill and my bill. Baker says we may take

up 2411 later this afternoon . . . Biden is ready to go on it. . . . About my bill, I hear some rumbles. What's the situation? Is there any precedent—not that I would do it—but could I come over to your markup if I wanted to? No problem? Well I might come over to be there just to answer questions. When is the markup? . . .

If he could help nudge it through the subcommittee, he remained optimistic about the support he would get from Chairman Peter Rodino in moving it through the full Judiciary Committee. "Rodino is in favor of it. He wasn't at first, but he is now. . . . He will help." As things turned out, Specter would need the help.

On December 9, I watched the House subcommittee members consider their equivalent of S 1688, HR 6386, introduced by Rep. Ron Wyden (D-Ore.). It was an informal markup session, at the end of an unrelated hearing. It took place from 11:45 to 1:15, with no more than five outsiders in attendance at any one time. Chairman Hughes and Republican members Harold Sawyer (Mich.) and Tom Kindness (Ohio) began the discussion. Democrats Robert Kastenmeier (Wis.), Dan Glickman (Kan.), and John Conyers (Mich.) plus Republican Hamilton Fish (N.Y.), came as the discussion proceeded. Representative Wyden was there from the beginning. The senator from Pennsylvania came in about a quarter of the way through and left shortly before the vote.

Viewing the event exclusively from the Specter position, the crucial ingredient was the palpable effort of Chairman Hughes to bring the proceedings to a successful conclusion. It was obvious that several subcommittee members had not paid any attention to the bill, which meant that Hughes had to allow a fairly free-form discussion. On the other hand, he had to step in on occasion to move things gently toward a vote. As he did so, his own preference in favor of the bill became clear. We cannot know just how much his support influenced other subcommittee members. Nor, indeed, can we begin to explain the position of any other House member. But Hughes—along with ranking minority member Sawyer—deserves the lion's share of the credit for the 4-3 vote by which the career-criminal bill passed the House subcommittee.

From the beginning of the discussion, Sawyer sought to make it clear, as the price of his support, that there had to be an absolute veto in the hands of the local prosecutor. In so doing, he placed a word that had been avoided in the Senate—*veto*—squarely at the center of the discussion. Once assured by Hughes, with a nod from Specter, that "a local veto" did exist, he said, "I'll go for it, though I am not enthusiastic about the bill." He did yeoman service later in the discussion, however, when the clarity of the relationship between federal and local jurisdiction was repeatedly questioned by others. "The feds will never, under normal circumstances, get their hand on a robber or burglar unless the locals hand them over," he stated. To another questioner, he replied, "If the DAs are opposed, it shows they don't understand it." In the end, Sawyer voted Fish's proxy, too, in favor of the bill.

A third vote in favor came from Glickman, who had come to the meeting convinced, as he put it, that "this is a very useful piece of legislation; there is nothing harmful about it at all." Although Sawyer's unenthusiastic acceptance may well have been influenced by Specter's personal lobbying effort, Glickman's acceptance may have been influenced by a quite different relationship with the senator. Said Specter afterward, "My father and his grandfather were junk dealers together in Wichita, Kansas. He was more supportive than he might have been under other circumstances."

The biggest disappointment to the Specter group was the negative vote of former FBI agent Tom Kindness. "He didn't seem to have a very good grasp of the bill. He hadn't done his homework," said one. On the jurisdictional matter, he vacillated throughout the discussion between the position that "a local veto" was needed and the position that it might be so strong that it constituted an invasion of federal prerogatives. Hughes, Sawyer, and, later, Specter tried to resolve his doubts, but to no avail. With a tacit admission that he could not figure it out, he adopted a "plague on both your houses" posture and voted against it.

The "no" votes of Kastenmeier and Conyers were ostensibly determined on procedural grounds. What lay behind their argument is not clear—perhaps some serious concerns about the possible encroachment on civil liberties. Both men maintained that the bill had not been adequately considered. Kastenmeier argued that it came too late in the session to be taken up properly by the full committee. Conyers argued that *his* subcommittee had legitimate jurisdiction over the bill, too, and it had not had time to hear all its own witnesses. Hughes reminded them both that his subcommittee *had* held a "sensitive," "exhaustive" hearing, that all committee precedents had been observed, that "you're either for it or against it," and that "I think it is incumbent on us to act on it." When they did, the two Democrats voted against it.

Arlen Specter's participation in all this was minimal, but his presence was testimony to his continuing personal effort to nurture his idea to fruition. He first entered the discussion when Kastenmeier was pressing Sawyer to explain the bill's rationale. "Is it permissible for me to speak?" Specter asked Hughes. "I've been sitting here wanting to say something, but I'd like to step in if it is all right." Hughes replied, "It's very informal." Then Specter explained the huge prosecutorial workload in big cities, the resulting inadequacy of sentencing, and the need for extra leverage in coping with repeat offenders. He answered a few more of Kastenmeier's questions in a low key, informational exchange.

Specter entered the discussion for the second and last time when Hughes came under heavy obstructionist fire from Conyers, who criticized Hughes's hearings as inadequate, called for additional hearings before Conyers's own subcommittee, and suggested a postponement of the markup. Hughes gently but firmly told Conyers that he had had plenty of time and notice; Conyers replied that he had never seen the Senate record or the House record. At that point, Hughes mentioned Specter's hearings, called the bill "one of Senator Specter's major initiatives," and looked over invitingly at the senator. Specter spoke up, saying that his subcommittee had, indeed, heard "several dozen witnesses" over "a four-day period" and had spent "lots of time" in hearings. Conyers shot back:

> Senator, if you're suggesting that your hearings are adequate for this body, I want to point out to you that it has absolutely nothing to do with the responsibilities of this body.

"I want to be helpful" replied Specter.

> In the closing days of the session, there are so many things to be done. I'm trying as hard as I can, consistent with appropriate practice, to consult with everyone. I sent copies of our report to everyone. I'm not suggesting anything about your responsibilities. I wouldn't do that.

The bicameral byplay ended. And the intense, combative prosecutor had been the one to hold his tongue. The restraint was a further indication that he had learned, against his instincts, to observe institutional protocol. "He was just great," said a staffer afterward. "He was angry and he started to blow, but he held back. He was very tactful." Specter may not have helped his cause, but he had avoided an exchange that could have damaged it.

The House subcommittee meeting was the last event in the life of the career-criminal bill that I was able to observe myself or discuss soon thereafter with participants. The rest of the story has been pieced together by records, by correspondence, by telephone, and by interviews less closely connected in time to the events.

With its passage by the House subcommittee, career-criminal legislation moved into the domain of Judiciary Committee Chairman Rodino. "The only way we will pass the bill now," said a staffer,

> is by suspension of the [House] rules. That depends entirely on Rodino. He doesn't want to hold a [full committee] markup because he's sitting on many other bills. He certainly can't hold a markup for this one bill. . . . But he can, without a

markup, without a meeting, with just a signature, send a letter to the Speaker asking him to bring it up [on the floor] on suspension.

That was not to be.

Later, on the afternoon of December 9, with Specter as its floor manager, and with his committee colleagues praising the Pennsylvania senator for his "persistence," the Justice Assistance Act (S 2411) passed the Senate by a voice vote.[21] When Specter called Hughes "to give him the news and to pursue the next step on getting S 1688 through the House," Hughes reported that S 1688 had reached a dead end in the House. As Specter wrote, "He advised me that the prospects for S 1688 in the House were bleak because Chairman Rodino did not intend to call a full committee meeting and did not want to take the exceptional step of putting S 1688 on the suspension calendar."[22] Time had combined with his negative-to-lukewarm attitude toward the bill to render Rodino of no help at the point where his help was most needed.

In the same letter, Specter recounted the ensuing events.

> Up to that time, I had expected S 1688 to be passed by the House. When Bill Hughes gave me that information, I then decided to try to add on S 1688 to S 2411 so that the House would have S 1688 in conference. I checked with Senator Baker and found that we could hold S 2411 at the desk if we obtained unanimous consent not to engross it which was the next step before sending it to the House. Unanimous consent was obtained late on December 9 not to engross S 2411.
>
> When I sought to add S 1688 to S 2411, I found that many people wanted to add their own bills and it became a very complex matter. After working on the matter for several days, I finally found that I could not even send S 2411 to the House at all unless I added on legislation on Tylenol, pharmacy robbery, CIA agents and ultimately the entire crime package of S 2572. When that entire package was sent over on December 14 . . . it looked like S 2411 was so weighted down that it would sink. . . . The staffs met and were bogged down on the many differences on the many bills. It appeared, as of late yesterday afternoon [December 19], that the package was going to die. Senator Thurmond had talked to Chairman Rodino and that appeared to be the likely fate of the crime package.[23]

At that point, S 1688 had become a very small part of a very large package. Its provisions filled only one of the bill's thirty-four columns in the *Congressional Record*.[24]

But the persistent prosecutor—the manager of S 2411—had not given up. "As you know," his letter continued,

> I have been working closely with Congressman Hughes, and I
> called him late yesterday afternoon [December 19] and we
> arranged to meet at 7:30 PM, with the meeting expanded to
> include Senators Thurmond, Biden, Kennedy and Congress-
> man Hal Sawyer.... We finally got most of the problems
> worked out.

It was the view of the Senator's staff that "Specter organized the whole
thing. He made the meeting happen. The principals had to meet and cut
a deal or the whole thing would unravel." But it was also their view that
without the desire and the push of each of the other principals, the bill
would have died. Senators Thurmond and Biden, authors of the largest
part of the crime package, had a particularly large stake in the bill.

So it was a collective accomplishment by a group of individuals,
each of whom had his own reasons for acting. The senator from
Pennsylvania—driven by his strong desire to pass a career-criminal
bill—had worked within the context created by the desires of others. But
to the last, he had clearly played an entrepreneurial role. On December
20, Hughes maneuvered the conference report through the House. And
at 2:15 a.m. on the twenty-first, the Senate, by unanimous consent
adopted it also. [25] "Crime Bill Is Sent to President" read the *New York
Times* headline. [26] Arlen Specter's career-criminal bill had surmounted its
next-to-last legislative hurdle.

LOSING ADMINISTRATION SUPPORT: WINTER 1982-1983

From a brief note from the senator dated January 11, 1983, I learned
more about the progress of the career-criminal bill. "At the moment, we
are in the throes of trying to avoid a veto on the crime package," he
wrote. [27] Three days later, President Reagan, one of the earliest supporters of career-criminal legislation, vetoed the huge anticrime package.
Describing the bill as "a miscellaneous assortment of criminal justice
proposals ... approved in the waning hours of the 97th Congress," the
president listed two specific objections. First and "particularly," he
challenged (in four paragraphs) the creation of a cabinet-level antidrug
enforcement agency headed by a "so-called drug czar." But second (in
one paragraph), he objected to the career-criminal section of the bill. He
said:

> This provision includes an unworkable and possibly uncon-
> stitutional restraint upon federal prosecutions in this area, by
> allowing a State or local prosecutor to veto any Federal prosecu-
> tion under his or her authority, even if the Attorney General

approved the prosecution. Such a restraint on federal prosecutorial discretion and the delegation of Executive responsibility it entails raise grave constitutional and practical concerns. [28]

Subsequent interpretation by "a Justice Department official" made it clear that "concerns over ... the repeat offender" had influenced the administration's position on the bill. [29]

Ironically, the argument of the veto message was the same one Specter had made repeatedly in support of his original bill against a succession of objections by senators, House members, and the National District Attorneys Association. But he had been forced at every stage to give ground to these critics in order to salvage the framework of his bill. Finally, having agreed to a local veto, he had provoked an administration reaction. In the process of winning legislative support, he had lost administration support. As strenuously as he had worked to gather support, he had not secured a reliable base on which to build—not in the administration and not in the Congress. Predictably, however, he did not quit. If he could resolve the president's doubts about the "drug czar" provision, he believed, the bill would not be vetoed. The secondary objection to career-criminal was not, he thought, sufficient to bring down the bill.

He recalled later:

> When Meese told me there was a 99-1 chance of a veto, I started to lobby. . . . Mike Deaver promised me a meeting with the president before he made up his mind. And I got a forty-five minute meeting [with President Reagan plus Counsellor Meese, Attorney General William French Smith, Senators Thurmond and Biden, House members Hughes and Sawyer]. I carried the ball at the meeting. I began by deferring to Thurmond; but he looked down at his pad, so I carried the argument. We ended with Meese saying he thought we could work out a compromise by modeling the drug czar after the head of the CIA. The president was getting edgy to leave. I ended the meeting by saying to the president that I was sure he would like to have a compromise so that he could avoid the problem of a veto. He said he certainly would and we broke up.
>
> I immediately canceled my trip to Africa and started to lobby. I was the only person doing it—except for Thurmond. He was very helpful. When I called Bill Hughes, I found he had left the country. I got [William] Casey of CIA to agree. I got Cap Weinberger to agree. But I couldn't get Smith to budge. He has absolutely no knowledge of criminal matters, no understanding of what we are trying to do. He has no intellectual interest in the subject of crime. He said the bill was worse than nothing because it failed to take up bail and sentencing reform and

because of the drug czar. He didn't care one bit about career-criminal. He's impossible to deal with. [30]

The saga of the career-criminal bill ended where it began, with a lack of administration support. As long as there was any chance at all, Arlen Specter had continued his efforts on behalf of the bill—even with a huge legislative accretion on his back. But to his palpable frustration, he had been unable to surmount the last hurdle. And he had neither the time nor the arena in which to maneuver further. Not, at least, until the new Congress inaugurated a new legislative agenda.

Summing up Arlen Specter's fifteen-month struggle to pass S 1688, a staffer called it "a success story without a happy ending." And he added, "It proved to his colleagues that Arlen is a pusher, that he can get things done." The senator, too, saw it as a personal success. "Howard Baker thought it was a remarkable accomplishment to get two major bills passed. Not many of our guys did that well.... It wasn't like [Dan] Quayle's jobs bill where there was already a perception. I had to create interest in the career-criminal bill. I carried the ball the whole way."

In a December 1982 assessment of the freshmen Republicans, one of Baker's top aides named Specter as one of the four most promising members of that sixteen-member class. "He's stubborn. He sticks to things. All the good ones are stubborn." He had made progress toward the kind of senatorial reputation he had been seeking, as someone who can get things done. The personal qualities that had dominated his activity as prosecutor and candidate continued to dominate his governing activity. And his governing performance had taken on a pattern—individualistic, independent, tenacious—altogether very much of a one-man show. His accomplishment, his reputation, and his stylistic pattern all provided evidence that his adjustment period in the United States Senate was over.

Looking back on his efforts, Specter viewed it through his newcomer's eyes, as a learning experience. What had his fifteen-month saga taught him?

> I learned that the legislative process is not fast. There are a thousand pitfalls, and if one of them snaps, you lose. You can't rush it. So you learn to be patient. You keep the pressure on, but you don't get excited. You just keep coming back to people again and again till you get it done.

He had learned that the governing procedures are stacked against positive action, but that patience and determination will overcome that bias. Having learned something about the new legislative context, he had concluded that individual persistence held the key to success in that context. In other words, the persistent prosecutor style had been tried and found applicable. "You just keep coming back to people again and again until you get it done."

Still smarting from his defeat, however, he added a proviso:

> I wouldn't call it a learning process when you run up against someone like William French Smith. . . . When you have everybody together in the room and when Meese has the formula ready and when you've checked it out with [FBI Director William] Webster, with Casey, with Treasury Department officials, even with Cap Weinberger, and then you get someone who says "no." You don't learn anything by dealing with an irrational force.

He was understandably angry at the particular individual who stood in the way of a happy ending. But the personalization of his problem may have been an oversimplification of the factors involved in the defeat.

A top staffer, also a newcomer to Capitol Hill, took away a similar lesson about the inertial bias of the legislative process, but he cast a wider net of responsibility for their failure to conquer it.

> There are too many people in too many places who don't like the bill and are very opposed to it. We were not good at knowing how you get things done. Arlen is good at carrying things along by his brain and his experience. But so many people can do you in; and they are all invisible. Especially in the House . . . among staffers at all levels. We haven't done well with the invisible army of opponents.

Unlike Specter's reflection, the staffer's statement is a commentary on the limits of individual effort. And it acknowledges implicitly that more than one person's determination is needed for success in the legislature.

The staffer learned the importance of cultivating allies. That, we have repeatedly suggested, was an aspect of governing for which Specter had neither a natural instinct nor a special concern. And so, at every stage, he consistently overestimated the degree of support that existed for his bill. In addition, he avoided any close analysis of his support problems by assuming that the merits of the bill plus a personal explanation would overcome any problems. The result was that he had no allies. He had no one with whom he consulted frequently or with whom he shared information and credit.

"Bill Hughes was the closest thing we had to an ally," said a staffer afterward,

> but he was wishy-washy. His staff absolutely hated the bill. So one day he would be for it and the next day he'd be against it. Arlen would always think Hughes was for it. He would tell us "Hughes is for it"; but his staff would tell us he wasn't. Arlen

heard "commitment"; but Hughes' staff would tell us "he said he'll do the best he could" or "he said he'd try."

As it turned out, of course, Hughes not only tried but succeeded in getting Specter's bill out of his subcommittee. But his "commitment" to S 1688 was always highly conditional upon the success of S 2411.

The Specter-Hughes alliance of 1982 proved not to be a durable one. It was dissolved unilaterally the very moment Specter decided it was in *his* interest to do so. As he explained his action of December 9,

> I called Bill Hughes to tell him that we had passed 2411, and he said "Arlen, I hate to tell you, but I'm not going to be able to get a full committee meeting to vote on career-criminal." So I said, "Well, then, I'm going to send you 2411 with career-criminal on it." He understood. It was not a move I had ever thought of before. It was something I had to do under the circumstances. It was the only thing I could do. He knew it. He had been very good about getting 1688 through his subcommittee. That was his quid pro quo. [If I hadn't done that] 1688 would have died. But 2411 would have passed.

In his effort to salvage S 2411, Hughes was forced to carry S 1688 through the House. He did so, but not because of any remaining relationship with the senator from Pennsylvania. In the end, Hughes's S 2411 went down with Specter's S 1688.

We cannot know what Representative Hughes's thoughts were. But one obvious reaction would be anger at Specter for taking an action that prevented S 2411 from certain passage. According to Specter's staffers, that was precisely the reaction of the NDAA. They had never liked S 1688. Their only commitment was to S 2411; they believed S 2411 would have passed had it not been encumbered by S 1688. As a result, they were "sore at Specter" for what he did. "There is personal bitterness at Specter," concluded an aide, "because holding S 2411 at the desk torpedoed justice assistance money for local people." And NDAA will be "hell bent to screw us" in the future.

Hughes's reaction may not have been that strong. But he, too, could easily blame Specter for the loss of his most treasured piece of legislation. I have no idea whether he did or not. But it is indicative of Specter's understanding of how much his unilateral action had cost Bill Hughes that he did not reflect upon that dimension of their relationship. "Bill Hughes was very upset," he said after the presidential veto. "But he was more upset about the drug czar part of the bill than the career-criminal part. He was very good about it. He didn't say anything. We all have our separate agendas. That's the size of it." It was the summary of someone more attuned to the individualism of the legislative business than to its collective aspects. And Specter's ultimate lack of success may be as much a reflection on the limitations of his highly individualistic style as it is a reflection on the irrational stubbornness of the attorney general.

In early March, I returned to Washington for my first post-mortem on the demise of the career-criminal bill. I found the senator from Pennsylvania looking forward to a second attempt.

> We've introduced the bill again. I've gotten [the Justice Department] to agree to language that avoids the constitutional problem—even though there never was one. I've got Paul Michel out in Reno with the national DAs group. Strom has referred it to my subcommittee alone and not to Criminal Law. So I don't have that to worry about. I can get it out of the subcommittee, get it up in full committee, and get it passed on the floor. It's already passed the House subcommittee once, so that will help. And I know Rodino will hold a full committee meeting on it. The guy from Detroit—what's his name?— [Conyers] will fight it. But I think it will pass the Judiciary Committee and pass the House. It's a good bill. . . . We'll get it passed. And it could be the occasion of a big bill-signing ceremony with the president.

"So you're going to stick with it" I remarked. He said, "Of course I am. Are you kidding?" The politician I had met in 1980 was still alive and well in the Senate.

EPILOGUE: 1983-1984

At the conclusion of our March 1983 conversation, the senator from Pennsylvania smiled and said, "But we've got to start all over again." That, in accordance with his optimistic scenario, is what he did. On October 12, 1984, President Reagan signed into law an omnibus Comprehensive Crime Control Act that included the Armed Career Criminal Act of 1984. Almost three years to the day after Arlen Specter had introduced his bill, it became law. It had taken a long second effort in 1983 and 1984 to get the job done. The story of that second effort will not be told here, because I have no special vantage point from which to tell it. Nonetheless, certain general aspects of the second effort might help us further to understand the first efforts of 1981-1982.

When, in March, Specter and his staff spoke about their new bill, the contrast in attitudes within the enterprise was the same as before— the senator certain that individual effort would overcome all obstacles, his aides confident in the capacity of their boss but aware of his limitations in surmounting obvious legislative difficulties. "He still believes it's a magical solution," said a staffer. "He is so convinced it is a great idea that he assumes that he can get it done and that it will work well." Another commented, "He won't quit. And people will believe him more this year than last year." Specter agreed, "I learned a lot about legislative procedure with that bill. It will be easier next time because we already got it passed once."

But the staffers saw major problems ahead. For one thing, they believed that this time the NDAA would be openly opposed from the beginning.

> They asked for "mutual consent" and we put it in. Then they wanted it put in the body of the bill. I thought the NDAA was satisfied. But now they say, "We only wanted to make a bad bill better. We were always opposed to the whole thing." They only wanted to hate it less. It is their top priority to kill it.

Members of the staff further believed that they would encounter more trouble in the House.

> Hughes will have more opposition this time. Congress was caught sleeping. This time there will be better organized hostility.... Conyers will kill us. Kastenmeier is going to kill us. Rodino is going to let us die. He won't twist arms or take on the knife wielders.... How do we get past the choke points?

Furthermore, of course, they would have to do something different if the Justice Department's fatal objections were to be met. The skepticism of several interested parties had more than likely hardened into opposition.

These worries pointed to a changed context—one in which the novel idea of 1981-1982 had become more familiar and in which the earlier uncertainty and skepticism had hardened into certainty and opposition. The change registered itself inside the Senate, too. The tip-off came when Chairman Strom Thurmond decided to hold hearings on Specter's new bill (S 52) in the *full* committee and to preside over them himself. In that forum he immediately raised the jurisdictional question which he had raised in committee the first time around. He told the Justice Department's witness:

> I've studied the constitution all my life, and I've tried to differentiate between the levels of government. We should keep the Federal government out of the State's business. We're making an exception here, frankly. I am very dubious about the constitutionality of it. That is the reason—to protect the constitutionality of it—that we should certainly provide that the

State prosecuting attorney would have to either request a prosecution or concur in it.

Specter then advised the witness, "My recommendation is to concur with what Senator Thurmond is trying to accomplish here. [31]

Specter and Thurmond seemed agreed on the same "request or concur," "local veto" language that they had worked out before. Only this time, in order to meet the Justice Department objections that had killed the bill, Specter had put the jurisdictional language back in a congressional intent section. The idea was to leave some tiny potential for federal initiative (see Appendix). But that change meant that surely the NDAA and its legislative allies, like Edward Kennedy, would insist, again, that the "local veto" be strengthened by moving it into the main body of the bill.

To put it simply, Specter's main goal had been to create a new federal crime, to establish the idea of a federal role in dealing with violent street crime. Strom Thurmond, the NDAA, Kennedy, and others did not want to establish a new federal crime lest it erode local prerogatives. But to the degree that they "made federal jurisdiction absolutely dependent upon the consent of the pertinent State or local prosecutor," the Justice Department objected. [32] So the career-criminal bill was caught in a whipsaw; the more entrenched became the opposing positions, the more inexorable became the whipsaw.

Specter, however, remained characteristically sanguine about the bill's chances. "We're going to get the career-criminal bill out of the Senate soon," he said in a brief September conversation, four months after the hearings.

> I thought we had it ready in July, but Kennedy objected. We have our controversy with the DAs organization settled— mostly. We put the veto in the congressional intent section of the bill and not the main section. I think that will be all right. It should be on the floor next week. It will pass the Senate. The trouble will come in the House. It will take time. But I think it will be part of a deal, with the justice assistance legislation Bill Hughes wants. Or, there may be a big crime package. And if that happens, my bill will surely be a part of it. One way or another, we'll get it.

It was the kind of prognosis I had heard him deliver many times since the beginning of his effort, always with the same blend of determination and wishful thinking. In the end, he would get something, but not with the ease nor in the form that he predicted.

An indicator of some trouble for the bill was that it took nearly a year from the time of hearings in May 1983 until it reached the Senate floor in February 1984—five months longer than Specter's September estimate. Once on the floor, the career-criminal bill ran into more trouble than either Specter or his staff had ever imagined. NDAA advocate Edward Kennedy and states' rights advocate Strom Thurmond concentrated their opposition to the bill in the form of an amendment that restricted its scope to robberies and burglaries committed within *existing* federal jurisdictions and already being prosecuted in federal court. Only robberies and burglaries on federal property such as military installations or post offices or robberies of federally insured banks would be covered under the statute. If the category of burglary or robbery were committed and if the criminal had committed two prior robberies or burglaries of any sort, then the criminal would be prosecuted in federal court and the severe career criminal penalties would be assessed (see Appendix). [33] But the number of criminals involved would be minuscule and insignificant. In Specter's view, it would reduce his bill's effectiveness by 85 percent, so much so that "we might as well not even have it." [34] It was as fundamental an attack on the bill as could be made without killing it outright.

For Specter, the Kennedy-Thurmond amendment precipitated the first open fight in the life of his bill, and the first full-scale test of his Senate support. Up to now, all of his efforts had been small-scale persuasions, one on one or in small meetings out of public view. Now he was forced to defend his pet project before all of his colleagues and against two of the most powerful individuals in the Senate. It is ironic, but not surprising, that this most threatening opposition should come from the very twosome Specter had cited in his first press conference as putative supporters of his bill! That presumption had turned into perhaps the greatest of his misestimations of support. Now, he thought of them in terms of an "unholy alliance." [35] Neither individual had ever liked the bill; and both of them admitted that their positions had hardened since the previous year's agreement. Kennedy now supported the most extreme position of the NDAA. Thurmond now despaired of compromising with the Justice Department. [36]

Specter battled strenuously and alone against the amendment. It was another David-and-Goliath, newcomer-against-the-establishment confrontation, not unlike the summit resolution. But now he was enmeshed in the total legislative process and was dealing with more substantial political forces. And, he got no help—public or private. "What the Kennedy-Thurmond amendment does," he argued,

> is to change this legislative provision totally. . . . The whole intent of the career-criminal bill would be emasculated and gutted. The purpose of this bill is to bring the federal govern-

ment for the first time into the area of street crime. . . . [Under the amendment] the career-criminal bill can apply only if the robbery or burglary is committed on federal property; if it is now prosecutable as a federal offense. That does not cover a robbery at Fourteenth and K Streets; it does not cover a robbery or burglary on Capitol Hill; it does not cover a robbery or burglary now cognizable under the laws of the fifty states of the United States. . . . We do not even have a real career-criminal bill under the amendment. . . . That, simply stated, *guts and emasculates* the bill. [37]

The three protagonists rehearsed the arguments and positions taken by themselves and by others. Only one other senator participated in support of the amendment. The bill remained, for most, an esoteric and unimportant matter.

The amendment passed 77-12. [38] A miscellaneous assortment of eight Republicans and three Democrats voted with the senator from Pennsylvania. But not one member of his own subcommittee or of the full Judiciary Committee supported him in his showdown fight. It was his most crushing personal defeat. And it illustrated most convincingly some of the limits of individual effort in a communitarian institution.

As a witness before the House Judiciary Committee in June, Specter argued for his career-criminal bill in its preamendment form, predicting hopefully that if the jurisdictional language were kept in the intent section of the bill, it *would* satisfy the administration and *should* satisfy the NDAA. [39] But apparently the Senate amendment had fixed an entirely new framework for debate. There would be no expansion of federal jurisdiction, only the application of severe career-criminal penalties (fifteen years to life, heavy fine, no bail, no parole) to what were already federal crimes.

However, the House committee changed the criteria for prosecution and enlarged the scope of the bill. The solution was to focus on a different but more common federal crime—the possession of a gun by a convicted felon. That crime was already punishable under federal law by a maximum prison sentence of two years. The House bill stiffened that sentence according to Specter's prescriptions (fifteen years to life, heavy fine, no bail, no parole) for career criminals. That is, people who were convicted for possession of a gun and who had previously received three felony convictions for robberies or burglaries would receive a severe sentence. The triggering offense was to be the possession of a gun at other than the robbery or burglary. Like the Senate bill, it created *no new federal crime* and permitted no federal prosecution of anyone who could not be prosecuted already under existing federal law. [40] It was far more restrictive than Specter's original bill but easier for him to live with than the Senate version. On October 1, it passed the House in that form. Three days later, the House version was agreed to by the Senate. [41]

The Armed Career Criminal Act of 1984, in the form that it cleared the House, was eventually attached to a large omnibus anticrime bill, which was in turn attached to a continuing appropriations resolution in October. As sections 1801 and 1802 of Public Law 98-473, it consumed but one-half of one column of print in the *Congressional Record,* at the tail end of a bill that was eighty-five columns long. [42]

When Chairman Thurmond rose to manage the bill on the floor, he handed out the customary kudos to those colleagues who have "devoted their strenuous efforts to this endeavor." He singled out six Judiciary Committee Republicans for special praise. But Arlen Specter was not one of them. [43] The glaring omission, of someone whose efforts were nothing if not "strenuous," was either a commentary on the insignificance of his legislation or a subtle hint that the independent-minded freshman had a ways to go yet before he achieved that "good relationship with Thurmond" he believed he had already "worked out." Specter spoke in support of the large bill; he described the career-criminal portion of it as "a fair accommodation of the complex countervailing considerations which have been so thoroughly aired ... in the committee and on the floor of both Houses." [44] Whatever its costs or benefits, his long legislative struggle was over.

It was a moment of personal satisfaction and personal accomplishment. But it was not a moment of heady triumph comparable to the summit resolution. The result was so much less than he had wanted or worked for or expected. On the other hand, it had presented a far more rigorous and realistic test of his governing abilities than the summit resolution. He had persevered against the inertia of the full-length legislative process and against the activities of a variety of opponents. And he had, once again, proven the efficacy of individual determination and effort. His difficulties along the way, however, and the disappointing outcome suggest the limitations of his tendency to place such overwhelming reliance on doing it solo, in the manner of the independent prosecutor.

Two years later, Paul Michel recalled the struggle.

There was never any enthusiasm for the bill. No one loved the bill except Arlen. He did it all by himself until the very end in 1984, when some House member came up with the idea, in the middle of the night I think, of attaching the whole crime bill to the continuing resolution. That's what we did and that's how it went through. So, from A to Y it was Specter. Then Z was someone else. Nobody loved it ...

The Pennsylvania newcomer never persuaded anyone to like it or to help him with it. Some of the limitations lay in the subject matter, some in the context, and some in his own individualistic style.

Still, Arlen Specter produced a piece of legislation that treated the subject he had introduced and went by the name he had given it. He had shown entrepreneurial skill in breaking new ground. He was responsible for creating a legislative skeleton to which he could, later on, perhaps, add flesh, but for which he could, in the meantime, surely take the credit. In sum, he could do a lot by himself, but he couldn't do it all by himself. The next time he undertook a similar legislative effort, he would need a clearer idea of where his solo effort should leave off and a collegial effort begin. He had learned a lot; his adjustment period was over; but he was still learning. And his learning was still constrained by the stylistic preferences he had brought with him to the Senate.

His performance showed that he was not yet much of a legislative strategist, that he had not yet learned to deal with his colleagues in a way that allowed him to gauge his support and his prospects accurately. He had not yet learned to match his policy expertise with personal relationships that encouraged his colleagues to defer to that expertise. Still, there was plenty of evidence that his personal strengths in terms of drive and intelligence were present, should he decide to harness them to the subtler legislative arts. His career-criminal experience had been, in the final analysis, only his legislative baptism, the experience that signaled the end of his adjustment period in the Senate. He was, then, still at the beginning of a full-blown Senate career. What he had learned and how he would react to this experience would be revealed only in the years to come.

NOTES

1. *Congressional Record,* April 19, 1982, S3636.
2. Ibid., May 5, 1982, S4531.
3. Ibid., April 19, 1982, S3636-S3637.
4. Ibid., May 4, 1982, S4473-S4477.
5. Ibid., S4475.
6. Ibid., May 5, 1982, S4533-S4534.
7. Ibid., May 4, 1982, S4477.
8. Ibid., May 5, 1982, S4534; May 4, 1982, S4476.
9. Ibid., May 5, 1982, S4528-S4535.
10. Ibid., S4534.
11. Ibid., May 6, 1982, S4630.
12. Ibid., May 12, 1982, S4903. When Tower was nominated to be George Bush's secretary of defense in 1989, Specter supported him in a losing cause. For his

reflections at that time on Tower's "toughness" displayed "tenaciously, if not acerbically" during the summit fight, see Ibid., March 1, 1989, S1883. When Tower died in a place crash in April 1991, Specter gave a longer account of his "battle royal" with Tower on the summit resolution, in which he describes Tower as a "striking, tough opponent." See *Congressional Record*, April 9, 1991, S4163.

13. "Tentative Agenda," Senate Committee on the Judiciary, June 15, 1982, July 20, 1982.
14. Ibid., July 27, 1982.
15. See U.S. Senate, Committee on the Judiciary, Committee Report no. 9 of 585, on Armed Career Criminal Act of 1982, 97th Congress, 2d Session, September 24, 1982.
16. *Congressional Record*, September 30, 1982, S12719-S12723, S12732. The one vote against was Sen. John East (R-N.C.).
17. Letter from Arlen Specter to Richard Fenno, October 8, 1982.
18. Transcript, Senate Committee on the Judiciary, Executive Session, September 21, 1982.
19. *Congressional Record*, December 9, 1982, S14245-S14276.
20. U.S. House of Representatives, Subcommittee on Crime of the Committee on the Judiciary, Hearings on HR6386 and Similar Bills; Armed Robbery and Burglary Prevention Act, September 23, 1982, 6-21.
21. *Congressional Record*, December 9, 1982, S14276.
22. Letter from Arlen Specter to Richard Fenno, December 23, 1982.
23. Ibid.; See also *Congressional Record*, December 14, 1982, S14572-S14573.
24. *Congressional Record*, December 20, 1982, S15836-S15847.
25. Ibid., H10459; H10491- H10509, S15853.
26. United Press International, "Crime Bill Is Sent to President," *New York Times*, December 22, 1982.
27. Letter from Arlen Specter to Richard Fenno, January 11, 1983.
28. The veto message is printed in *Congressional Quarterly Weekly Report*, January 22, 1983, 180-181.
29. "Box score," *Congressional Quarterly Weekly Report*, January 15, 1983.
30. A similar, public account will be found in U.S. House of Representatives, Subcommittee on Crime of the Committee on the Judiciary, Hearing on Armed Career Criminal Act, June 28, 1984, 30-31.
31. U.S. Senate, Committee on the Judiciary, Hearings on Armed Career Criminal Act of 1983, May 26, 1983, 13.
32. Letter from Robert McConnell to Strom Thurmond, in *Congressional Record*, February 22, 1984, S1562.
33. Ibid., S1560-S1567.
34. Rich Scheinin, "Arlen Specter Always Told People He'd Be a Senator," *Philadelphia Inquirer*, April 15, 1984.
35. "Soft on Crime," *Wall Street Journal*, April 14, 1984.
36. For Kennedy, see *Congressional Record*, Feburary 22, 1984, S1560-S1562; for Thurmond, see pp. S1563-S1564.
37. Ibid., S1562, S1566-S1567.
38. Ibid., S1567.
39. U.S. House of Representatives, Hearing on Armed Career Criminal Act, 11-27.
40. Nadine Cohodas, "Repeat Offenders Targeted," *Congressional Quarterly Weekly Report*, September 22, 1984; *Congressional Record*, October 4, 1984,

S13080-S13081.
41. *Congressional Record,* October 1, 1984, 10550-10551; October 4, 1984, S13578.
42. Ibid., October 4, 1984, S13520-S13548.
43. Ibid., S13062-S13063.
44. Ibid., S13081.

4

Campaigning and Renewal

THE REELECTION CONTEXT

There was never much doubt that Arlen Specter would run for reelection. The Senate had been his lifelong ambition, and no one had worked harder than he to get there. In every sense, he had made a huge investment in a Senate career. Every utterance I heard—from "Wow, I made it! Here I am in the Senate. I really made it," in March 1981, to "It's a great job. I love it. It's still exhilarating just to be a United States Senator" in June 1982—bespoke immense career satisfaction.

Occasionally, in his first year, a staffer would mention reelection. "We think about reelection, and I work on it every week," said one in September 1981. "Every Thursday we bring some important people from the state here to have lunch with Arlen.... I'm not sure we'll ever benefit from it, though. He might get so frustrated with the place that he won't want to run." Another explained: "If I were Arlen I'd be so frustrated at the end of each day I'd ask myself, 'What good is it being a senator? What's the use when you can't pass the legislation that interests you?'" But they were projecting their own feelings onto him.

"Arlen takes a longer view," continued an aide. "He says that it's not a one-year job, that if you lay some good foundations you can accomplish things later." By mid-1982, despite his frustrations, this longer run perspective had come to dominate Specter's view of his career-criminal efforts—that he had the time, the patience, and the perseverance to see it through, that eventually the bill would become law; in the meantime, partial successes would, as he put it, "count."

For two years, reelection activity percolated beneath the surface, with such efforts as the Thursday luncheons and the preparation of a

129

forty-page in-house analysis of some 1980 vote patterns, setting forth "how Senator Specter can improve his electoral performance in Allegheny County in 1986." [1] He commissioned his first polls in June of 1981. But he waited until his Pennsylvania colleague John Heinz won reelection on November 2, 1982, before he made a visible move. Immediately after the election, he wrote a letter to "some seven hundred Republican supporters from his 1980 campaign ... [asking for] their continued support for 1986." [2] In early December, he invited fifty of these supporters to Washington for a money-raising luncheon. His four-year campaign to win reelection had begun.

When observers began to notice his reelection activity, they emphasized Specter's obvious attachment to his job. In 1984 a Washington journalist quoted him as saying, "I love being a Senator. I worked very hard to get here." [3] A local reporter traveling with him at home that same year found him "gushing ... about the *fun* he has been having in Washington since his election to the Senate in 1980." [4] In 1985, Specter explained to a national reporter:

> I had a rocky road getting here and I'm going to do my damnedest to stay here. This is a fascinating job, challenging, demanding, a great opportunity to serve. Every problem in the world comes to the U.S. government and every problem in the government comes to the U.S. Senate. [5]

This incumbent had fulfilled his lifetime desire for high public office, and he thoroughly enjoyed his job. In light of a political style that had always featured extraordinary resolve in the pursuit of his goals, it was obvious that no one was going to take his job away from him without a very, very tough struggle.

It also became obvious, early on, that some of Pennsylvania's best politicians were giving serious thought to taking him on. Given his widespread loser image and his narrow 1980 victory, Specter was deemed vulnerable from the very outset of his tenure. And he knew it. "All the politicians back home knock him around," said one close associate in September 1981, "so he's like Satchel Paige, looking over his shoulder to see who might be coming." Another commented at the same time, "I'm afraid he'll never feel legitimate, like he really belongs here, until he's been reelected." Besides his electoral record, there was the 800,000 Democratic registration advantage and continuing economic distress in the western part of the state to cloud his reelection outlook.

If the best measure of an incumbent's perceived vulnerability is to be found in the quality of his challengers, Specter ranked at the high end of the scale. Two of Pennsylvania's most promising young Democrats—forty-year-old state auditor general Don Bailey from Western

Pennsylvania and forty-two-year-old, six-term congressman Bob Edgar from suburban Philadelphia—geared up to fight a hard primary for the right to challenge him. What's more, the popular two-term incumbent Republican governor Richard L. Thornburgh thought long, hard, and openly about challenging Specter in the Republican primary.[6] To the very end of 1985, it looked as if serious campaigns would be launched against the newcomer from within as well as from outside his own ranks. The national Republican party, and observers generally, listed him among the most endangered Republican freshmen.[7] By the late spring of 1986, the nature, if not the extent, of the threat had been clarified. Thornburgh had decided not to run, and Edgar had defeated Bailey in a close primary.[8] For the next six months, therefore, a first-term senator, evincing an extraordinary determination to keep his job, would face an experienced and highly successful congressman primed to take it away from him.

From my vantage point, over Specter's shoulder, any treatment of his reelection effort will be grossly inadequate. That is because his effort rested heavily on the activity of his postadjustment years in office and because my close-in observation stopped at the beginning of those last four years. Besides, my observation focused inward on his governing activity and not outward on his home activity. Since, however, our interest extends to the relationship between the two activities and the two contexts, and since our interest extends also across the entire electoral cycle, I shall extend the coverage—sketchily and episodically—to the full length of Arlen Specter's six-year term. And I shall trace from a distance—aided only by a couple of quick campaign visits—his successful reelection effort.

Given what we know about his two-year adjustment period, the question presents itself whether the threads I have used to weave the governing story are relevant to the reelection story as well. The answer is yes and no. In terms of political style, yes; in terms of legislative achievement, no.

GOVERNING ACHIEVEMENT AND REELECTION

I shall address the negative answer first. That is, it would be of special interest if Arlen Specter's expenditure of effort on the career-criminal bill had paid off in terms of tangible electoral support, or if some new strategic lessons he learned as a result of that legislative experience had been transferable to the conduct of his campaign. But there is no evidence that either was the case. He was certainly proud of his accomplishment, and it certainly had a place in his campaign. But it did not shape or dominate the campaign, and it had no discernible impact on the outcome.[9]

The achievement did give him something positive to talk about— especially in the period before the campaign against his opponent heated up. Specter had kept up an active interest in the implementation of his career-criminal legislation after its October 1984 enactment. In the months immediately following, Specter held national and statewide hearings at which he brought together federal and local prosecutors to discuss the problems of implementation and at which he talked these officials into cooperative arrangements. Given the jurisdictional vagaries that dominated the bill's legislative history, it is not surprising that implementation problems centered on the practical working relationships between officials at the two levels of responsibility. In the first year of the act's existence, "thirteen defendants were charged as armed career criminals" and "eleven defendants were convicted under the statute as armed career criminals."[10] The act's sponsor was not satisfied. Specter's mission was to wring from his witnesses praise for the leveraging potential of the act and promises of future cooperation on a few test cases.[11]

Specter's bird-dogging activity led him to propose a change in the act. "Based on the testimony presented at these hearings by victims, sheriffs, U.S. Attorneys, police, local prosecutors and other criminal justice officials, I am convinced," he said, "that we must expand the law to apply to ... additional classes of career criminals."[12] Specter's amendment (S 2312) expanded the "predicate crimes" under the act from robbery and burglary to "a crime of violence or a serious drug offense."[13] The new bill was passed by the Senate on September 30, 1986, and by the House of Representatives a month later.[14] It was of additional help, therefore, that when Specter talked about his legislation late in the campaign, he was able to include murderers, rapists, and, especially, drug dealers as eligible targets under the career-criminal statute.

Specter's hearings in New York City, Washington, Miami, Dallas and Los Angeles were beneficial in this substantive sense.[15] But his meetings with officials in Pennsylvania had visible political benefits, for they allowed him to generate favorable and widespread publicity at home during the early campaign season. One weekend a month, for the first four months of 1986, he held a joint press conference with a local district attorney and the relevant U.S. attorney in one of the state's major media markets. They would publicly agree on the need for federal-local cooperation under the act and the need to bring drug-related offenders within the scope of the act.

In Philadelphia in January, Harrisburg in February, Pittsburgh in

March, and Scranton in April, the senator's crime-fighting efforts received local newspaper (and, we assume, television) coverage. A sampling of the resulting headlines reads:

> At Least 15 Years Sought for Habitual Criminals
> Prosecutors Join in Crackdown
> Specter Prods Use of New Federal Crime Fighting Law
> Expand Crime Law, Specter Is Urged
> Lawmen Support Expanded Career Criminal Law
> Local Law Enforcement Officials Back Specter on Armed Criminals
> Law Enforcement Reps Call for Longer Jail Terms[16]

To increase the visibility of his kickoff Philadelphia appearance, the office issued a press release—"Sen. Specter Says U.S. Attorney's Office and DA's Office Agree to Implement the 'Career-Criminal' Bill"—which read:

> Flanked by U.S. Attorney Edward Dennis and District Attorney Ron Castille at a press conference, Sen. Specter said that the two prosecutors will formulate a new cooperative effort by their offices to use this new federal statute to combat career criminals in the Philadelphia area ... to identify incoming cases which may be suitable for federal prosecution under the career criminal statute.... 'If the criminal population awaiting trial in the state courts sees some of their fellow criminals being sent by the DA's office to the federal courts and getting 15 year sentences, I believe that many of them will be happy to plead guilty for lesser sentences in the state courts,' he said.[17]

The statement represented an accurate comment on what he wished to accomplish in terms of policy, and the press conferences increased the chances that prospective constituents would notice.

We have no way of accurately gauging the amount or the quality of local press coverage given to Specter's career-criminal bill over its lengthy legislative life. What is noteworthy is that from the very outset of that undertaking, beginning with his initial press conference, the Specter enterprise worked to generate publicity for it. As such, their effort was indicative of a changing emphasis on the pursuit of publicity. At each milestone, his office issued a press release—more than for any of his other first-term endeavors. His office put out these titles:

> Specter Urges House Subcommittee on Crime to Support this
> "Career Criminal" Bill [September 22, 1982]
> Senate Judiciary Committee Gives Final Approval to Specter's

Career Criminal Bill [September 24, 1982]

U.S. Senate Passes Specter's "Career Criminal" Bill [September 29, 1982]

Specter's Two Anti-Crime Measures Win Final Congressional Approval [December 21, 1982]

Specter Reintroduces Six Anti-Crime Bills at Start of 98th Congress [January 26, 1983]

Senate Judiciary Committee Gives Approval to Three Specter Anti-Crime Bills [June 16, 1983]

Specter's Tough Sentencing "Career Criminal" Bill Passed by U.S. Senate [February 23, 1984]

Specter Tells House Crime Subcommittee His "Career Criminal" Bill Badly Needed [June 28, 1984]

Specter's Tough Sentencing "Career Criminal" Bill Is Passed by Congress [October 4, 1984].

Scattered evidence suggests that these bootstrap efforts produced minor and mixed results. The state's largest paper, the *Philadelphia Inquirer*, appears to have given the entire effort the back of its hand.[18] A reporter for the *Patriot-News*, on the other hand, gave the bill serious, thoughtful coverage from beginning to end—and was the only journalist to do so.[19] Some small newspapers printed the press releases verbatim.[20]

The bill never became a major story. And there is no evidence that it penetrated to the electorate. When asked directly in early 1986 whether they had "read, seen or heard anything about Arlen Specter" recently, no voters mentioned his anticrime activity. And when asked, "What issues or problems has Arlen Specter worked on the hardest in the U.S. Senate?" 5 percent of the responses fell into a catch-all "social issues" category, the only one in which crime might have fit. The "don't know" answers to these two questions totaled 76 percent and 73 percent, respectively. When Specter's pollsters asked respondents to rank a list of seven issues in terms of importance, crime was not even one of them. Nor did the pollsters include career-criminal matters in a question asking for a ranking of four secondary issues.[21]

In a later poll, however, pollsters did include "reducing crime" in a battery of nine issues about which respondents were asked whether the issues would be "handled better" by Specter or Edgar. Respondents chose Specter as his preferred crime-reducer by 48 percent to 19 percent. The difference of 29 points between the two gave Specter his third biggest advantage among the nine issues. The preference for Specter was greatest on the "fighting terrorism" and "foreign affairs" issues and virtually the same for the "federal budget deficit" issue.[22]

In sum, the voters of Pennsylvania did not picture Specter spontaneously as a crime fighter; his campaign consultants did not treat crime as a major issue in the campaign. Yet they did treat it as a distinctive issue. And when they presented the crime-fighting issue directly to the voters, the preference for Specter was strong and clear, although not extraordinarliy strong relative to other issue areas.

Specter's media campaign began before the May primaries. During that period, nine sixty-second television commercials played statewide, in rotation. One spot was devoted to the career-criminal bill. The documentary-style spot was shot against a background of outdoor street scenes. A policeman, with "Fraternal Order of Police, Philadelphia" written beneath him on the screen, begins: "On TV crime shows, the series ends when the prisoner's led away in handcuffs. In real life, the prisoner often times goes free." A second policeman, sitting in a parked car with "Philadelphia Detective" on the screen says:

> One of the most frustrating things I have dealt with as a detective was to see those criminals that should have been punished, that committed crimes over and over and over again, that they were given a slap on the wrist. And now, thanks to Arlen Specter, we have a bill with some teeth in it.

As he speaks, the following words appear on the screen: "70% of all crimes committed by repeat offenders." Near the end of his comments, Senator Specter is seen talking to the policeman through the car window. It is the only glimpse of the bill's author during the spot—and he does not speak. A third man, with the printed description, "District Attorney of Lancaster County," says:

> We all like to talk about doing something about serious crime. But Senator Arlen Specter has done something about it. Drawing on his past dedication to public safety as a district attorney in Philadelphia, Senator Specter has given local prosecutors a very strong tool to remove armed career criminals—repeat offenders—from our streets.

As he speaks, there appears on the screen the following: "wrote Armed Career Criminal Act" and "15 year mandatory sentence for repeat offenders." The ad ends with the campaign slogan flashed on the screen: "Arlen Specter. Out front . . . Fighting for Pennsylvania."

The career criminal television ad was the most direct, the most visible, and the most widely distributed presentation, at home, of that particular governing accomplishment. The ad was played again in the fall, but only in Philadelphia, where it could trigger memories of Specter's performance as DA and could help offset his opposition to gun control.

In the eyes of its author, the passage of the bill was the second most important achievement of his first term. As he put it, when we talked near the end of the campaign:

> I would have to rank my work on arms control first—my [three] summit resolutions and the press I've gotten [from them]. [Kenneth] Adelman mentions it whenever I see him. [George] Schultz knows about it. I've talked to the president about it. It's important that those resolutions came from someone like me. Career criminal would have to come right after arms control.... It was a major achievement. You know how hard I worked, how I had to persuade Strom Thurmond that it would not infringe on states' rights. It took me four years to pass it and then two years more to get an amendment to it. The amendment will enlarge the scope and the usefulness of the legislation. I think of it as a landmark bill. For the first time, it brings street crime within the jurisdiction of the federal government. It was an issue I was familiar with and could jump right into. It was my first big issue.

Nothing in the television ad gave such prominent treatment to the career-criminal bill as his special senatorial achievement, as evidence of his legislative ability or his leadership in the Senate. Less conspicuous still was the treatment of the bill in his bread-and-butter campaign brochure—in which career-criminal legislation is listed in the thirty-seventh paragraph out of forty-two about first-term achievements. In short, the bill did not receive a degree of campaign attention remotely commensurate with Specter's own assessment of it.

For the accomplishment of Specter's adjustment-period goals in Washington, the career-criminal bill was of major importance. For the accomplishment of his reelection goals at home, however, it was of minor importance. In the home context, we may best think of it as having a distinctive but strictly secondary influence on the campaign. Specter himself, when asked about its importance to the campaign, said, "It's had a good reception—a limited reception, but a good one." Most likely, it made a small, positive, and not easily distinguishable contribution to the overall favorability rating of the candidate.

POLITICAL STYLE AND REELECTION

CHANGES IN STYLE

Implicit in the relative lack of attention to a major personal achievement was Specter's assumption that the keys to his reelection lay elsewhere.

Not surprisingly, Specter's electoral strength was assumed to come from the same political style that had superintended his career and gained him the office in the first place. Furthermore, that style had been employed during five years in the office and was expected to buttress the natural advantages of his incumbency—including favorable name recognition and the performance of constituent services. It was believed that Arlen Specter's persistent prosecutor style—hard working, tenacious, independent—would allow him to exploit those opportunities successfully. In these respects, then, the elements of the governing style we observed during the saga of the career-criminal bill were the same ones we would expect to find highlighted in his reelection campaign.

There was one important change in emphasis. Specter's early adjustment period had been marked by his decision to eschew the distinctive media orientation of his years as district attorney and as a candidate in favor of a tend-to-business, learn-the-ropes, keep-a-low-profile approach to the Senate. He did not issue press releases; he did not hold press conferences. He sought, instead, to establish himself as a serious, substantive senatorial work horse. As we have seen, he was widely credited with this kind of legislative performance by the Pennsylvania scorekeepers. Toward the end of his first year, at about the time of his press conference on S 1688, however, he began to abandon that early decision and to return to his earlier mold.

The change was picked up first by a Washington reporter for several Pennsylvania newspapers. His article of March 1982 stated: "Specter has begun returning to the high profile approach he took as Philadelphia's district attorney ... [He] calls a news conference practically every time he introduces a bill and he holds a press availability for Pennsylvania reporters every month or so." [23] The article ran statewide under such headlines as these:

Specter Making More Noise
Arlen Specter Coming Out in the Senate
Senator Specter Casts off His Invisibility
Senator Specter Raises Low Profile, Quiet Year
Visible Specter Cautious
Specter Maintains Caution Along with Higher Profile

Specter had been impressed, he told his interviewer, with the power of the media in setting the Senate's agenda and the need, therefore, to attend to that power.

At that point, Specter was beating a steady return to the strong media orientation of his earlier career; we have traced one path of that retreat in his press activity on the career-criminal bill. It was not, however, his most visible path. "I'm groping to find a major, substantial issue that could become the subject of an investigation," he said during a conversation in late January.

> I want to find something that would command attention. I'm under no illusion that I can have a Kefauver or a McClellan type investigation. My subcommittee doesn't have a very broad jurisdiction. There isn't too much I can do without the approval of others. But I'm trying to find something that will have a substantial impact.

This thought spawned a three-year string of investigatory subcommittee hearings—many of them quite deliberately intended to "command attention."

Consider a sampling:

Juveniles and Dangerous Drugs [January 1982]
Abuse of Juveniles in Public Care and Detention [February, May 1982]
Exploited and Missing Children [April 1982]
Problems of Runaway Youth [July 1982]
Child Pornography [December 1982]
Child Kidnapping [February 1983]
Gang Violence and Control [February 1983]
Parental Kidnapping [May 1983]
Serial Murders [July 1983]
Relationship Between Child Abuse, Juvenile Delinquency and Adult Criminality [October 1983]
Crime and Violence in the Schools [January 1984]
Child Sex Abuse Cases [May 1984]
Pornography: Women and Children [September 1984]
Teenage Suicides: Cause and Effect [October 1984]
Investigation of Dr. Joseph Mengele [March 1985]
Missing Children: Private Sector Initiatives [May, July 1985)

Specter was correct in surmising that none of these investigations would make him a household word on the order of Estes Kefauver or John McClellan. But his hearings did put the spotlight on a steady succession of sex offenders, pornographic movie stars, abused children, suicidal young people, abnormally violent individuals—and even a perpetrator of the Holocaust. And as such, they did "command attention."

As far as the three nightly network news programs are concerned, it appears that his investigations produced a total of six scattered instances of publicity. The first was a hearing on the sexual abuse of juveniles in the Oklahoma prison system in February 1982 (see Chapter 3). The second and third bits of attention, both on ABC, stemmed from his

October 1984 hearings on teen suicide and corporal punishment in the schools. The final three instances, one on each of the three networks, were outgrowths of an investigation into the crimes of Nazi Joseph Mengele.

Specter's expressed hope for a substantial impact apparently went unfulfilled. But he was able to use the hearings to capture publicity. We cannot, with this summary, capture the indirect effects of the hearings. They might, for example, help account for the gradual increase in the number of Specter's appearances on the three nightly network news programs, from one in 1981, to six in 1982, to four in 1983, to thirteen in 1984 and seventeen in 1985.[24] Also, major network news summaries tell us nothing at all about other television, magazine, and newspaper outlets that were available and, perhaps, responsive. So we can be certain only that Specter's investigations commanded some attention, not how much.

What the Pennsylvania newcomer did reap from his investigative activity, however, was a whirlwind of negative press commentary on the hearings themselves—as being a superheated publicity effort by one of the Senate's emerging show horses. From liberal, conservative, and in-between sources alike came unflattering judgments reminiscent of the critiques levied against Specter's performance as Philadelphia's district attorney.

Indeed, in a 1985 *New Republic* article, a Philadelphia journalist argued that Specter's Senate record of investigations without legislative results matched exactly his DA's record of investigations without indictments. As a senator, he wrote, "[Specter] is the model of how to build a Senate career through manipulation of the media." He described Specter as "an intelligent freshman senator of moderate political instincts who has received an unprecedented amount of highly favorable media coverage." Acknowledging the low-profile reputation of Specter's adjustment period, the author argued that "Specter now has the best of both worlds. His new reputation in no way hinders his old penchant for showboating." He quoted a Specter staffer as saying, " 'There's the big four, the four major subjects that Specter knows will rope in the television cameras: kids, sex, drugs and violence.' " The author repeated the comment of a Thurmond aide: " 'The subjects he chooses are not even the remotest bit related to anything to do with juvenile justice.' " Specter's "antics," concluded the reporter, show "his emphasis on style over substance." [25]

A 1985 *Wall Street Journal* analysis argued similarly that "Mr. Specter has emerged as one of the capitol's most artful generators of publicity." But the writer drew from his observation of Specter's performance an even more negative conclusion—that the newcomer had earned precisely the reputation among his fellow senators that he had tried deliberately to avoid during his adjustment period. "His legislative achievements are limited and he seems to have failed to win the trust of his colleagues," the author wrote. "The result is Mr. Specter's reputation among his colleagues as, in Sam Rayburn's characterization, a legislative show horse rather than a work horse." He described Specter's record in terms of "publicity grab" and "political gamesmanship." [26] He was being portrayed as a hyperindividualistic member of the Senate, and minimally attentive to the communitarian side of the institution.

Both journalists emphasize the obvious reelection benefits of publicity-seeking behavior. Indeed, they explain Specter's actions largely in terms of his desire for reelection. The *New Republic* author wrote: "If the justifications for the publicity are dubious, the benefits are worthwhile. After the Mengele hearings, Jewish groups in Miami and Los Angeles held fund-raisers for Specter's 1986 reelection campaign, raising tens of thousands of dollars." And the *Wall Street Journal* article was headlined, "Sen. Arlen Specter Succeeds in Getting Headlines in an Effort to Boost His Reelection Chances."

A third unflattering judgment came from a conservative columnist.

> It is hard to know how to regard Specter. If politics were baseball, Specter would be termed a "journeyman.". . . If politics were the movies, Specter might be the Marx Brothers—all of them. He has used his prosecutor's instincts and his judiciary subcommittee entertainingly to investigate Mengele, the dead Nazi; to interrogate Linda Lovelace, the retired porn queen; to celebrate Bernhard Goetz, the subway vigilante. Other guests have included Captain Kangaroo, some of John Hinckley, Jr.'s jurors and Cathleen Webb, the "rape victim" who decided she wasn't.

Without attributing these activities to the senator's reelection effort, the author concluded that Specter's career had been one of "failing upward," that "Specter is a survivor and probably will survive." [27]

These criticisms emanated from "inside the Beltway"—from Washington insiders. The immediate question for Specter was not their effect on his reputation in Washington, but their effect on his reelection chances at home. His campaigners were sufficiently concerned to include in their March 1986 survey this question: "Would learning the following about Arlen Specter make you more or less likely to vote for him: that he aggressively seeks news coverage for himself and his legislative proposals?" When 43 percent responded "more likely" and 31 percent responded "less likely," and when the patterns followed the other major lines of cleavage between the candidates, the campaign strategists concluded that the Washington criticism would be hard for an opponent to exploit at home. It seems that they were correct, since the thrust of the challenger's campaign went in another direction.

So, too, did the main thrust of local journalists writing primarily for local audiences. The two longest personality profiles of 1984 took as their theme how much Specter had changed from his DA days, with their media-oriented intensity. They portrayed, instead, "the new Specter," a man who was "more mellow," "more low key," "less pressured," "less aggressive." They called him "a smash hit in the Senate," "a round peg in a round hole." [28] Clearly, the local observers had a different point of view.

"The evolution of intensity and drive is a fascinating subject. . . . Compared to my DA days, I'd say I'm limp," said Specter. His specific reaction to the Washington criticism was simply that there was nothing to exploit in the first place. "We made a conscious decision in the first six months not to hold press conferences, and we didn't," he explained during my October 1986 visit.

> After that, we acted normally. We got media attention because we held some hearings that were very provocative. They involved sex, children, and pornography. We developed those through the subcommittee. . . . The hearings were provocative. That's all there was to it. Edgar began by talking about the showboat thing, but it just disappeared. It didn't wash.

Whatever the validity of this explanation, the absence of any repercussions in Pennsylvania from the criticism generated in Washington illustrates at least that there remains a degree of separation and distinctiveness between the two arenas in which senators operate.

The contrast may also illustrate the different standards used by the media and the voters in assessing legislators. Specter's early adjustment style obviously hewed more closely to the biases of the media scorekeepers than did his later, more publicity-oriented style. As Specter himself once noted, "The press wants you to answer their questions, but they hate themselves for the coverage they give you. They want you to answer their calls, but they have a paranoia about being used. You can't avoid that reaction." Part of that reaction is a propensity to turn against legislators whom they believe have manipulated them to gain excessive publicity. If, indeed, there was any trace of the Washington criticism to be found in Pennsylvania, it appeared on the editorial page of the newspapers at endorsement time.[29] Editors tend not to like a publicity-seeking legislative style. But this is an occupational reaction, and it reflects an "insider" relationship of no great interest to the voters—so it seems from the Specter experience.

With respect to his change from the low profile of the first year to the higher profile of the next five years, people within the Specter enterprise believed that the first year game plan was simply a temporary adjustment to the Senate's communitarian expectations. They believed that Specter's natural political style had always had a strong media orientation and would reassert itself after a while.

Near the end of the first year, one staffer exclaimed: "Everything is so Hollywood here. I can see it in the way everyone behaves—in the way Arlen behaves. The media is the only thing that counts." Shortly before the senator began his series of investigations, in the second year, another aide noted: "Arlen has not gotten a lot of press. He'd like to. But he doesn't have that dash, that charisma that the media likes." In the middle of his effort to get the career-criminal bill passed in the Senate, a staffer said: "He thinks it ought to carry on the merits. He wants the press to recognize the merits and do his work for him. You can't do it through the press. They won't do that for you. He still thinks the press is everything."

With his reelection campaign in its final week, a long-time associate looked back on the spate of scorekeeper criticism and said:

> The press was absolutely right about his drive for media. These are smart people. They can't be fooled no matter how hard he tried to rationalize it. But that's one thing he said he would do differently. It's one of the few mistakes I've heard him admit— that he went too far with the pornography thing, Linda Lovelace and the rest. . . . But Arlen believes strongly that you can't do anything unless you have the public with you and the only way you move the public is through the media.

In 1983, he was "the heaviest user" of the radio taping service of the Senate Republican Conference, mailing three radio spots per week back to the state's sixty radio stations.[30] In 1984, he was the Senate's second heaviest user of the franking privilege.[31]

To characterize Arlen Specter's political style, in preparation for an analysis of its importance to his reelection campaign, we need to think of it as including the robust media orientation he brought with him to the Senate and not the abstinence from the media that he exercised during his first year there. That is true whether or not his publicity-seeking activity in Washington and the criticism he received for it there affected his reelection.

STYLE AND INCUMBENCY

Based on scattered survey data and my three visits to Pennsylvania (in June 1982, November 1985, and October 1986), it is my strong impression that the familiar elements of Arlen Specter's political style—the energy and the independence, the persistence and the individualism—provide the keys to his campaign and to his reelection. The benefits of this style surely had been registered well before the campaign against Bob Edgar began. The incumbent went into the campaign with a favorable reputation and held it to the end. That is, of course, what successful incumbents typically do: they spend five years gaining name recognition and favorable job ratings, and they spend nearly that long collecting money to help them capitalize on and advertise and protect those advantages.

Table 4-1 displays a five-year progress report for Arlen Specter. It shows a marked improvement in terms of the ability of voters to recall his name, in terms of their approval of his job performance, and in terms of their feelings toward him. In the last two cases, the improvement holds fairly steady; and the level of unfavorable answers remains consistently low.

Specter's pollsters, who had been charting his progress, saw these trends as very encouraging. With respect to the thermometer ratings, they said, "Specter's major strength is the very low level of negative perceptions of him across all major voting groups, including Democrats." They described his job ratings as "high even for an incumbent U.S. Senator" and described the five-year improvement in this measure as "quite dramatic." In the March 1986 survey, Specter ran more than 30 points ahead of both of his prospective Democratic rivals. Furthermore, reported his pollsters, "Specter was not hurt by the threat of a primary challenge from Thornburgh." [32] All the survey evidence pointed to a substantial, if not solid, incumbency base on which to build a reelection campaign.

Recalling the 1980 campaign, and the victorious candidate's reflections on that campaign, we can locate one crucial source of this incumbency base. Just as Specter campaigned personally and energetically "in all sixty-seven counties" and just as he looked forward to keeping steadily in touch with his constituents, so, too, did he set for himself a strenuous schedule of personal visits back home. From the beginning of his term he was enthusiastic about establishing an accessible home style.

In his end-of-the-year newsletter, December 30, 1983, he was able to say "I have visited all of Pennsylvania's sixty-seven counties, and have held open house-town meetings in all sections of the state." Indeed, he visited every one of the sixty-seven counties during his first two-year cycle and again during his second two-year cycle. By the middle of 1986, he had conducted "more than 265 town meetings" across the state, as he made clear in a campaign brochure. According to

TABLE 4-1 Voter Perceptions of Arlen Specter, 1981-1986

			Thermometer Rating[c]			
	Name Recall[a]	*Job Approval*[b]	*Favorable (100-51)*	*Neutral (50)*	*Unfavorable (49-0)*	*Never heard of*
March 1986	48%	70%	57	21	12	10
August 1985	52	73	60	19	10	11
September 1984	37	56	—	—	—	—
October 1983	34	57	—	—	—	—
February 1982	23	48	—	—	—	—
June 1981	16	48	39	24	13	24

Source: "Pennsylvania Statewide Study," *Market Opinion Research*, March 1986.

[a] Question: "Can you tell me the names of the U.S. Senators from Pennsylvania?" (first and second mention combined).

[b] Question: "Do you approve or disapprove of the way Arlen Specter is handling his job as U.S. Senator?"

[c] Question: "Using a 0-100 scale, how would you rate your feelings toward Arlen Specter?"

his March 1986 survey, 37 percent of Pennsylvania's citizens recalled that Specter had visited their "area of Pennsylvania in recent months."

"If you are going to be a senator," he exclaimed after a day on the road in June 1982, "you have to get around and you have to like it. You have to show people you care.... My problem is that I've been around too much! When I go to Harrisburg or New Castle or Oil City or Hazelton or State College, I know the people, I know the roads, I know the restaurants." In addition to the number of his visits, he also emphasized their distribution. "We're on the right track and going according to plan with Pennsylvania," he said in his second year, "eleven visits to Pittsburgh, two visits to Erie, eight visits to Harrisburg ... I think a visit in the first year is worth five visits in your last year."

After a talk to the Harrisburg Chamber of Commerce later that year, he elaborated: "People appreciate it when you come around when you don't have to, when you're not running. A guy came up to me today and said spontaneously, 'You didn't have to be here. I feel much better about government after hearing you speak today.' " A top member of the 1980 campaign staff, in attendance at the speech, was more pointed in his comments afterward.

Those guys will become the core of the Harrisburg area fund-raising committee for the campaign.... They want to see him and feel they have access. That's one of the things I learned in fund raising during the campaign. People would say to me,

"We never see Arlen except when he's asking for money." The magic of this weekend is that he went to the meeting even though he wasn't running. And he'll do it again next year.

Specter, too, believed that his personal efforts at home would eventually pay off in electoral benefits.

Table 4-2 charts both the grand total of county visits for each year of his term and the number of visits per year for each of the ten most visited counties. The record suggests a continuation of the energetic, omnipresent, individualistic political style that helped Specter achieve success in his 1980 campaign and in his governing activity. It suggests a good deal of attentiveness to his constituents overall, a sharp reelection-related increase in attentiveness over the second half of the electoral cycle, and particular attentiveness both to his Philadelphia base and to his targets of opportunity in the western and northeastern regions of the state. All in all, the record suggests that this first-term senator was determined to make the most out of his incumbency in solidifying his support at home.

Incumbents capitalize on their advantages, also, by demonstrating—or claiming—an ability to deliver tangible benefits to their constituents. In their response to a survey question asking them which of three "qualities" are "most important" in their senator, Pennsylvanians placed "power and influence in Washington to get things done for Pennsylvania" above "keeping in touch with people in Pennsylvania" by 45 percent to 34 percent. Arlen Specter was unable to demonstrate his "power and influence in Washington" with a leadership role in the passage of major legislation. His own major piece of legislation, the career-criminal bill, had a very minor impact among the voters. But he did try to demonstrate his "power and influence" by focusing on actions taken to obtain, extend, or protect certain recognizable benefits to certain recognizable constituencies.

His claims in this regard were made plausible by his membership on the Senate Appropriations Committee, through which most of the divisible, distributive government benefits must pass. On the campaign trail, he carried with him six pages of appropriations bestowed on localities or groups in the state—disaster relief for farmers and homeowners, allocations for bridge repair, Urban Development Assistance Grants, defense contracts, research facilities, educational subsidies, and the like. Of equal importance—given the administration's determined drive to reduce budgets—was evidence of his ability to stop reductions and save jobs otherwise marked for extinction—in the Conrail system, the Philadelphia navy yard, and Amtrak. "Someone asked me the other day," he said on a swing through the western part

TABLE 4-2 County Visits

	1981	1982	1983	1984	1985	1986	Total
Total yearly visits	72	105	99	194	226	333	1,029
Ten most visited counties							
Philadelphia	13	10	21	30	33	87	194
Allegheny (Pittsburgh)	10	16	16	25	24	40	131
Dauphin (Harrisburg)	8	9	9	7	19	32	84
Luzerne (Wilkes-Barre)	2	4	6	14	9	14	49
Lackawanna (Scranton)	2	1	2	11	12	11	39
Lehigh (Allentown-Bethlehem)	2	4	2	6	7	9	30
Montgomery (Philadelphia suburb)	0	3	3	2	4	15	27
Erie	1	2	2	6	4	11	26
Lancaster	2	3	1	3	6	11	26
Delaware (Philadelphia suburb)	0	3	1	2	3	13	22

Source: Staff memo to Senator Specter on County Visits, December 1986; for Philadelphia 1981, compilation by R. Fenno.

of the state in 1985, "what I thought my greatest accomplishment as a senator has been, and I said 'helping to get and keep jobs for Pennsylvania.'" In 1986, he told a reporter, similarly, that his "major accomplishment" in the Senate had been "a thick compendium of jobs and funding for Pennsylvania."[33]

There is nothing spectacular or unusual about Specter's constituency-oriented record. All legislators engage in credit claiming.[34] Under the best of circumstances, it is difficult for an opponent to refute it. But the tactic seems to have given unusual strength to this particular incumbent because he went on the offensive with it—by combining his tangible achievements with reinforcing reminders of his compatible political style. His campaign slogan became "Senator Arlen Specter. Out Front ... Fighting for Pennsylvania." In Washington, claimed his campaign brochure, "Arlen Specter displays the same activism, independence, and tenacity that earned him a solid reputation in his eight years as Philadelphia's District Attorney. [And] while he fights for Pennsylvania in Washington, he also stays in touch with Pennsylvanians." Wrapped in this largely stylistic package, his "power and influence in Washington" get magnified. It becomes easy to assume that this kind of senator must be responsible for these kinds of achievements—that he must be especially good at "fighting for" his constituents. The sum becomes greater than the parts. And the incumbent gains an important initial advantage over his challenger.

OBSERVATIONS AND REFLECTIONS:
WESTERN PENNSYLVANIA, NOVEMBER 1985

If there was one element within his statewide constituency that provided the acid test of Arlen Specter's ability to parlay his incumbency
into an initial electoral advantage, it was the western part of the state. As
a region it was Democratic, anti-Philadelphia, and now economically
depressed.[35] From the beginning of his 1980 campaign—indeed, from
the beginning of his three statewide campaigns—Allegheny County and
the surrounding area had been his weak spot. And from the beginning
of his term, he was determined to devote special attention to it. It was
the only area for which he commissioned a detailed electoral analysis.
During his first three years in the Senate he visited Pittsburgh about as
often as he visited Philadelphia. "I have a good base in eastern
Pennsylvania," he told a reporter in the summer of 1985, "because the
DA's job is very high-profile if you're active, as I was. But to get known
in the western part of the state . . . you have to travel." [36]

For two days in November 1985, I traveled with him in western
Pennsylvania—in Oil City, Brookville, Indiana, Point Marion, Uniontown, and Pittsburgh—to try to capture the flavor of his efforts there.
He drove over three hundred miles to hold two open house-town
meetings and three fund-raisers, to make two speeches and three
inspection tours.

Near the beginning of his remarks at his Uniontown fund-raiser, he
brought together the two pillars of his incumbent's strength:

> I have spent a good deal of time in the western part of the state,
> for many reasons. The most important reason is that there has
> been so much need for help from Washington, D.C. Western
> Pennsylvania has not shared in the economic recovery; and the
> steel industry and the coal industry have been very hard hit. It
> has taken the special attention which I have tried to provide,
> being on the Appropriations Committee. It's a great committee
> to be on—amazing how many friends a fellow can earn, having
> a hand in the distribution of $980 billion. But western Pennsyl-
> vania needs the help and we'll be back next month with the
> Charleroi-Monessen Bridge, one bridge of the many, many
> which we have helped bring the funding for. And the funding
> we have, $404 million, for the lock rail system in downtown
> Pittsburgh. They ran short and [we gave it] a little extra push
> and came into town just a couple of weeks ago . . . and brought
> another $21.8 million. That kind of assistance is really neces-
> sary given the very unique problems which western Pennsyl-
> vania has. And I'm not unmindful of the fact that in the west
> there is a certain distancing from the city of Philadelphia, and

it's necessary for someone who has Philadelphia County under his name on the ballot to spend a little extra time and a little extra push in western Pennsylvania, and I've tried to do just that.

He struck the same notes of personal attention and constituency service whenever he had the chance.

In his Brookville open house, he emphasized a benefit he worked to salvage for the area. "One of the items that's very important here in Jefferson County is coal," he said,

and we had quite a battle last week. It didn't make the newspapers, but if it had gone the other way, you would have heard a lot about it. There was an effort made to eliminate the requirements that U.S. military bases overseas burn American coal. . . . We won the fight last week. And that's very important for bituminous-coal-producing Pennsylvania and anthracite-producing Pennsylvania.

At a luncheon in Indiana, he talked at length about his ongoing fight to keep Conrail from being sold to the Norfolk and Southern Railroad:

Conrail is vitally important to Pennsylvania because of the 15,000 jobs it has, corporate headquarters, rail repair yards, services 2300 shippers, and at the top of the list is coal. If [your] coal were shipped on the Norfolk Southern, it would cost at least $4 a ton more. . . . I stay in constant touch with the people here [who are] very apprehensive that, were they to gain control of Conrail, it would be very difficult for Pennsylvania coal to compete.

In Pittsburgh he closed his comments at a fund-raiser with this: "I know you've seen a great deal of me in western Pennsylvania in the last five years, and I intend to keep that up."

As he had during his 1980 campaign, Specter repeatedly invoked his prosecutorial experience. His career as district attorney seemed nearly as close to the surface and almost as basic to his persona as it had been six years before. At his first open house, in Oil City, a questioner said that whenever she complained about corrupt trucking officials who were forcing drivers to work an illegal number of hours, "everyone sends me to someone else." Specter replied:

Bring it to your United States senator and he won't pass it to anyone else. That's what I'm here for. As DA, I prosecuted many cases—murder, robbery, rape. I've dealt with people like this before. We'll find out what these people are up to, unless they are willing to commit perjury.

He opened his town meeting in the county courthouse in Brookville saying, "It's a great pleasure to be here and to see this lovely courtroom. I feel very much at home in courtrooms. What I'd like to do now is impanel a jury and see if we can't try a case here this morning." At the end, he remarked, "I used to be district attorney, as some of you may know—tried a lot of cases in courtrooms like the one we're in today."

The next day, in speeches at Duquesne and at a victims' advocacy group luncheon he often invoked his earlier credentials. "When I was district attorney of Philadelphia . . ." or, "I recall that when I became assistant DA back in October of 1959 . . ." or, "I've had experience as a prosecuting attorney . . ." or, "When I became DA of Philadelphia . . ." or "Let me talk again from my experience as district attorney." As we drove in the car, he reminisced about past cases. The prosecutorial perspective seemed as dominant as ever.

Moreover, people who introduced him mentioned his prosecutorial past: ". . . reputation as a tough prosecutor . . ." and, "vigorous prosecution of criminals as DA." He was described as "a fighter," but with reference to his fights in Philadelphia, not his career-criminal fight in Congress. The standard biographical handout, from which the introductions were typically taken, was as much devoted to Specter's pre-Senate record as to his Senate performance. Indeed, the career-criminal bill was given only one sentence—in the eighth paragraph out of ten, on the second page of two in his basic resume. Altogether, his performance conveyed the strong impression that the connections between senator and constituents still depended heavily on the prosecutorial persona. Specter was a senator. He talked about what he had done as senator. But his achievements in the Senate would not yet suffice to give him a strong and distinctive senatorial reputation.

This condition was highlighted, also, by the appearance of a campaign feature I had not observed in 1980—the heavy reliance on his Republican senatorial colleague, John Heinz. This reliance was, of course, a western Pennsylvania phenomenon, since Heinz's home was Pittsburgh. And perhaps in that area Specter had ridden coattails in 1980. But the relations between the two men, who had fought a bitter primary in 1976 and who had been on opposite sides in Specter's next two primary fights, had grown more cooperative and respectful during their six years together in the Senate. So there was now a solid basis for asserting close mutual support—which Specter certainly did.

At Brookville: Senator Heinz and I have been fighting for that and we won . . . [coal for military bases]

Senator Heinz and I have held hearings . . . [Grace Commission]

	Senator Heinz and I have gotten into this fairly deeply . . . [IRS performance]
At Uniontown:	Senator Heinz was here on Thursday and I was here on Friday [flood damage]
	I know that John Heinz shares my concern on these problems . . . [budget cuts]
At Duquesne:	Senator Heinz and myself, for example, are unwilling to vote to raise the debt ceiling unless . . . [deficit]
	Senator Heinz and I have worked on appropriations for targeting . . . [homeless]
At Point Marion:	Senator Heinz and I have been touring the area the last few days . . . [flood damage]
At Pittsburgh:	John Heinz and I were together today . . . [veterans day ceremony]
At Indiana:	I hope you'll be prepared to support John Heinz in 1988. I suppose I've just made John's reelection announcement. I can't do that. Then again, since I don't speak for him and he can deny it, I guess I'll go ahead and do it.

Near the end of the second day, Specter turned to his district staff chief and smiled. "Did I mention John Heinz too many times?"

The strategy was as rational as it was transparent, for the two-termer Heinz was a more popular and more secure senator than the newcomer. And he was beloved and invulnerable in the western area. Nonetheless, it is a commentary on Specter's own lack of an established senatorial persona that he should need to couple himself so closely with his colleague. Specter's pollsters used Heinz as the standard against which to measure Specter's political strength; all their comparisons argued for the coupling strategy I observed. In their March 1986 analysis, they concluded, "Western Pennsylvania should be considered the front line of the 1986 contest: . . . The Specter campaign should make good use of John Heinz in this area as well as developing an advertising message with a regional focus." It called for the same aggressiveness and the same tactics in the region that the candidate himself had been pursuing since the beginning of his term.[37]

Carried out over a five-year period, the kind of performance I observed had produced important gains for Specter in the area. His

March survey revealed: "Specter's performance in Western Pennsylvania is . . . 11-22 points (depending on the measure) ahead of the normal Republican vote in this heavily Democratic area." [38] And a comparison of his June 1981 and his June 1986 ratings on unaided name recognition, job approval ratings, and "feeling thermometer" scores shows improvement in each category in Allegheny County. Moreover, the scores show a larger net increase, over the five years, for Allegheny County than for the state as a whole (Table 4-3).

Specter's disproportionate effort in the west appears to have paid off in a disproportionate improvement in his standing there. On the evidence, he appears to have used his incumbency effectively to strengthen his support in his politically weak area. On the other hand, Table 4-3 also shows that his various ratings in the west still remained well below those in the rest of the state. That meant, of course, that his special concern for western Pennsylvania would have to continue.

In terms of Specter's preparation for the longer reelection haul, there were indications during the trip that he had seized yet one more incumbency advantage—the chance to raise money. One established pattern of modern senatorial elections is that incumbents normally "out-raise" and out-spend challengers. Frequently, the financial advantage of the incumbent is sufficiently large to discourage prospective opponents from entering the race. Arlen Specter had proven to be a formidable fund raiser—$91,000 in 1983, $313,000 in 1984, and $2.4 million in 1985.[39] But he had not yet, apparently, preempted all opposition.

The central question pervading every political conversation during the trip was whether or not the governor—with his Western Pennsylvania base—was going to enter the Republican primary. Predictions varied, and uncertainty prevailed.[40] Specter expressed his familiar determination. "If we have to fight a primary, we will," he said privately. "And we will win. I think I can beat him. So does [consultant-pollster] Bob Teeter. But it will take every bit of our money. Then we'll have to start all over again raising enough money to run in the general election." When he was asked about Thornburgh, he would allude to his own financial advantage. "I have no idea what his thinking is. We're just carrying on the way we do day by day. We've now raised $3 million. And I would think that the longer he waits, the harder it will be for him to organize a campaign." He hoped that it was already too late for a potential opponent to overcome his financial lead. And he believed others would see that such was the case.

We started our fund-raising campaign right after the 1982 elections, and we signed up a lot of people. We have over

TABLE 4-3 Five-Year Improvement, Allegheny County

	Name recall			Job approval			Thermometer Ratings Favorable (100-51)			Unfavorable (49-0)		
	6/81	6/86	Diff.	6/81	6/86	Diff.	6/81	6/86	Diff.	6/81	6/86	Diff.
Statewide	16	42	+27	48	72	+24	39	60	+21	13	11	−2
Allegheny County	13	44	+31	33	67	+34	22	56	+34	19	15	−4
Allegheny County Differential			+4			+10			+13			−2

Source: "Pennsylvania Statewide Study," *Market Opinion Research,* March 1986 and June 1986.

fifteen hundred people enrolled in the $1000 for Arlen Specter Club. These people who have given don't want to give again. They won't like financing a primary and then a general election. I'm sure they are telling Thornburgh not to run.

At his large Pittsburgh fund-raiser, he was introduced by the Republican party's top woman official—herself a Pittsburgh native and a longtime Thornburgh ally—with a strong and pointed endorsement. "We are extremely fortunate to have a wonderful senator, Arlen Specter, and I think we are here tonight because we care what happens to Arlen Specter, because we think he's done a beautiful job of representing Pennsylvania and want him back again, for Pennsylvania." The evening netted him $100,000 and a strengthening of support in the governor's backyard. We have no way of knowing how much of a factor Specter's fund-raising prowess and his huge financial head start was in Thornburgh's eventual decision not to run. But it must have had an effect.

THE CAMPAIGN

INCUMBENT AND CHALLENGER

The campaign between Arlen Specter and Bob Edgar began in May. A look at it will help us to understand further the Pennsylvania newcomer's political career. Specter entered the campaign with a substantial incumbent-style lead over his opponent and never relinquished it. In March, before the Democratic primary, Specter led Edgar in a hypothetical pairing 62 percent to 28 percent. In June, after Edgar's primary victory, Specter's lead in terms of vote intentions held at 60 percent to 31 percent. In the middle of October, under a strong attack by his challenger, the incumbent's lead remained strong at 57 percent to 39 percent.[41] And on election day, the voters of Pennsylvania reelected Specter with 56 percent of the vote. The contest was never close.

Some observers believed it would be. Their belief rested on a lack of appreciation for the incumbency advantage as it dovetailed so nicely with the home style of the incumbent. Particularly, they did not understand Specter's long-term build-up of support in the west. They gave too little weight to Specter's simple question, "Why should people in southwestern Pennsylvania vote for [Edgar]? They don't know him. You couldn't give him a geography test he'd pass in southwestern Pennsylvania." [42] They operated with standard assumptions about political geography until the game was virtually over.

A July 1986 analysis carrying the headline "Glimmers of Trouble for Arlen Specter" began, "Into the summer doldrums drops this growing perception among Republican and Democratic politicians alike: Arlen Specter is in trouble." Informed opinion, says the author, predicts "a race that will tighten until Election day, [and] a win by either Specter or Edgar by only 2 or 3 percentage points . . . a squeaker." "How could the incumbent be in such a jam?" he asks. His explanation begins by quoting a "political consultant" in denigration of Specter's attentiveness to home. "I'd give Arlen a fifty-fifty chance of winning. His problem is that he's spent six years not as a Senator but as a candidate. He's like a woman who spent all her time wooing people—until a prettier girl came to town." Blacks, liberals, and independents, says the consultant, will be attracted to the prettier girl. The author then invokes conventional wisdom: "This year Specter faces a challenge from his own back yard"; "western Pennsylvania is the most problematic area for Republicans this year"; and "if Edgar wins in the west and battles Specter to a draw in the east, the race may well turn on how well the incumbent does in the middle." [43]

In September, a former Philadelphia reporter proffered a similar analysis. "Edgar is from the Philadelphia suburbs . . . and will cut into Specter at home. When these two easterners go into the other major population center, the hard-hit steel region of southwest Pennsylvania, the presumption will be with the Democrats." He, too, pictured Specter as "busily . . . advertising his own successes at constituent service," but attributed no special potency to that effort.[44]

Bob Edgar, too, worked off the same premises. In his primary campaign against westerner Don Bailey, he took the view that "any Democrat this fall could carry Bailey's base in economically struggling western Pennsylvania." [45] And after the primary he told a leading Pittsburgh political columnist that the election would "be won or lost in terms of political geography." Edgar's plan was this:

> He will carry Philadelphia BIG over Sen. Specter. He also will sharply reduce, if not overcome, the traditionally large Republican vote in the Philly suburbs. He will neutralize the customary GOP margin in Central Pennsylvania. Then he will amass a winning majority in Western Pennsylvania, where the principal issues—job losses and plant shutdowns—favor the Democrats. [46]

"My consultant tells me," Edgar assured a Philadelphia reporter, "that if I fell asleep today and woke up on Election Day, I'd get 45% of the vote." [47] He had accepted the conventional wisdom, and he had taken confidence from its time-honored tenets.

In addition to political geography, Edgar was relying on the vote-getting abilities of a well-organized and intensely loyal coalition of issue-oriented groups—the grass-roots coalition that had seen him through the primary. He explained his primary victory as an organizational victory—for his sixty-seven county committees, eight field offices, a paid headquarters staff of twenty-eight and about seven thousand "highly motivated, energetic" volunteers from environmental, nuclear freeze, women's, civil rights, and labor groups. [48] Throughout his campaign against Specter, he claimed a similar advantage.

> My field staff is better than his. We've spent two years building the best field staff in Pennsylvania. We decided you can't win this campaign only on TV. We spent two years identifying the environmental voters, the peace voters, the civil rights voters, the women voters. We think none of the intensity of my supporters and the lack of intensity for Specter shows up in the polls. The conventional wisdom on polls may fall flat for not calculating the effect of our field organization. [49]

Edgar's comments are illuminating for anyone who would understand Arlen Specter's political strength. For Specter did not have an organization of intense issue-oriented believers. Indeed, he did not have any "field organization" at all worthy of the name. His campaign was not fueled by the enthusiasm of likeminded volunteers. His campaign was a highly individualistic effort, based on the unremitting hard work of one man over a long period of time—traveling the state, meeting people, raising money, buying media. A veteran Philadelphia editor said it best: "Arlen Specter [is] the hardest working candidate I have ever known. [He] takes nothing for granted." [50] His support was broad, but not deep and intense. And he had behaved in Washington in a manner that had kept it that way—identified with no great emotional cause, boasting no glamorous legislative triumph. His opponent, surrounded by cause-oriented organizers, was operating under a starkly different set of organizational premises.

With his geographical and organizational premises in hand, Edgar needed only to decide what he wanted to say to the Pennsylvania electorate. We have no idea what the challenger's polls told him about the Pennsylvania electorate or suggested he should say to them about the incumbent. We do know, however, what Specter's surveys of March 1986 told *his* campaigners about these matters. And, judging by Edgar's eventual campaign message, both camps must have been receiving the same polling information.

Specter's pollsters identified his strength as his low level of negative voter perceptions; and they identified his weakness as the low level of intensity among his supporters. This combination, they believed, would lead any challenger to "decide it was necessary to attack Specter" and would "leave voters vulnerable to appeals by Specter's opponent." Accordingly, they set about to isolate "soft Specter voters" for special attention. But their analysis of voter sentiment on issues led them to believe that there were no identifiable issues on which the incumbent was vulnerable or on which the election could be made to turn. They concluded, therefore, that "this is unlikely to be an issue driven election . . . we can expect voters to make their decisions based much more on personality and performance assessments rather than issue judgments." They advised Specter, accordingly, to emphasize his accomplishments, and they launched a media campaign that pictured him "getting results." [51]

His first set of TV commercials advertised his legislative achievements: his avian flu appropriation for poultry farmers;[52] his unfair foreign competition bill for business; his antiterrorism bill; his job-saving efforts at the Philadelphia Navy Yard and on Conrail;[53] his support for locks, dams, and bridges on the Monongahela River; his summit resolutions; his missing children's center bill; his support for Dr. Leon Sullivan's job training programs; his success in placing a federally funded software engineering institute in Pittsburgh; his career-criminal bill. For Specter the campaign began with an illustrated, repetitious, recitation that "my record is one of producing for Pennsylvania in a tangible way." [54]

Bob Edgar, following the prescriptions implicit in Specter's survey information, initiated an immediate, hard-hitting, head-on "attack" on Specter, focused on his "personality and performance." Specter's Senate voting record, Edgar told the voters, revealed "an opportunist with a big political ego who tries to be all things to all people," "a boatsman

tacking his sails to every little shift in the political winds."[55] He focused
the attack on several salient issues—the MX missile, apartheid, Star
Wars—for which Specter's record either was or could be seen as
inconsistent. And he charged the incumbent with a record of expedi-
ency and flip-flopping rather than conviction and constancy. "There is
an Arlen Specter on both sides of every single issue," he said at one
point. "There are two Arlen Specters," was another reported charge.
Similarly, "[He] talks one way and votes another." [56]

An early TV commercial depicted "the two faces of Arlen Specter . .
one normal, the other shadowy and distorted," while the flip-flops of
his voting record were listed. A later commercial featured a cracking,
crumbling bust of Specter's head, while a recitation of his inconsisten-
cies revealed that "he's not all he's cracked up to be." [57] Edgar had a
strong liberal record in the House. But, he explained, "the wisdom,
whether right or wrong is you first have to peel the voters off your
opponent." [58] He never stopped trying. His effort may not have been as
well financed as it needed to have been to get his negative message
across. But he did spend $4 million and run an extremely well organized
campaign. It received sympathetic press treatment.[59] But it did not work.

It did not work, in the broadest sense, because the incumbent was
simply too strong. In Specter's view, it was "a paper wad bouncing off a
Sherman tank." [60] Near the end of the campaign, Specter said:

> The reason I've been able to withstand Edgar's negative on-
> slaught is because people know who I am. Even when Edgar
> was gaining in the polls, he never dented my "favorables" or
> my "unfavorables." I've been to Pittsburgh and Scranton and
> Wilkes-Barre so many times in the last six years that I can't
> count. People feel they know me.

In an endorsement interview with a Philadelphia paper that same day,
he was asked about his reputation as a showboat. And he explained why
that "wouldn't wash."

> Edgar can't use that against me because of all the damn things
> I've done. I've brought jobs and money to Pennsylvania. I've
> been in every county in the state at least four times. I've been
> the most visible senator Pennsylvania ever had. I've been hard
> working and successful. I've got "spilkus"; in yiddish that
> means excessive energy.

It was a media question and an incumbent's defense.

But Edgar's "negative onslaught" did not work in the narrow sense
either, because the attack ran up against the most solidly established
element of Arlen Specter's political persona—his independence. First as
a prosecutor, later as a candidate, and finally as a senator, he had

cultivated a reputation as someone who "calls 'em as he sees 'em," who makes up his own mind and charges ahead. Of course, one person's independence is another person's inconsistency. And one person's judgment call is another person's opportunism. Indeed, Specter's polls showed that people would be "more likely" to vote for him (66 to 16 percent) if they learned that "he often takes an independent position" but "less likely" to vote for him (52 to 24 percent) if they learned that "he sometimes changes his mind on important issues." [61] So the campaign became largely a contest to determine which interpretation of Arlen Specter's behavior would prevail.

In this contest, the challenger had what prosecutor Specter liked to call "the laboring oar." He had to make the case against the incumbent. Specter argued that "a senator who represents Pennsylvania has to be independent, and given Pennsylvania's problems he has to be very independent." [62] Calling himself "the most independent" Republican senator, he asserted, "My vote is not determined by President Reagan, and I shy away from such labels as liberal or conservative . . . because the real role of a U.S. Senator is a judgment call." [63] He further argued that "People here . . . understand that a Pennsylvania Republican can be reelected only if he shows some independence and pursues a moderate course." [64] As a practical matter, that meant voting with the Reagan administration on some matters and voting against the Reagan administration on other matters. As his home state observers had noted at the outset, he was "the one up there on the tightrope." But the evidence was that he had kept his balance.

During his term, he had been most often assailed by the conservative right wing of his party. And it was they who had fueled the Thornburgh primary boomlet.[65] Now, during the campaign, he was being assailed from the other side by the liberal Edgar. Conservatives blasted him for opposing judicial appointees like William Sessions and Clarence Manion; Edgar blasted him for supporting William Rehnquist. Specter's pollsters found Pennsylvania's voters placed him "almost midway between [the] Republican and Democratic" parties. "One of Specter's major political strengths," they concluded, "is that he is not a partisan figure." [66] Journalists agreed that he had "a steely grip on the center" and that "for six years he has been . . . somewhere near the middle . . . acquiring an independent image of the type absolutely required of a Republican who runs for office in a state with an 800,000 Democratic registration majority." [67] Washington observers often gave Specter top billing in articles about Republican senatorial independence.[68] In sum, the incumbent's reputation for independence was sufficiently well fixed to create an extremely heavy burden of proof for the challenger.

During the month of October, Specter launched a counterattack of his own. In his speeches, he argued that Edgar was a "far out, left-wing" Democrat, "outside the mainstream in Congress, outside the mainstream of the Democratic party and outside the mainstream of the most liberal branch of the Democratic party. He is really off the board." [69] On television, he presented a second wave of nine new commercials. Three of them attacked Edgar's record directly. Two of them featured John Heinz stating that "Arlen and I have worked together," and criticizing Edgar in general terms. "No wonder Bob Edgar is distorting Arlen Specter's record. He just can't compete." Or, "when someone lets ambition get in the way of integrity, that's a shame." Two other commercials touted Specter's accomplishments in foreign policy, namely, his summit resolutions. And two more played exclusively in western Pennsylvania.

Specter, as usual, put his greatest faith in the power of the media. "All campaigns are media campaigns," he said. "This one may even be more of a media campaign than last time, because we have more money." He raised $6 million, compared with $1.6 million in 1980. And a top campaigner summarized their media strategy. "We stayed on top of him [Edgar] all the time" he said.

> If he went on TV with 400 [rating] points, we went right on with 600 points. If he went on with 800 points, we went right on with 1,200 points. If he ran an ad that needed answering, we came right back with an ad alluding to his. We believed we had to do that to keep the Democrats from coming to him. And we had the money to do it. We never let him get started.

With a campaign treasury of $4 million, Edgar could not keep up the pace and was forced off the air at several key points. Otherwise, the pattern of attack and rebuttal continued at all levels of the campaign during its final month. By all accounts, the climax of the campaign was their one debate, in mid-October, during which both men took off the gloves and slugged away.[70] It provided a surfeit of emotion but, like the rest of the campaign, it had no traceable effect on the outcome.

EXPLANATION OF GOVERNING ACTIVITY

Bob Edgar's attack forced Arlen Specter to explain his Washington behavior. That is the link electoral competition forges between governing and campaigning at the end of the electoral cycle. Specter's explanations of his most criticized votes retained sufficient plausibility to increase the challenger's burden. That is to say, when they did not convince they usually confused. And confusion benefits the incumbent.

On the matter of the MX missile, where Specter had clearly changed positions from antiadministration opposition to proadministration support, he covered his switch with a highly publicized and highly plausible assertion of his independence. As the administration battled for Senate support for the MX missile in 1985, a "White House official" said that

> if [a] senator doesn't support us on the MX and he wants a fund raiser in the next three or four months, he's not going to get a fund raiser. If the President's going to go out and raise a million bucks for an incumbent that's going to be up for reelection, we can expect a little support for him here. . . . going up and raising a million bucks for Arlen Specter goes a long way towards him having an easier time raising his money. If he's not there with us, let him raise his own money.

Specter's immediate reaction was that "I'm prepared to raise my money by myself if somebody's talking about a quid pro quo. I have been told an early fund raiser by the president was set for me this spring and nobody raised the question of a quid pro quo." [71] In yet another context, he was expressing his familiar, instinctive, loner's aversion to any quid pro quo. And, as one aide put it, it "got his back up."

Four days later he told the president at lunch that "those remarks were very destructive and debilitating to a senator's independence and integrity." Then he went to the Senate floor to announce his support *for* the MX, and to announce, also: "So that there will be no doubt about my motivation on my vote, I shall not have President Reagan come to Pennsylvania or elsewhere to help me raise campaign funds." [72] "I just died when I heard that," said his campaign manager. "It cost us a million dollars. But Arlen thought his independence was at stake." Specter himself said later, "I think I might have reflected on that a little more—found a way to assert my independence without costing me a million dollars. But I felt very keenly about it. I thought it was very intimidating, very unfair. I reacted instinctively." [73] But it was an instinctive reaction that served—certainly in the public press—to underline more his independence than his inconsistency. [74]

Another issue stressed by Edgar and picked up in Philadelphia's black community involved Specter's "flip-flop" votes on sanctions against South Africa. At one point, he supported presidentially proposed mild sanctions in place of congressionally proposed strong sanctions; later he supported those same strong sanctions. Edgar argued that these votes reflected less than staunch opposition to apartheid. Specter argued that they reflected "judgment calls" as to how best to proceed against apartheid—first encouraging the president when he took some action, later supporting stronger measures when the earlier action failed to produce results.[75]

During our western Pennsylvania swing in late 1985, he talked about the first vote in the context of his relations with the president. "I've tried to help him out," said Specter.

> I backed him on his South African initiative. Politically, I would have been better off voting against him. But I thought he deserved support. He had gone 90 percent of the way. And it is better to have the chief executive do something that is 90 percent effective than to have the legislature make a 100 percent declaration that will never be implemented.

It was a pragmatic argument that might have appealed to administration supporters if they thought about it (which they probably did not), but more likely would not appeal to the black community if they thought about it (which they probably did). They were encouraged to do so by a pamphlet calling Specter South Africa's "friend in Pennsylvania." [76]

"We won't do as well with the blacks in Philadelphia as we did," he admitted late in the campaign.

> Edgar is a liberal Democrat and that will help him. Flaherty was more to the right. So the contours are different this time. Congressman Bill Gray is working hard for Edgar and circulating some scurrilous literature amounting to an accusation that I'm responsible for killing babies in South Africa. That will hurt us in the black community. I'm not sure how much.

He added, "I think I have the best civil rights record in Philadelphia. That's too strong—I have as good as any. That goes back to my record as DA." In this situation, Specter's rebuttal centered on his strong civil rights record at home and in Washington.

At the top of the Washington list, he displayed his vote against the president's nomination of William Bradford Reynolds, chief of the Justice Department's Civil Rights Division, to the second-ranking position in the department. Reynolds was strongly opposed by civil rights groups and strongly supported by right-wing conservative groups. As Specter explained to reporters:

> The Reynolds vote was an extremely tough vote. I knew I was putting my life in my hands by opposing him. I had a meeting here with the whole conservative branch of the party ... about 20 people ... and there was no misunderstanding as to the consequences if I opposed [him].[77]

The conservatives "couldn't wait to come into Pennsylvania to denounce me," he said. It was a vote the angry conservatives never forgot, and

their highly publicized wooing of Thornburgh was followed by venge-
ful statements of nonsupport.[78] National observers wrote about "infuri-
ated administration officials," saying that Specter had "gone too far";
yet, they noted, "Specter's independence has won him considerable
local press coverage." [79] To a group of black politicians in Pittsburgh,
Specter argued that his willingness to "put my political life on the line"
in the Reynolds case was sufficient warrant for believing his interpretation of his position on apartheid.[80] Some black politicians continued to
support him; others did not.

And so it went—attack, counterattack, rebuttal, and explanation—to
the end of the campaign. By the time of the debate, reports indicated
that the specific arguments about votes and issue positions had become
so detailed and complex that they were impossible to follow.[81] The more
that condition prevailed, the easier it was for the incumbent to make
plausible explanations and the harder it became for the challenger to
make his case stick. For a couple of days in the last week of October, I
joined the Specter campaign. At that point, he had been told by his
managers to "just relax" and "stay out of trouble." Not surprisingly, he
was keeping up a full schedule. But he and his staffers talked a little
about his efforts to cope with the Edgar attack.

For Specter, the campaign was his introduction to the explanatory
process at home as it follows the governing process in Washington. In
his efforts to maintain his balance, he had sometimes given a procedural
vote to the administration while saving a subsequent substantive vote to
register his true position. For the party leadership, it is always easier to
get a favorable vote on a procedural matter. And for individual
legislators it is a time-honored way of staying in balance on a political
tightrope.

Specter's first, and hotly disputed, apartheid vote, for example, had
been a vote against cloture (that is, against ending debate), not a direct
vote against sanctions. Similarly, Specter had voted in the Judiciary
Committee in favor of reporting some controversial nominations, which
he later voted against on the floor. But the Edgar flip-flop attack had
taught him, he now said, the costs incurred by such behavior.

> I made a political mistake by voting against those nominations
> on the floor but voting in committee to send them to the floor. I
> don't think the committee should be part of the bottling-up
> process. Philosophically and institutionally, I think I'm right.
> But I've learned a lot about politics in the last six years. And
> one thing I've learned is that you have to worry about how and
> what you do can be explained or twisted. I always thought if
> you did what was right, the explanation would take care of
> itself. But I find that you have to worry about the explanation

of everything you do. That was a very new concept for me.

It was a lesson about the connective tissue between governing and campaigning that can be taught only by a reelection experience.

The lesson was not only that explanation at home was necessary, but also that an explanation that might be totally satisfactory in Washington—such as procedure versus substance—might not be adequate at home. For someone who had never before held legislative office, nor run before for reelection on a voting record, learning about the explanatory process was a climactic step in the adjustment process.

One of his staffers reflected, further, on Specter's explanatory style:

> He can explain anything he does or any vote he casts, sometimes in the most roundabout, convoluted way. It makes sense to him and he can't understand why everyone can't see it the way he does. It's "Now I've told you. That's it. Of course, you understand." But people don't understand, and they feel he is manipulating them.... It's a matter of style with Arlen, the way he does things as much as what he does.

That is, Specter's explanations conveyed the attitude that he knew what was right; that he intended to charge ahead; and that he had only so much time and energy to expend bringing others along. It becomes both doubly difficult and doubly essential to bring people along when your position is confusing in the first place. And, admitted a campaign staffer, Arlen's legislative behavior *was* confusing in the first place. On the MX missile, the aide said: "He wants to have it both ways. He didn't take a stand. I wish he'd say more often, 'Some things are sacred and I won't budge.'" For the outcome of the campaign these explanatory problems did not matter. But, in the longer run, they presented a challenge for the Pennsylvania newcomer.

For most of the time I traveled with him, Specter was accompanied by half a dozen Pennsylvania reporters. And, immersed as I was in the entourage, I observed yet another aspect of his explanatory style. It was something I had also observed in the 1980 campaign, and it did not seem to have changed. Arlen Specter was not comfortable with his state's reporters and had not established a good working relationship with them. He behaved dutifully with them, but not warmly or openly. Of course, he needed them to convey his explanations to a wider public. And, given his extreme reliance on the media, he needed them to supply him with favorable publicity. But he did not give much of himself in return. He struck the same stance with them at home that he struck with his colleagues in the Senate—wary of anything that smacked of a quid pro quo, uncertain of whom to trust, placing his faith in individual efforts. So he kept the reporters at arms length. "He always tells us how fascinating the legislative process is," complained one reporter, "but he never tells us how he does it."

For his part, Specter often complained about problems on the other side of the relationship. "The press guys covering the campaign" he had said in 1980, "aren't as sharp as I had expected. I guess I shouldn't have expected Phi Beta Kappas. The story of my campaign is the media . . . and the media figures are all available to the public . . . if anyone wanted to dig for them." A year and a half later, on a home visit, he said, "The trouble with the media here is that turnover is too high. That's especially true of the TV people. They never stay long enough to learn anything about Pennsylvania." A couple of years later, he told a journalist that "for years he had been subjected to a mass psychoanalysis by amateurs." But that treatment was itself the result of their inability to get close to him, the result of his "privateness." [82] Specter's complaints conveyed the sense that his style of explanation— "Now I've told you. That's it. Of course, you understand"—ought to suffice. And if it did not, well, that was the fault of the reporters who asked the questions in the first place—and they did not have the competence to probe further.

The reporters took a different view—that in the absence of any convincing explanation or any special expenditure of time and energy on the senator's part to elaborate his views, they would remain disbelievers. In private conversation, they agreed with Edgar's interpretation completely. Specter, they believed, flip-flopped on the issues; sufficient proof of that fact was that they were never able to pin him down on what he stood for. Their view seemed to be that he was manipulating the voters just as he was manipulating them. They recognized the political advantage in such a stance. "Specter never makes any enemies," said one. "Everyone leaves annoyed but not angry." This pragmatism was not a style that appealed to them as journalists. And Specter had done nothing to show them the principled conduct they admired, nor had he extended himself to breach this natural occupational divide.

All this grousing took place in the evening's aftermath of an incident on the campaign trail in suburban Philadelphia. Riding with a staffer and three reporters in the first car of a two-car caravan, Specter had ordered his driver to speed up in thick traffic, with the result that the two reporters following in the second car got separated from him and caught up with him only after the afternoon's events were over. The problem had been compounded by the fact that only the senator knew where he was going. For me, it was a campaign equivalent of the many solo performances I had observed in the Senate. But to the reporters it was a literal enactment of his determination to keep his distance from them. These two had lost most of their opportunity to interview him. "I've never seen a statewide campaign as poorly organized and as totally messed up as this one" said one of the day's losers, a ten-year veteran of political reporting.

From their conversation—not from the content of their reporting—I detected a very unsympathetic view of Specter's candidacy. It was something in the nature of a repayment for his lack of communication with them. And although the tension did not contribute to the election outcome, it did not help the candidate. At the least, it kept the reporters from seeing the strengths of his candidacy and kept them fixated instead on the voting record contretemps. At the most, it meant that he might lose the benefit of the doubt in the future, that when he needed the reporters "to make his case for him," they would not. Whatever the case, we should think of this relationship, too, as one more test of the limits of an individualistic, go-it-alone political style.

PATTERNS OF SUPPORT

As a substantive matter, the essential question for the campaign was: Which of the general arguments being used by the two candidates were appealing to which elements in the Pennsylvania constituency? Newspaper endorsements came late in the campaign and tended to reflect the argumentation of the campaign. Some endorsement patterns, therefore, may provide a clue about how the two conflicting interpretations of Arlen Specter's behavior were playing to the electorate.

Edgar's liberal voting record, his issue-oriented campaign organization, and his attack on Specter probably appealed most to people who were strongly likeminded on the issues to begin with and to people who had no reason to know about or think well of Arlen Specter. Both sorts of voters were Democrats. The two Philadelphia papers—both of which switched from the 1980 Specter endorsement to support Edgar—represent the issue-oriented, interested segment of Democratic opinion. To begin with, the city papers disapproved of Arlen Specter's aggressive, publicity-oriented style on purely occupational grounds. On top of that, they valued liberal issue purity above legislative pragmatism.

Editors at the *Inquirer* tended to make more of their reactions to style, while those at the *News* tended to make more of their preference for issue purity. The *Inquirer* had long been viewed, within the Specter enterprise, as ranging between unsympathetic and hostile to Specter as a politician and to the furtherance of his career. At the *News*, skepticism regarding Specter's issue positions—on gun control, the MX missile, apartheid—was palpable during the board's hectoring endorsement interview. Both boards bought into Edgar's "inconsistency" argument and rejected Specter's "independence" explanations. The *Inquirer* claimed that Specter was "forever in a quandary, weighing the political consequences of his 'independence.'" The *News* said, "Charges that Specter can be found on different sides of the same issue at different times are accurate far too often." Both praised Edgar positively as "the better choice for the job" and "the right choice for the U.S. Senate." [83]

On the other hand, Specter's assertions about his independence, and his defense of that governing style, appealed to newspapers in the Republican suburbs around Philadelphia. While leaning toward conservative positions, they opposed extremism and were attracted to the idea of a legislator who did not follow the party line. They either applauded or understood Specter's record of support (mostly) and opposition (prominently) to "their" administration. And they even tended to be sympathetic to the thrust of his more notorious opposition votes. The editors of the *Bucks County Courier Times* praised him for his "solid record of moderation, insight and political independence ... [which redounded] to his credit and our benefit.... An admirable independence has become the Specter signature." They concluded, after praise of Edgar, "It takes a knockout punch to dislodge an incumbent who is doing a good job," and that Edgar could not deliver it. [84]

The *Pottstown Mercury* in Montgomery County, began its endorsement: "As a liberal Republican in a Democratic state, Arlen Specter has had to balance his ideals with loyalty to President Reagan.... [He] has done well, helping the President on major issues, but reserving his independence on social programs." And, they wrote approvingly, "Specter has been able to see both sides of an issue and has changed his vote as new circumstances arise." [85] It was to the people in the large suburban areas, where the core Republican vote is cast, that Specter had been directing his argument for balance and independence. These are the voters who had to buy into that interpretation if he was to be reelected. The neswpapers' endorsements suggest that he succeeded.

The main argument that Specter directed to western Pennsylvania was not reflected in the city and suburban papers we have discussed. In this part of the state, Edgar's attack was largely irrelevant; Specter's appeal for support rested most on his attentiveness to the area. In the final days of the campaign, his appeal was carried to the region by John Heinz in a commercial that began: "For six years, Arlen Specter and I have worked side by side for western Pennsylvania." It went on: "Where was Bob Edgar when we needed him" to help with relief for the United Mine Workers, or lock and dam repairs on the Monongahela River? "Where western Pennsylvania is concerned, Arlen Specter was right on those issues and Bob Edgar was dead wrong." Simultaneously, another ad showed several men talking by the Monongahela River.

Arlen Specter came and saw the condition of our bridges and came to our meeting, they said. Now we have the Charleroi bridge and the Mon City bridge is on the way, they said. "To us a bridge is like a baby being born."

Judging by some editorial response, the arguments took hold. The *Greensburg Tribune-Review* endorsement began this way:

> Sen. Arlen Specter has done his homework. Few senators spend as much time listening to people and responding as Pennsylvania's Specter. He has constantly zig-zagged across the Commonwealth to touch and feel the fabric of the land. He worked in the Mon Valley when they needed him. He got relief for victims of the tornadoes and floods in western Pennsylvania . . . he has grown close to the people he represents in his travels.[86]

From the *Uniontown Herald Standard*—we had stopped in Uniontown for a 1985 fund-raiser—came this endorsement recommendation:

> On the purely parochial basis of what is best for southwestern Pennsylvania, we believe that Specter has demonstrated a concern for our special problems and has labored mightily to understand them through constant visits and conferences over a period of years. Edgar, on the other hand, has made only relatively few campaign trips. . . . When a person has done an overall good job, it requires an extraordinarily strong case to justify turning him out of office. We do not believe such a case has been made.[87]

It was exactly the sentiment the incumbent had worked so tirelessly to elicit.

Arlen Specter won reelection by over 450,000 votes (56 percent), carrying all but five of the state's sixty-seven counties. He lost Philadelphia by 60,000 votes (43 percent); but he still carried 30 percent of the black vote there, cutting nearly in half Edgar's predicted 100,000 vote margin. He carried all four suburban counties by 184,000 votes (64 percent), including two Edgar had predicted he would win: Delaware by 24,000 (56 percent) and Bucks by 52,000 (64 percent).[88] He carried eight out of the eleven counties of southwestern Pennsylvania, including Allegheny County. Edgar could not carry "Bailey's base" there, as he had so confidently assumed. Looking only at Specter's other most visited counties (see Table 4-2) he carried Dauphin by 21,000 (65 percent), Luzerne by 800 (50.1 percent), Lackawanna by 7,000 (54 percent), Lehigh by 14,000 (60 percent), Montgomery by 75,000 (69 percent), Erie by 12,000 (57 percent), and Lancaster by 48,000 (75 percent).

CBS network exit polls showed that Specter won 87 percent of the Republicans, 59 percent of the independents, and 27 percent of the

Democrats. Viewed a bit differently, he won votes from 69 percent of the conservatives, 57 percent of the moderates, and 33 percent of the liberals. He won 18 percent of the black vote. Of all those who voted for him, 45 percent picked "past performances" as their major reason; 29 percent picked "control of the Senate," and 21 percent picked "character." The election was described as a "lopsided victory" for Specter and a "crushing defeat" for Edgar—the more so for a Republican in a Democratic state, and on a day when a Democrat was elected governor. Arlen Specter had secured a renewal of statewide support and a secure hold on the legitimacy that went with it. He was, at last, a pure winner.

In his election night analysis, Specter repeated his familiar themes—attentiveness at home, independence in Washington. "One thing I concentrated on at all times," he explained, "was being very visible in the state. People in the state knew who I was and what I was trying to do. If you look at Allegheny County, that was the story. If you look at Lackawanna . . ." He explained further that "I think people really appreciated the fact that I traveled throughout the state to listen to their problems. I've listened to both Republicans and Democrats." And he continued with that inclusionary theme. "I think people have appreciated the fact that I don't just vote the party line, that I listen to what they have to say before I vote." And he added, "There is no expectation on the part of the party that I will vote other than my conscience and for the interests of Pennsylvania. I will remain independent in my views and my votes." [89]

As he looked forward to returning to the Senate—this time as a member of the minority party—he stressed the advantages of his independence:

> Centrists, moderates are very important in the Senate, because if you have people on opposite sides, it is the people in the center who sometimes bring the parties together and are willing to look at the facts. . . . I can talk to Joe Biden and I can talk to Ed Meese. There aren't too many people who can do that.[90]

Early Wednesday morning, Specter left his home in Philadelphia and took the train back to Washington to begin again. At home he would never again be identified as a loser. In Washington he would never again be identified as a newcomer.

CONCLUSION

These chapters about Arlen Specter have been about a political career and a political style. They are about the longevity of the career and the durability of the style, and about the effects of the one upon the other. Specter's early career was an up-and-down one; but his career built gradually toward ultimate success, viewed in terms of his 1986 victory. "It all builds," he said in 1984. "I could never have been elected to the Senate if I hadn't made the runs in '76 and '78." [91] When we talked late in the campaign, the senator stressed again the necessity of his long, slow, often painful cultivation of an electoral base in the state.

> When I was elected district attorney, I was the only Republican who succeeded citywide; and I had a hell of a fight to do it. Then I ran a hard campaign against Heinz, when he outspent me. But I set the stage for the Senate campaign. I don't think you can run statewide without going through that kind of effort—or without money. I began with a strong base; the Philadelphia area casts 40 percent of the state's votes. But the rest of the state doesn't like Philadelphia. And I had other liabilities. My political philosophy was not attuned to that of many Republicans. So I needed to build an underpinning— which I had developed by 1980.

Similarly, in the aftermath of his 1986 victory, his campaign manager observed, "Arlen Specter has not been campaigning for one year or two years or six years. He's been campaigning for twenty years." Census Bureau figures showed that of the thirty-four states with Senate contests in 1986, Pennsylvania was the one with the highest percentage of its current population born in the state.[92] Pennsylvania voters have a lifetime to size up their politicians, and they appear to take a while to do so. An observer once described Philadelphia as "a grind it out city, in a grind it out state." [93] Grinding it out takes time.

If these observations are at all accurate, an understanding of what happened in 1980 and 1986 requires a long perspective. While it is true that politics is played at the margins and in the here and now, it also is played over time. In this sense, it is developmental and accumulative. In Arlen Specter's case, we must understand the process by which he developed and accumulated a political "underpinning." Then we must give this underpinning great weight in explaining his current activity.

Thus, the slow accretion of an electoral base out of his sequence of electoral wins and losses has great bearing on his 1980 success. Similarly, the slow accretion of his several incumbency advantages has great bearing on his 1986 success. "It wasn't the campaign that did it," he said afterward. "It was six years of going around to every little town, getting all those grants." Nothing he has achieved has come quickly or easily. He has never been the beneficiary of a movement or a cause or a historic moment or a welling up of intense support for any reason or from any quarter. Whatever he is doing at the moment will be a tiny increment sustained and shaped by a huge base of previous effort.

In the case of someone with a long political career, the temptation is particularly great to study that career in terms of behavioral changes over time. Surely Arlen Specter did change. But it is the continuity of his behavior that is more striking and more diagnostic. The continuity was expressed partly in his interests, but mostly in his political style— prominently displayed as district attorney and carried forward into his candidacy and, then, into his behavior as a senator. The elements of that style are hard work, aggressiveness, intelligence, publicity consciousness, persistence, and independence—above all, perhaps, persistence and independence. The overall result was an especially individualistic political style, which we have found dominating his entrepreneurial efforts on the career-criminal bill.

At our end-of-the-campaign conversation, Specter reflected on the relationship between the success of his career and the durability of his style:

> I'm thought by some people to be too aggressive; but I believe that you cannot penetrate to the guy at home unless you work extra hard at it. I've been criticized as being ambitious; but long ago I decided to agree with that, and to take the position that that is what this country was founded on. I had no money and I haven't played games with the political leaders. I've taken on a lot of long-shot battles. The evaluators may raise an eyebrow, but the guy in the street doesn't care about aggressiveness. You have to work like hell to make your case. I've done it by dint of sheer persistence. It's like digging into the side of a granite mountain with your fingernails.

The summary would apply just as well to his electoral activity as to his governing activity. His style has been a constant that has operated at home and in Washington and has produced similar patterns of behavior in both places. Style is also the constant that binds together the several stages of his career. Given his ambition, it is his style that has superintended his career, in every place and at all times.

Specter's style has led to success whenever individual effort matters—and has even enlarged the sphere in which individual effort can be made to matter. But it has been less successful in matters that require collective effort. That is true whether we are talking about behavior at home or in Washington, about coalition building in the Senate, or organizing his office and his campaign, or building relationships with the media. Arlen Specter may be as hard working and as smart as any person in the Senate. But his tendency to go it alone in the face of tasks requiring collective action continually tests the limits of individualism and often impairs relationships with others. "Arlen Specter is the smartest man on the Judiciary Committee," said an aide in late 1986. "And that's how he's gotten by there. But there's a lot more than IQ that goes into success in the Senate."

Near the end of his fifth year, after listening to a long monologue on two cases he had won in the courtroom, I asked the senator to discuss the difference between the legal and political systems. "They are the same in a lot of ways," he reflected.

> The legal process is a spider web. Every rule in the web has its purpose. You try to use each rule to give your client a break. The political process is a labyrinth, too. But the difference is that you have to do so much consultation and persuasion with your colleagues. So it takes a long time to get anything done. With the career-criminal bill, as you know, we had to be absolutely relentless about it.

Relentlessness came naturally to him. Consultation did not.

At the end of the first two years of governing activity, the newcomer had learned a great deal but still had much to learn. Four years later, in the eyes of his associates, the development of his consultative talents remained incomplete. Based on the first term, his staff offered generalizations concerning difficulties we had observed during the career-criminal struggle.

> When he's dealing with others, he's so sure he's right that he hears what he wants to hear. And he doesn't hear what people are saying to him. If another senator says, "I'll take a look at it" or "I'd like to help you," he comes back and says so-and-so is on board. Then the senator's staff person will call and say, "my guy never committed himself." I don't know how many times he has slowed up what we were trying to do by not really listening to what people were telling him.

A longtime associate placed his collegial shortcomings in a career-long perspective:

> He's grown—I suppose everyone does—but not as much as I'd like to see. It's still hard for him to realize that you need to engage in a quid pro quo. I tell him, Arlen, you want an awful lot from other people. You have to be willing to give them something in return. But he doesn't want to owe anyone anything. That's very basic for him. I wish he were more malleable. But that's like changing someone's batting stance after twenty years. That desire for independence was shaped by his earlier career. His long career and many failures left him

very distrustful of others, a person who finds it very difficult to work with others.

None of these comments should be taken to minimize the adjustment Specter made to the Senate nor what he had accomplished there. He had displayed an effective style but a limited one. His adjustments and his accomplishments rested largely on his ability to exploit the individualistic possibilities of the institution. Even his one major concession to the Senate's communitarian tendencies ended in a reversion to his older, more natural go-it-alone posture. He came to view the Senate as preeminently a place where individualism, not collegiality, had to be accommodated to.

As Specter expressed it at campaign's end,

> The Senate is a fascinating place. The best description I've heard was when James Kilpatrick said that the Senate is a place where the presiding officer is called *President* Pro Tem, and where, when someone gets up and says "Mr. President," forty heads turn. Jesus Christ, the elbows are so sharp in there. Everybody is jockeying to get media. It's not a snake pit. It's a rhinoceros pit.

The combination of clashing egos and his own do-it-yourself style made accommodation to the individualistic Senate easy for him. But it did not alter the need for him to develop greater collegial skills, if he was to succeed at governing.

Looking toward his second term, I asked him what kind of a reputation he would like to achieve. His answer was modest and low key—as if it were not within his control.

> I don't pose that question for myself. It's not a question I ask myself. I just tend to business and go about the work of the Senate. I have a tendency to speak on a selective basis on the floor on matters where I have done my homework and am prepared. I think I have the reputation among my colleagues that when I speak I know what I'm talking about.

He did not think of himself as someone who would make a reputation by making floor speeches. His achievements as a senator would have to come from some other of the Senate's activities.

A top aide described his posture this way:

> Arlen is not an agenda person. He never sets out his priorities. So he never knows what he wants and what to give up when he's in battle. He just rolls along doing whatever interests him at the time. . . . In the heat of battle, he's like a Sherman tank.

Not one of the new M-1 tanks. Not a maneuverable tank, just one that keeps right on coming and doesn't change course.

It is a familiar picture. It is the persistent prosecutor inside the independent-minded senator, blending a maximum of hard work and intelligence—plus a newly won legitimacy—to the total completion of whatever task he has undertaken. Only the future would determine the task and set him on course.[94] As he applied himself to his work, his senatorial reputation would presumably take care of itself. From all that we have observed, it would be a reputation resting on some new equipoise of his natural, time-tested individualism and his continuing, trial-and-error adjustments to the senatorial community.

NOTES

1. Memorandum, "Precinct Targeting and Election Analysis of Allegheny County, Pennsylvania," Political Targeting, Inc., May 25, 1982.
2. Milton Jaques, "Sen. Specter Begins Plan to Run Again," *Pittsburgh Post-Gazette*, November 16, 1982.
3. Vera Glaser, "People to Watch," *Washingtonian* Magazine, December 1984.
4. Rich Scheinin, "Arlen Specter Always Told People He'd Be a Senator," *Philadelphia Inquirer*, April 15, 1984.
5. James Dickenson, "What Makes Arlen Run Scared?" *Washington Post Weekly Edition*, July 22, 1985.
6. Shirley Uhl, "State GOP Faces Slugfest," *Pittsburgh Press*, November 10, 1985; Richard Cohen, "The $2 Million Campaign," *National Journal*, September 7, 1985.
7. Paul Taylor and David Broder, "Here's the Morning Line on the 1986 Senate Races," *Washington Post Weekly Edition*, September 16, 1985; William Schneider and Eileen Quigley, "GOP Senators May Avoid 6 Year Itch," *National Journal*, May 25, 1985; Rob Gurwitt, "GOP Aims to Elude Senate Takeover Bid in '86," *Congressional Quarterly Weekly Report*, July 20, 1985; Rob Gurwitt, "Many 1986 Senate Candidates Tailor Bids to Local Moods," *Congressional Quarterly Weekly Report*, August 23, 1986; *U.S. News and World Report*, July 28, 1986; Jack Germond and Jules Witcover, "Seven Pivotal Races May Decide Senate Control," *National Journal*, August 30, 1986.
8. Rhodes Cook, "Pennsylvania Democrats Wage Family Feud," *Congressional Quarterly Weekly Report*, May 3, 1986; Rhodes Cook, "Edgar Shows Broad Appeal in Senate Primary," *Congressional Quarterly Weekly Report*, May 24, 1986.
9. For a very different story, see Richard F. Fenno, Jr., *The Making of a Senator: Dan Quayle* (Washington, D.C.: CQ Press, 1988), chap. 4.
10. Memorandum, "The First Year Under the Comprehensive Crime Control Act of 1984," Department of Justice, January 1986, 64-65.
11. See, for example, U.S. Senate, Subcommittee on Juvenile Justice of the Committee on the Judiciary, "Hearing on the Implementation of the Federal Armed Career Criminal Act," New York, December 21, 1984.
12. "S 2312, Armed Career Criminal Amendments," *Congressional Record*,

April 16, 1986, S4235-S4236.

13. Ibid.; See also U.S. Senate, Subcommittee on Criminal Law of the Committee on the Judiciary, Hearings on the Armed Career Criminal Act Amendments, May 14, 1986.

14. In the House it was a small part of the Anti-Drug Abuse Act of 1986, Public Law 99-570, October 22, 1986. Funding for the enforcement of the drug portion of Specter's act began at $2.5 million in 1987 and had risen to $58.5 million by 1990.

15. Hearings on the Implementation of the Federal Armed Career Criminal Act were held by the Subcommittee on Juvenile Justice in New York City on December 21, 1984, in Miami on January 10, 1985, in Dallas on February 11, 1985, and in Los Angeles on February 13, 1985.

16. *Philadelphia Inquirer*, January 17, 1986; *Patriot-News* (Harrisburg), October 3, 1986; *York Daily Record*, February 14, 1986; *Pittsburgh Press*, March 24, 1986; *Greensburg Tribune-Review*, March 25, 1986; *Scranton Tribune*, April 22, 1986; *Wilkes-Barre Citizens Voice*, April 22, 1986.

17. Press Release, January 16, 1986. The story is found in Steve Lopez, "At least 15 Years Sought for Habitual Offenders," *Philadelphia Inquirer*, January 17, 1986.

18. On one of the most important days in the life of the career-criminal bill, when the administration finally announced its support in a hearing before Specter's subcommittee, the *Inquirer* story was headlined "Specter, Heinz and Phila. DA Press Crime Bills." The lead paragraph read "House and Senate bills intended to help curb the nation's crime rate commanded the attention yesterday of Pennsylvania's two Republican senators and Philadelphia's Democratic district attorney." Michael Hobbs, "Specter, Heinz and Phila. DA Press Crime Bills," *Philadelphia Inquirer*, March 19, 1982.

19. Mick Rood of the *Patriot-News*. See footnotes Chapter 2. Also Mick Rood, "Bill Hits 3-Time Robbers," *Patriot-News*, October 1, 1982. He was the only reporter to attend the later hearings on the bill's implementation.

20. For example, "U.S. Senate Okays 15-Years-to-Life Sentences for Habitual Criminals," *Delaware Valley News Eagle*, October 6, 1982.

21. Unless otherwise specified, the poll results reported herein are from "Pennsylvania Statewide Study," *Market Opinion Research*, 2 vols., March 1986. See vol. 2, 107-108. Only quotations will be cited by page number hereafter.

22. "Pennsylvania Statewide Study," *Market Opinion Research*, June 1986, 305-310.

23. Bill Sternberg, "Specter Making More Noise," *Connellsville Courier*, March 19, 1982.

24. Compiled from volumes January 1981 through October 1986 of *Vanderbilt University Television News Index and Abstracts*, Vanderbilt University Library, Nashville, Tenn.

25. Murray Waas, "Media Specter," *New Republic*, September 30, 1985.

26. David Shribman, "Sen. Arlen Specter Succeeds in Getting Headlines in an Effort to Boost His Prospects for Reelection," *Wall Street Journal*, October 25, 1985.

27. George Will, "Where Geography Beats Ideology," *Indianapolis Star*, October 31, 1986.

28. Michael Levin, "The Washington Senator Who Doesn't Always Play Ball,"

Pennsylvania Gazette, October 1984; Scheinin, "Arlen Specter Always Told People He'd Be a Senator."

29. For example, "The Senator has left himself open to a charge of 'political gamesmanship.' . . . Both Highly Qualified," *Scranton Times*, October 25, 1986. The phrase is from Shribman, "Sen. Arlen Specter Succeeds in Getting Headlines."
30. Scheinin, "Arlen Specter Always Told People He'd Be a Senator."
31. Steve Blakely, "Senators' Mail Costs Disclosure: Cranston Tops List," *Congressional Quarterly Weekly Report*, December 14, 1985.
32. "Pennsylvania Statewide Study," vol. 1, (March 1986), 29, 30, 57.
33. Richard Cohen, "Arlen Specter," *National Journal*, April 12, 1986. See also Richard Cohen, "Good Times for GOP?" *National Journal*, June 21, 1986.
34. The classic study is David Mayhew, *The Electoral Connection* (New Haven: Yale University Press, 1974).
35. Paul Taylor, "In Pennsylvania, the Democrats Can't Lose—But They Usually Do," *Washington Post Weekly Edition*, September 8, 1986; Richard Cohen, "Transition Politics," *National Journal*, October 11, 1986; Thomas Ferrick, "Lacking Hot Issues, Candidates Get Personal," *Philadelphia Inquirer*, October 12, 1986; Ellen Hume, "Democratic Party's Crisis over National Identity Takes Center Stage in Pennsylvania Senate Race," *Wall Street Journal*, April 29, 1986; Cook, "Pennsylvania Democrats Wage Family Feuds."
36. Dickenson, "What Makes Arlen Run Scared?"
37. "Pennsylvania Statewide Study," vol. 1 (March 1986), 35.
38. Ibid.
39. Brooks Jackson and Robert Taylor, "GOP's Deep Pockets Help the Republicans in 1986 Senate Races: In Pennsylvania, Sen. Specter Spends Heavily, but Lack of Funds Hurts His Rival," *Wall Street Journal*, October 13, 1986.
40. Uhl, "State GOP Faces Slugfest."
41. Figures taken from Specter's polls. A confirming result can be found in the *Pittsburgh Post-Gazette*'s survey. Tom Waseleski, "Casey, Scanton Close; Specter Leads Edgar," *Pittsburgh Post-Gazette*, October 1, 1986.
42. Bob Dvorchak (Associated Press), "Specter Blasts Opponent's Ads," *Indiana Gazette*, October 27, 1986.
43. Thomas Ferrick, "Glimmers of Trouble for Specter," *Philadelphia Inquirer*, July 7, 1986; see also Dottbest Lipson, "Pol. News of 1986: Senator Arlen Specter May Be in Trouble, Big Trouble," *Philadelphia Magazine*, August 1986.
44. Taylor, "In Pennsylvania, the Democrats Can't Lose."
45. Cook, "Pennsylvania Democrats Wage Family Feud."
46. Shirley Uhl, "How Edgar Plans to Win," *Pittsburgh Press*, August 3, 1986.
47. Frederick Cusick, "Big Firms Benefited from Specter Tax Vote, Edgar Says," *Philadelphia Inquirer*, September 5, 1986.
48. Carolyn Acker, "Edgar: Organization Was Key," *Philadelphia Inquirer*, May 22, 1986.
49. Marcia Coyle, "Specter Counters Attacks on Voting Record," *Morning Call* (Allentown), October 28, 1986.
50. Tom Fox, "A Campaigning Pol Returns to His Roots," *Philadelphia Inquirer*, October 12, 1986. See also Fox, "Jim Crowley is Still in There Kicking," *Philadelphia Inquirer*, October 24, 1982. For similar editorial judgments, see "Specter Favored," *Erie Times-News*, October 26, 1986; "Both Highly Qualified," *Scranton Times*, October 25, 1986.
51. "Pennsylvania Statewide Survey Study," vol. 1 (March 1986), 30, 31, 106.

52. See John Forester, "Senate Incumbent Recollects His Roots on Farm in Kansas," *Reading Times,* October 18, 1986.
53. See Milton Jacques, "Conrail, Amtrak on Track for Fewer Lines," *Pittsburgh Post-Gazette,* October 12, 1981; Douglas Feaver, "Conrail Sale Sidetracked by Politics," *Washington Post Weekly Edition,* May 26, 1986.
54. James O'Toole, "Specter Likes Man-in-the-Middle Role," *Pittsburgh Post-Gazette,* October 6, 1986.
55. Dickenson, "What Makes Arlen Run Scared?" United Press International, "Edgar Says There's Two Specters," *Danville News,* September 23, 1986.
56. United Press International, "Edgar Says There's Two Specters"; Dan Meyers, "Sorting Fact, Fiction in Senate Race," *Philadelphia Inquirer,* October 3, 1986; Jeff Barker (Associated Press), " 'Negative' Fuss Troubles Edgar," *Indiana Gazette,* October 27, 1986; Thomas Ferrick, "Edgar, Specter Joust in TV Debate," *Philadelphia Inquirer,* October 15, 1986.
57. Joe Hart, "Specter Counters Claims," *Delaware County Daily Times,* October 5, 1986; Dvorchak, "Specter Blasts Opponent's Ads."
58. Marcia Coyle, "Edgar Campaigns Against Specter's Record," *Morning Call* (Allentown), October 27, 1986.
59. Ibid.; Will, "Where Geography Beats Ideology"; Uhl, "How Edgar Plans to Win"; David Marziale, "Edgar Playing Catch-Up for Senate," *North Penn Reporter* (Lansdale), October 23, 1986; Ferrick, "Edgar, Specter Joust in TV Debate." Marcia Gallagher, "Edgar: Don't Take Bashing Personally, Arlen," *Philadelphia Daily News,* September 5, 1986.
60. Joe Hart, "Specter Breaks Silence on Dem Attacks," *Delaware County Times,* September 7, 1986.
61. "Pennsylvania Statewide Survey," vol. 2 (March 1986), 130, 133.
62. O'Toole, "Specter Likes Man-in-the-Middle Role."
63. Doris O'Donnell, "Specter's Self-Description: 'Most Independent,' " *Greensburg Tribune-Review,* May 29, 1986.
64. Dickenson, "What Makes Arlen Run Scared?"
65. Marziale, "Edgar Playing Catch-Up for Senate"; Uhl, "State GOP Faces Slugfest."
66. "Pennsylvania Statewide Study," vol. 1 (March 1986), 82-83.
67. Dickenson, "What Makes Arlen Run Scared?"; Cohen, "Transition Politics"; Shirley Uhl, "GOP Has Edge in State Races," *Pittsburgh Press,* May 26, 1986; Shirley Uhl, "Specter's Nimble Nays," *Pittsburgh Press,* June 29, 1986.
68. Paul Taylor, "18 Republicans Find Strength in Political Independence," *Washington Post,* March 30, 1986; Steven Roberts, "Republican Family Feud Deepens as 1986 Looms," *New York Times,* August 4, 1985.
69. "Voter's Guide," *Pittsburgh Press,* October 28, 1986; see also Gary Rotstein, "Specter Countering Edgar's Attacks," *Pittsburgh Post-Gazette,* September 24, 1986.
70. Sandy Grady, "The Great, Hour-Long Senate Race," *Philadelphia Daily News,* October 15, 1986; Gary Rotstein, "Specter, Edgar Trade Harsh Charges in TV Debate," *Pittsburgh Post-Gazette,* October 15, 1986; Shirley Uhl, "Low Blows," *Pittsburgh Press,* October 15, 1986; Ferrick, "Edgar, Specter Joust in TV Debate."
71. Bernard Weinraub, "22 GOP Senators Pressed to Back Reagan Programs," *New York Times,* March 15, 1985.
72. *Congressional Record,* March 19, 1985, S3161-S3162.
73. O'Toole, "Specter Likes Man-in-the-Middle Role."

74. Dan Balz, "One Senator's Road to a Yes Vote on the MX Missile," *Washington Post Weekly Edition*, April 1, 1985; Taylor, "18 Republicans Find Strength in Political Independence."
75. Meyers, "Sorting Fact, Fiction in Senate Race"; O'Toole, "Specter Likes Man-in-the-Middle Role."
76. Coyle, "Specter Counters Attacks on Voting Record."
77. O'Toole, "Specter Likes Man-in-the-Middle Role."
78. "Periscope," *Newsweek*, September 16, 1985, April 14, 1986; "The President's Angry Apostle," *Newsweek*, October 6, 1986.
79. Richard Cohen, "Running Without Reagan," *National Journal*, December 7, 1985.
80. Marty Willis, "Specter Commands Black Politicians," *New Pittsburgh Courier*, July 19, 1986.
81. Ferrick, "Edgar, Specter Joust in TV Debate."
82. Sheinin, "Specter Always Told People He'd Be a Senator."
83. "Edgar for U.S. Senate from Pa.," *Philadelphia Inquirer*, November 2, 1986; "For U.S. Senate," *Philadelphia Daily News*, October 22, 1986.
84. "Specter for the Senate Because of Solid Record," *Bucks County Courier Times*, October 27, 1986.
85. "Specter for the Senate," *Pottstown Mercury* (Pottstown), October 28, 1986.
86. "Re-elect Sen. Specter," *Greensburg Tribune-Review*, October 26, 1986.
87. "Senator: Specter," *Uniontown Herald Standard* (Uniontown), October 29, 1986. Similar arguments about incumbency are made in: "Specter Rates Another Term," *Beaver County Times* (Beaver), October 29, 1986.
88. Uhl, "How Edgar Plans to Win"; on the black vote, see Kendall Wilson, "Money, Incumbency Give Specter Clout," *Philadelphia Tribune*, November 7, 1986.
89. James O'Toole, "Specter Views Role as Bridge to Democrats," *Pittsburgh Post-Gazette*, November 6, 1986; Kenn Marshall, "Specter Credits Reagan, with Whom He Doesn't Always Agree," *Harrisburg Evening News*, November 5, 1986; Kenn Marshall, "Specter Back to Work the Day After Election," *Harrisburg Evening News*, November 6, 1986.
90. David Marziale, "Specter Envisions Role as Peacemaker in New Senate," *North Penn Reporter* (Lansdale), November 6, 1986.
91. Sheinin, "Arlen Specter Always Told People He'd Be a Senator."
92. "Senate Control Will be Determined . . . By Votes in These 34 States in 1986," *National Journal*, December 7, 1985.
93. David Nyhan, "As Philadelphia Goes, so Goes the Nation," *Boston Globe*, September 25, 1980.
94. In the post-1986 period, Senator Specter's most highly publicized and most highly praised governing performance was another triumph of individual effort—and closely related, once again, to his pre-Senate career. In the fall of 1987, he was a central figure in the Judiciary Committee's confirmation hearings on the intensely controversial nomination of Judge Robert Bork to the United States Supreme Court. Specter's prominence was equally the result of his pivotal vote—eventually cast against the nomination—and of his conduct as an interrogator. Among observers, both local and national, and among those who disagreed with his decision as well as those who agreed with it, there was praise for his performance.

"Although we may disagree with his decision . . . we must applaud the senator's deep and intellectual probing. . . . Senator Specter, the former

Philadelphia district attorney, has cruised along a path much of his own charting.... The nation cultivated a widely expressed respect for the manner in which this Republican questioned and probed Judge Bork." ("Senator Specter's Wise Demeanor," *Morning Call* (Allentown), October 8, 1987.) "Despite our enthusiasm for the nominee, we have to credit the senator with doing his homework.... He asked the most probing questions during Judiciary Committee hearings. ... Specter reached his decision through a thorough examination of the nominee." ("Specter's Vote on Bork," *New Era* (Lancaster), October 6, 1987.) "Specter emerged as the committee's shining light.... I believe he made the wrong decision. But ... Specter's brillant questioning and gracious manner throughout the hearing brought honor to his state and to his nation." (Bill Thompson, "Specter: A Bright Spot in a Bad Week," *Fort Worth Star-Telegram*, as reprinted in the *Times Leader* (Wilkes-Barre), October 4, 1987.)

Noteworthy is the reaction of two papers opposing him in 1986. In an editorial entitled "Arlen Specter's Finest Hour," one wrote that "Pennsylvania's Arlen Specter—Yale law graduate, former district attorney—has done his constituents proud by providing some of the most intelligent and penetrating questions."(*Philadelphia Inquirer*, September 22, 1987.) The other opined that "Specter questioned Bork with a piercing intensity and a fierce thoroughness that impressed his peers and the public." (*Philadelphia Daily News*, October 18, 1987.) From outside the state came a similar judgment: "Senator Arlen Specter ... showed the eager curiosity that is the essence of intellectualism ... and so won the respect of the nation." (A. M. Rosenthal, "A Victory for the Conservatives," *New York Times*, reprinted in the *Patriot-News*, October 12, 1987.)

In his summary article on the Bork affair, one of Washington's most respected congressional reporters singled out Specter—alone among committee members—for praise. "The performance by U.S. Senator Arlen Specter, considered the committee's most skilled questioner, propelled the Pennsylvania Republican into the national spotlight, earning him renewed respect among his colleagues and name recognition around the country." (Steven B. Roberts, "White House Planners Look Beyond Bork," *New York Times*, reprinted in *Morning Call* (Allentown), October 11, 1987.)

Appendix: Annotated Chronology of Career–Criminal Legislation

OCTOBER 1, 1981 Senator Arlen Specter introduces three crime-control bills. All referred to Judiciary Committee.

S 1688: Career Criminal Life Sentence Act of 1981 (short title).

S 1689: Incarceration of State Prisoners Sentenced to Life as Career Criminals in Federal Institutions.

S 1690: Rehabilitation Requiring States to Provide Prisoners A Trade Before Paroling Them.

Official title of S 1688: A bill to combat violent and major crime by establishing a federal offense for continuing a career of robberies or burglaries while armed and providing a mandatory sentence of life imprisonment.

Key provisions of S 1688 as introduced:

Sec. 2(a) Whoever commits, conspires, or attempts to commit a robbery or a burglary in violation of the felony statutes of a State or of the United States while using, threatening to use, displaying or possessing a firearm, after having been twice convicted of a robbery or a burglary in violation of the felony statutes of a State or the United States is a career criminal and upon conviction shall be sentenced to imprisonment for life.

Sec. 4 It is the intent of Congress that in exercising its jurisdiction under this Act, the United States should ordinarily defer to State prosecution. However, if the Attorney General or a United States Attorney, in consultation with appropriate State or local officials, determines that there is a significant Federal interest in the case and the State authorities are unlikely to secure a sentence of imprisonment for life, then Federal prosecution may be brought.

OCTOBER 26, 1981 Hearings held by Subcommittee on Juvenile Justice.

NOVEMBER 13, 1981 Meeting with President Reagan.

DECEMBER 10, 1981; JANUARY 28, 1982 Further hearings held by Subcommittee on Juvenile Justice.

179

MARCH 18, 1982 Administration formally supports S 1688.

MAY 20, 1982 S 1688 polled out of subcommittee favorably, with three yes votes and two absentions. List of eleven "findings" pertaining to problem and need added to bill by subcommittee member Charles Mathias.

SEPTEMBER 21, 1982 S 1688, as amended, is reported out of the Senate Judiciary Committee, unanimously.

Short Title: Armed Career Criminal Act of 1982.

Official Title: A bill to combat violent street crime by establishing a federal offense for continuing a career of robberies or burglaries by using a firearm to commit a third or subsequent offense and providing a mandatory minimum sentence of between 15 years and life imprisonment.

Key provisions:

Sec. 2(a) Any person who while he or any other participant in the offense is in possession of a firearm, commits, or conspires or attempts to commit robbery or burglary in violation of the felony statutes of the State in which such offense occurs or of the United States—

(1) may be prosecuted for such offense in the courts of the United States if such person has previously been twice convicted of robbery or burglary, or an attempt or conspiracy to commit such an offense, in violation of the felony statutes of any State or the United States, and

(2) shall, if found guilty pursuant to this section, and upon proof of the requisite prior convictions to the court at or before sentencing, be sentenced to a term of imprisonment of not less than fifteen (15) years nor more than life and may be fined not more than $10,000.

Sec. 4(a) It is the intent of Congress regarding the exercise of jurisdiction under this Act that ordinarily the United States should defer to State and local prosecutions of armed robbery and armed burglary offenses. However, if after full consultation between the local prosecuting authority and the appropriate Federal prosecuting authority, the local prosecuting authority requests or concurs in Federal prosecution and the Attorney General or his designee approves such prosecution to be appropriate, then Federal prosecution may be initiated under this Act.

"Findings" eliminated from the bill.

SEPTEMBER 23, 1982 Hearings on HR 6386, the House version of the career-criminal bill, before Subcommittee on Crime of House Judiciary Committee.

SEPTEMBER 24, 1982 Senate considers S 1688. Kennedy Amendment moves intent section, involving federal/local jurisdiction, from section 4 to section 2(e) of the bill. Bill passes 93-1.

DECEMBER 9, 1982 House Subcommittee on Crime Reports out HR 6386, career-criminal bill, to House Judiciary Committee, by 4-3 vote (Specter participates). House Judiciary Committee fails to act on the bill.

DECEMBER 9, 1982 S 2411, Justice Assistance Act of 1982, providing federal assistance to state and local jurisdictions for justice activities, is passed by voice vote in the Senate. Specter is floor manager for bill. House of Representatives had passed similar bill, HR 4481, in February 1982, by vote of 289-73.

DECEMBER 14, 1982 In the Senate, S 1688 is tacked onto S 2411 as one of several amendments.

DECEMBER 20, 1982 S 1688 remains intact in report of the conference committee of Senate and House Judiciary Committee members. Report recommends a package of anticrime bills to both chambers. Anticrime package HR 3963 passes both chambers.

JANUARY 14, 1983 President Reagan vetoes HR 3963.

JANUARY 26, 1983 Arlen Specter introduces S 52, the Armed Career Criminal Act of 1983.

Key provisions of S 52: Same as S 1688 except for rewording of intent section 2(e), regarding federal/local jurisdiction, as follows.

Sec. 2(e) Ordinarily, armed robbery and armed burglary cases against career criminals should be prosecuted in state court. However, in some circumstances such prosecutions by state authorities may face undue obstacles. Therefore, any such case lodged in the office of the local prosecutor may be received and considered for federal indictment by the federal prosecuting authority, but only upon request or with the concurrence of the local prosecuting authority. Any such case presented by a federal investigative agency to the federal prosecuting authority, however, may be received at the sole discretion of the federal prosecuting authority. Regardless of the origin of the case, the decision whether to seek a grand jury indictment shall be in the sole discretion of the federal prosecuting authority.

MAY 26, 1983 Hearings on S 52 before Senate Judiciary Committee.

JULY 20, 1983 S 52 reported to Senate by Judiciary Committee, unanimously.

> **Key provisions:** Intent section no longer part of the operative section 2 of the bill, but has been returned to section 4, with the following wording:

> > An offense under this section shall not be prosecuted unless the appropriate State prosecuting authority requests or concurs in such prosecution and the attorney general or his designee concurs in such prosecution.

FEBRUARY 23, 1984 S 52 passed by Senate 92-0. Kennedy-Thurmond Amendment passes 77-12.

> **Key provisions:**

> > *Sec. 2(a)* Whoever carries a firearm during the commission of a robbery or burglary offense which may be prosecuted in a court of the United States, or commits such an offense with another who carries a firearm during the commission of such offense, or attempts or conspires to do so, shall be fined not more than $25,000 and imprisoned not less than fifteen years.

> > *Sec. 2(b)* An offense under this section shall not be prosecuted unless the United States proves beyond a reasonable doubt that the defendant has been convicted of at least two offenses described in subsection (c) of this section.

Intent section eliminated entirely, since bill now pertains only to robberies or burglaries which are otherwise subject to federal prosecution.

FEBRUARY 24, 1984 Senate passes Comprehensive Crime Control Act, including Armed Career Criminal Act.

SEPTEMBER 25, 1984 House attaches Senate crime package to HJ Res 648, the continuing appropriations resolution for FY 1985.

OCTOBER 1, 1984 House passes HR 6248 Armed Career Criminal Act of 1984.

> **Bill: as eventually signed into law:**

> > *Section 1202(a)* of title VII of the Omnibus Crime Control and Safe Streets Act of 1968 (18 U.S.C. App. 1202(a)) is amended by adding at the end "In the case of a person who receives, possesses or transports in commerce or affecting commerce any firearm and who has three previous convictions by any court

referred to in paragraph (1) of this subsection for robbery or burglary, or both, such person shall be fined not more than $25,000 and imprisoned not less than fifteen years, and, notwithstanding any other provision of law, the court shall not suspend the sentence of, or grant a probationary sentence to, such person with respect to the conviction under this subsection, and such person shall not be eligible for parole with respect to the sentence imposed under this subsection."

Sec. 3. Section 1202(c) of title VII of the Omnibus Crime Control and Safe Streets Act of 1968 (18 U.S.C. App. 1202(c) is amended:

(1) by striking out the period at the end of paragraph (7) and inserting a semicolon in lieu thereof; and

(2) by adding at the end of the following "(8) 'robbery' means any felony consisting of the taking of the property of another from the person or presence of another by force or violence, or by threatening or placing another person in fear that any person will imminently be subjected to bodily injury;" and

"(9) 'burglary' means any felony consisting of entering or remaining surreptitiously within a building that is property of another with intent to engage in conduct constituting a Federal or State offense."

OCTOBER 4, 1984 Senate passes HR 6248.

OCTOBER 11, 1984 Armed Career Criminal Act is passed by House and Senate as part of the continuing appropriations resolution HJ Res 648.

OCTOBER 12, 1984 President signs HJ Res 648, including Armed Career Criminal Act in the form that it passed the House.

Index